Murray Walker's 1991 GRAND PRIX YEAR

Photography
John Townsend

Murray Walker's 1991 Grand Prix Year is published by Hazleton Publishing, 3 Richmond Hill, Richmond, Surrey TW10 6RE, in association with FOSTER'S.
Typeset by Surrey Typesetters, Stoneleigh, Surrey.
Colour reproduction by Masterlith Ltd, Mitcham, Surrey.
Printed in England by Fulmar Colour Printing, Croydon, Surrey.

ISBN: 0-905138-90-2

PUBLISHER: Richard Poulter
EXECUTIVE PUBLISHER: Elizabeth Le Breton
EDITOR: Simon Arron
DESIGNER: Michèle Arron
PHOTOGRAPHER: John Townsend
PRODUCTION MANAGER: George Greenfield
PRODUCTION CO-ORDINATOR: Deirdre Fenney
GRAND PRIX STATISTICS: Maurice Hamilton

DISTRIBUTORS
UK & OTHER MARKETS
George Philip Limited
59 Grosvenor Street, London W1X 9DA

NORTH AMERICA
Motorbooks International
PO Box 2, 729 Prospect Avenue
Osceola, Wisconsin 54020, USA

AUSTRALIA
Technical Book & Magazine Co. Pty
289-299 Swanston Street, Melbourne, Victoria 3000

Universal Motor Publications
c/o Automotive Motoring Bookshop
152-154 Clarence Street, Sydney 2000

NEW ZEALAND
David Bateman
'Golden Heights', 32-34 View Road, Glenfield, Auckland 10

CONTENTS

13
13
'Don't you just hat

U JUST LOVE IT.

1991 DRIVERS

Driver	Country	Team	No. GPs
Michele Alboreto	I	Footwork	153
Jean Alesi	F	Ferrari	39
Julian Bailey	GB	Lotus	7
Fabrizio Barbazza	I	AGS	-
Michael Bartels	D	Lotus	-
Gerhard Berger	A	McLaren	115
Eric Bernard	F	Lola	31
Mark Blundell	GB	Brabham	14
Thierry Boutsen	B	Ligier	137
Martin Brundle	GB	Brabham	83
Alex Caffi	I	Footwork	56
Ivan Capelli	I	Leyton House	78
Andrea de Cesaris	I	Jordan	165
Pedro Chaves	P	Coloni	-
Erik Comas	F	Ligier	13
Bertrand Gachot	B	Jordan, Lola	15
Olivier Grouillard	F	Fomet, AGS	25
Mauricio Gugelmin	BR	Leyton House	58
Mika Häkkinen	SF	Lotus	15
Naoki Hattori	JPN	Coloni	-
Johnny Herbert	GB	Lotus	15
Stefan Johansson	S	AGS, Footwork	79
Nicola Larini	I	Lamborghini	40
JJ Lehto	SF	Dallara	23
Nigel Mansell	GB	Williams	165
Pier-Luigi Martini	I	Minardi	70
Stefano Modena	I	Tyrrell	58
Gianni Morbidelli	I	Minardi, Ferrari	19
Roberto Moreno	BR	Benetton, Jordan, Minardi	24
Satoru Nakajima	JPN	Tyrrell	74
Riccardo Patrese	I	Williams	224
Nelson Piquet	BR	Benetton	204
Emanuele Pirro	I	Dallara	37
Eric van de Poele	B	Lamborghini	1
Alain Prost	F	Ferrari	184
Michael Schumacher	D	Jordan, Benetton	6
Ayrton Senna	BR	McLaren	126
Aguri Suzuki	JPN	Lola	28
Gabriele Tarquini	I	AGS, Fomet	24
Karl Wendlinger	A	Leyton House	2
Alessandro Zanardi	I	Jordan	3

1991 WORLD CHAMPIONSHIP

	Drivers	Pts
1.	Ayrton Senna	96
2.	Nigel Mansell	72
3.	Riccardo Patrese	53
4.	Gerhard Berger	43
5.	Alain Prost	34
6.	Nelson Piquet	26.5
7.	Jean Alesi	21
8.	Stefano Modena	10
9.	Andrea de Cesaris	9
10.	Roberto Moreno	8
11.	Pier-Luigi Martini	6
12.	JJ Lehto	4
	Bertrand Gachot	4
	Michael Schumacher	4
15.	Mika Häkkinen	2
	Martin Brundle	2
	Satoru Nakajima	2
18.	Aguri Suzuki	1
	Emanuele Pirro	1
	Julian Bailey	1
	Eric Bernard	1
	Ivan Capelli	1
	Mark Blundell	1
24.	Gianni Morbidelli	0.5

	Teams	Pts
1.	McLaren-Honda	139
2.	Williams-Renault	125
3.	Ferrari	55.5
4.	Benetton-Ford	38.5
5.	Jordan-Ford	13
6.	Tyrrell-Honda	12
7.	Minardi-Ferrari	6
8.	Dallara-Judd	5
9.	Lotus-Judd	3
	Brabham-Yamaha	3
11.	Lola-DFR	2
12.	Leyton House-Ilmor	1

1991 GRANDS PRIX

Race	Winner	Pole Position	Fastest Lap
USA	A Senna	A Senna	J Alesi
Brazil	A Senna	A Senna	N Mansell
San Marino	A Senna	A Senna	G Berger
Monaco	A Senna	A Senna	A Prost
Canada	N Piquet	R Patrese	N Mansell
Mexico	R Patrese	R Patrese	N Mansell
France	N Mansell	R Patrese	N Mansell
Great Britain	N Mansell	N Mansell	N Mansell
Germany	N Mansell	N Mansell	R Patrese
Hungary	A Senna	A Senna	B Gachot
Belgium	A Senna	A Senna	R Moreno
Italy	N Mansell	A Senna	A Senna
Portugal	R Patrese	R Patrese	N Mansell
Spain	N Mansell	G Berger	R Patrese
Japan	G Berger	G Berger	A Senna
Australia	A Senna	A Senna	G Berger

1991 DRIVERS
Who have won a GP, been on pole or set fastest lap

Grand Prix Wins		Races Contested	Pole Positions	Fastest Laps
44	Alain Prost	184	20	35
33	Ayrton Senna	126	60	17
23	Nelson Piquet	204	24	23
21	Nigel Mansell	165	17	22
6	Gerhard Berger	115	8	14
5	Michele Alboreto	153	2	5
5	Riccardo Patrese	224	7	10
3	Thierry Boutsen	137	1	1
0	Jean Alesi	39	0	1
0	Andrea de Cesaris	165	1	1
0	Bertrand Gachot	15	0	1
0	Mauricio Gugelmin	58	0	1
0	Roberto Moreno	24	0	1
0	Satoru Nakajima	74	0	1

DURING 1991 ...

* Ayrton Senna became the first driver to win the first four World Championship Grands Prix in a season and subsequently became the youngest-ever three-times world champion. His image, however, was greatly tarnished by his admission that his 1990 first-corner collision with Prost at Suzuka had resulted from his decision to ''go for the lead regardless of the consequences.''
* Cesare Fiorio was fired as the Ferrari team manager.
* At Phoenix the Honda V12 engine won first time out.
* Pirelli won its first GP (Piquet/Canada) since Mexico 1986 (Berger/Benetton).
* Porsche's return with Footwork was a demeaning failure.
* Pedro Chaves failed to pre-qualify for all the 14 races he attended with the Coloni team.
* The long-established Ligier, Footwork and Brabham teams sank to the depths of having to pre-qualify after Britain.
* The new Jordan team was impressively successful.
* Amidst dismay the French GP moved from the Paul Ricard circuit to Magny-Cours.
* Amidst acclamation the Spanish GP moved from Jerez to Barcelona.
* With great success the British GP was held for the first time on the much-revised Silverstone circuit.
* Some 13 different makes/types of engine were used — Ford HB and DFR, Hart V8, Honda V10 and V12, Renault V10, Ferrari V12, Lamborghini V12, Judd V8 and V10, Ilmor V10, Porsche V12 and Yamaha V12.
* John Barnard resigned from Benetton.
* Harvey Postlethwaite left Tyrrell for Mercedes-Benz.
* Nigel Mansell became the 'winningest' English Grand Prix driver by scoring his 17th GP victory in France.
* Tom Walkinshaw's TWR organisation bought 35 per cent of Team Benetton.
* At Hockenheim, McLaren lost leadership of the constructors' World Championship for the first time in 40 races.
* Soichiro Honda, founder of the great motor sport oriented organisation, died at the age of 84.
* Bertrand Gachot was sentenced to 18 months' gaol for assaulting a London taxi driver with CS gas. The sentence was eventually reduced on appeal, Bertrand having spent two months inside.
* Michael Schumacher, replacing Bertrand Gachot in the Jordan team, made an impressive Grand Prix debut in Belgium, qualifying seventh.
* Two weeks after his Belgian debut, Schumacher was centre of another F1 controversy, leaving Jordan to drive for Benetton.
* Max Mosley replaced the unpopular Jean-Marie Balestre as president of FISA, becoming the first British subject to hold motor sport's most prestigious and influential post.
* Before Adelaide, Alain Prost's open criticism of Ferrari led to his dismissal from the team.
* The Australian GP was the shortest World Championship event of all time, red-flagged after 14 torrential laps.

PREFACE

Childhood pals Roberto Moreno and Nelson Piquet formed a happy alliance at Benetton.

For a while, there was concern that the 1991 Grand Prix season might not happen. For political reasons, some people believed it was wrong to go motor racing whilst a major war was being waged in the Gulf. And with worries about terrorist strikes, especially at air travellers, there was a view that it was foolhardy and irresponsible to do so. Further to aggravate an unhappy and worrying situation, a worldwide recession was making things very tough indeed for a money-hungry sport, with the result that a lot of the teams had far from full budgets.

But life goes on. Undeterred by its problems, the Formula One world progressed its preparations for a new season which showed promise of topping even the superb 1990 championship in terms of excitement, razor-sharp competition, unpredictability and mechanical variety.

Some 18 teams had made entries for 34 drivers, which meant that the dreaded eight o'clock Friday morning pre-qualifying sessions would have to be held for the eight Fondmetal, Dallara, Coloni, Lamborghini and Jordan drivers, thus reducing the would-be qualifiers to 30. A contentious ruling by FISA had seen the Larrousse-Lola team's 11 well-earned 1990 points disallowed for an infringement of the car registration regulations, but it was allowed to avoid pre-qualification.

In all, 16 drivers remained with their 1990 teams, but there were major moves, new faces, three welcome returnees to Grand Prix racing and a lot of departures. The mercurial Jean

Alesi had switched from Tyrrell to Ferrari for only his second full season of F1. Nigel Mansell had left the Prancing Horse to return to Williams. Stefano Modena was out of Brabham and into Tyrrell. Thierry Boutsen, rejected by Williams, had gone to Ligier. By signing for Benetton, Roberto Moreno had at last got the top-team drive that he deserved and JJ Lehto, Nicola Larini and Bertrand Gachot had transferred, respectively, to Dallara, Lamborghini and Jordan, whilst Andrea de Cesaris was to drive for his eighth GP team — Jordan.

To general acclaim, Martin Brundle returned to Brabham for a third go at Grand Prix racing, having added victory at Le Mans for Jaguar in 1990 to his 1988 World Sportscar Championship title. His team-mate would be ex-Nissan Group C racer and Williams F1 tester Mark Blundell — thereby creating a commentator's nightmare! The popular Stefan Johansson, out of Formula One since the San Marino race in 1990, had found himself a seat with AGS (his ninth team). 1990 British Formula Three Champion Mika Häkkinen (like his Finnish countryman JJ Lehto, a protégé of Keke Rosberg) was to make his Formula One début driving for Lotus. Frenchman Erik Comas, the 1990 European Formula 3000 Champion, was to be Ligier's second new driver. Britain's 1990 Formula 3000 Champion, Pedro Chaves from Portugal, was to drive for Coloni. Eric van de Poele increased Belgium's representation to three by signing for Lamborghini.

Even before the season started, Nigel Mansell had something to celebrate, picking up an OBE in the New Year's Honours List.

Murray's nightmare! Martin Brundle and Mark Blundell (seen leading Moreno and Modena in Phoenix) teamed up in the new-look Brabham team, to develop Yamaha's fledgling V12 (inset).

But ten of 1990's Grand Prix drivers were out. Sadly, one of them was the ebullient and enormously popular Derek Warwick who, understandably disenchanted with Lotus after a disastrous 1990, had been overlooked for a replacement drive despite his experience, success and lion-hearted ability. There are very few with Derek's personality, likeability and qualities of leadership. Grand Prix racing needs people like him and he would be greatly missed. So would Benetton's Alessandro Nannini, still recovering from the effects of the helicopter accident which had severed his right arm. Miraculously, it had not only been replaced but had knitted together well enough for Sandro to be optimistic about rejoining his team. But time alone would tell. 1990's other casualty Martin Donnelly, grievously injured in Spain, was similarly making an astounding recovery and intended to be racing for Lotus again, but until he could his place would be taken by 1988 Tyrrell driver Julian Bailey. There was no such hope though for David Brabham, Yannick Dalmas, Paolo Barilla, Philippe Alliot, Claudio Langes, Gregor Foitek and Bruno Giacomelli, all of whom had slithered down the greasy pole.

There were major changes on the engine front, too. A new Honda V12 for McLaren, to replace the dominant Honda V10 which had enabled them to win the constructors' championship for the past two years. The Ferrari V12 for Italy's Minardi team (the only rival constructor ever to be supplied by Maranello). Lamborghini V12s for Ligier and Lamborghini. Porsche V12s for the Footwork (né Arrows) team. A very serious new V12 from Yamaha for Brabham. A greatly improved Renault RS3 V10 for Williams. Developed Honda V10 units for the new, and very impressive, Tyrrell 020. From Ilmor, the tremendously successful British supplier of engines for America's Indycar racing, a brand new V10 for Leyton House's new Chris Murphy-designed car. For Dallara, the exclusive use of John Judd's new V10. Ford had further improved its HB V8 engine, which had powered Benetton to victory in the last two 1990 races, and was to supply it not only to Benetton but also to Irishman Eddie Jordan's new team (a tremendous coup for the irrepressible Irishman). But there's a reverse side to every coin. Lotus and Larrousse-Lola were downcast at the fact that their loss of Lamborghini power to Ligier and Lamborghini

Despite its newness, much was expected of the Jordan chassis. Bertrand Gachot and designer Gary Anderson swap notes.

meant that they'd have to use the less powerful Judd and Ford DFR V8s.

So what else was new? Plenty! Following changes of ownership we had to learn to call the Arrows team 'Footwork' and Osella 'Fondmetal'. The unsuccessful Eurobrun and Life teams had disappeared, to be replaced by the Italian Lamborghini and Anglo/Irish Jordan organisations. Lotus had been completely reconstructed after nearly going under. Thank heavens it hadn't, but with new management, new personnel, a new and inexperienced driver, number one driver Martin Donnelly still recovering from his awful 1990 crash, less powerful engines and new sponsors, it was now one of the lesser teams, in sad contrast to its glory days under Colin Chapman.

There were other changes too. A win would now earn the driver and his constructor ten points in their World Championships, and all of a driver's points scored in the 16 races would count (if that had been the case in 1988, Alain Prost would have been champion rather than Ayrton Senna). Three of those races would be held at very different locations, with the French GP moving to Magny-Cours (very unpopular), the Spanish race to Barcelona (very popular!) and the British round being held on the much revised Silverstone. In order to reduce downforce, new aerodynamic rules had been introduced requiring smaller front wings and the rear wing to be mounted further forwards. However, winter testing had shown that, as usual, the designers had beaten the legislators and that the cars would be faster rather than slower! And with the refusal of Ferrari's fuel supplier, Agip, to agree to the universal use of unleaded petrol, the evil and environmentally unfriendly special qualifying brews would stll be legal — a black mark for Formula One which was both unnecessary and undesirable.

Although McLaren had again won both championships in 1990 and '89, their six victories had been matched by Ferrari, whilst Williams and Benetton had both won twice. It looked as though the racing would be even more competitive in 1991, with five teams capable of winning and several others in with a chance. With a meticulously developed 642 version of its successful 1990 V12 car, and Prost and Alesi to drive it, Ferrari was going to be stronger than ever. But how would the two Frenchmen get on with each other in the highly charged, political atmosphere that always exists at Maranello? No problem like that at McLaren, where everyone pulls in the same direction and the V12 Honda was already producing more power then its championship-winning V10. Bad news for the competition, but very good news indeed for World Champion Ayrton Senna and his team-mate Gerhard Berger — especially for the lanky Gerhard, as McLaren had now been able to produce a car that really fitted him. But Ferrari and McLaren were going to have to fight far more than in 1990 to beat the Williams, Benetton and Tyrrell

Spot the sponsor. Pedro Chaves' deal with Coloni was a low-budget affair.

After the traumas of 1990, the experienced Peter Collins led the refettled Lotus team into 1991. During the winter, its continued participation had been in some doubt.

drivers. The very British Nigel Mansell (deservedly awarded the OBE in the New Year's Honours List) was psychologically at ease back in the Williams team that he knew, liked and could motivate far more than the alien Ferrari organisation — especially as he was now the undisputed number one driver. In the 1990 car, he had been enormously impressive in the winter tests and comfortably fastest of all at Paul Ricard. He liked the new Williams semi-automatic gearbox ("better than Ferrari's!") and was confident that the 1991 FW14 with its new Renault V10 would enable him to be totally competitive. And nor was his team-mate, the vastly experienced Riccardo Patrese, to be overlooked.

The Benetton drivers had every reason to be confident too. Nelson Piquet, fired up after his 1990 wins in Japan and Australia, and the underrated Roberto Moreno would have an innovative all-new car, masterminded by the brilliant John Barnard and powered by a further-developed version of the race-winning Ford HB V8. But their possible joker would be the fact that this year they'd be driving on Pirelli tyres, specially designed for their car. Pirelli had made giant strides in 1990 and was hungry for a win. But that win might well come from the combination of the gifted Stefano Modena and his Honda V10-powered, Pirelli-shod Tyrrell.

Brief reprieve. Stefan Johansson rejoined the F1 trail you with the financially straitened AGS team, but only for two events...

Jean Alesi had taken two brilliant second places for the team in 1990, propelled by the worthy but lesser-powered Ford DFR V8. With Honda grunt, surely the talented Modena could go one better in '91?

The top five teams had to be the favourites, but strange and unpredictable things can happen in Formula One. There were other very promising combinations, all of them new and under-developed but, given the right circumstances, capable of being on the podium. Like Ivan Capelli in the Ilmor-powered Leyton House, the hungry-for-success Martin Brundle in the Brabham-Yamaha and Pier-Luigi Martini in the Minardi-Ferrari. It was going to be fascinating to see who came out on top!

Popular evergreen Riccardo Patrese stayed with Frank Williams for his 15th season of Grand Prix racing.

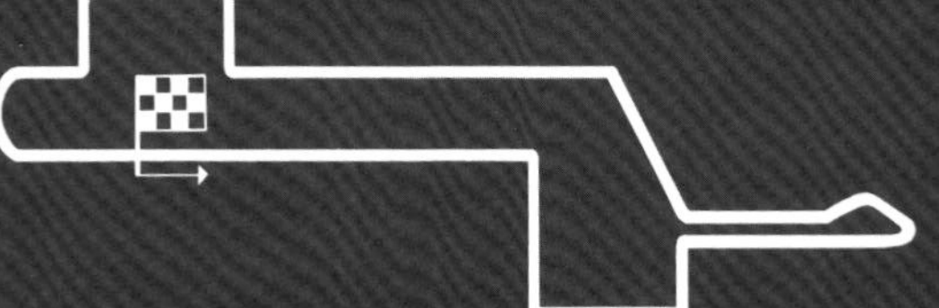

USA

March 10 1991 Circuit: Phoenix

Watching brief. Despite his stated pre-race reservations about the power of Honda's V12, Ayrton Senna was in majestic form in the United States.

Phoenix Arizona was a good place to be during the weekend of March 9/10 1991. After a cold and dreary winter in Europe, the weather was superb, a hot sun burning out of a clear blue sky, and the atmosphere was euphoric. For America was bursting with pride because of the successful conclusion of the Gulf War, which had brought a crushing victory. Her self-respect was restored, the flags were out and her victorious troops were on their way home.

That was the good news. But for the Grand Prix people, there was less joy. Although this was the Arizona desert city's third World Championship race, its concrete-walled street circuit was still a bad joke, even though it had been improved by the elimination of several of its short 'point-and-squirt' straights and right-angled bends. But the track was still unsuitable for 200mph single-seaters, and the city continued to be largely ignorant of and, at best, apathetic about the great sporting contest which was closing some of its streets.

Never mind! Another Grand Prix season was beginning and it promised to be the best we'd had for years. The winter tests, which had raised so many intriguing possibilities, were over. Now we'd see who really was the best! And right away we had a surprise. When

Ayrton Senna and Gerhard Berger had briefly tested the new McLaren MP4/6 at Imola only a week before the car's first race, they hadn't been too complimentary. ''Not enough power,'' they said. In Phoenix, Gerhard revealed that, like the previous year, he still hadn't got room for his feet. With the Ferrari and Williams drivers delighted with their well-tested new cars, the general impression was that this time McLaren really had left it too late and that they'd suffer for doing so. We should have known better.

Senna was fastest in Friday's free practice, just missed taking provisional pole position on Friday (Alesi did so with an edge-of disaster lap in his Ferrari, and achieved his 53rd pole on Saturday with a scintillating 1m 21.434s (102.208 mph) — over a second faster than Prost, who was second on the grid. ''My motivation remains the same,'' said Senna, impressively fit and relaxed after three months away from it all in his beloved Brazil, ''and that is to win every race. With every point counting this year, reliability will be the key to success. Historically that favours McLaren and Ferrari. Our car is much better than last year but it needs development, especially in view of the much improved competition.'' That may have been so, but already it was looking depressingly clear to his rivals in Phoenix that yet another victory for Ayrton was virtually a foregone conclusion.

Behind Senna and Prost, the two Williams-Renaults held row two of the grid with Riccardo Patrese ahead of Nigel Mansell. Riccardo may have been number two in the team, but he certainly wasn't deferring to Nigel and was in very impressive form. Piquet and Alesi were next — Nelson for his first race in a Benetton using Pirelli tyres, and Jean for his race début in a Ferrari, a major responsibility with the eyes of Italy on him. Then came Berger, who had been in pole position in 1990 but was only seventh this time. Behind him was the warming sight of Roberto Moreno (Benetton-Ford) and the two very impressive Dallara-Judd V10s of Emanuele Pirro and JJ Lehto (which had pre-qualified first and second). Martin Brundle was a contented 12th for his return to Grand Prix racing, newcomer Mika Häkkinen a superb 13th in his

''Here Ken. Your horoscope says both your cars will finish in the points.'' Messrs Tyrrell and Ecclestone confer.

Lotus-Judd V8, Bertrand Gachot an excellent 14th for the new Jordan-Ford's first Grand Prix and Mark Blundell qualified 24th for his initial Formula One race. It was going to be interesting, particularly as it seemed unlikely that the race would go the scheduled 82 laps before the two-hour limit was reached.

But, to be honest, there wasn't much interest in the race for the lead because there wasn't one. Phoenix 1991 was another copybook demonstration by Ayrton Senna of how to drive the opposition into the ground. It was not only his 27th Grand Prix win, to equal the second-best-ever record of Jackie Stewart but it was, if my research is correct, his 16th green light-to-chequered flag victory. A brilliant achievement with, doubtless, more to come. No, it was the race for the places that made the day.

As Senna blasted off into the lead at the start, Prost held second ahead of Mansell, Patrese, Alesi and Berger followed by Piquet, Moreno and Modena in the Tyrrell-Honda. On lap one Alesi demoted Patrese to fifth and, by lap ten, Senna was a crushing ten seconds ahead of Prost and looking totally in control. No contest! Patrese was the man to watch. After harrying Alesi for lap after lap he retook fourth on lap 16 and then set about Mansell. On lap 20 he, Prost and Nigel were together. On lap 22 Riccardo dived up the inside of his team leader, overshot the corner and rejoined sixth with Mansell, thanks to a masterful avoidance, retaining his third place. Undaunted by his 'off', Riccardo got his head down and charged. On lap 30 he passed a struggling Berger and closed on Alesi, but sadly neither he nor Mansell had got long to go. For suddenly we had the depressing sight of Nigel waving Alesi and Patrese past on the main straight as his semi-automatic gearbox gave up in its first event. Maybe not altogether unexpected in an unraced car, but a real disappointment. But the inspired Riccardo kept up the pressure. On lap 43 he was up to third behind Prost as Alesi came in for new tyres. Now that *was* unexpected for, before the race, Goodyear's Lee Gaug had firmly predicted that, even on his company's softest D compound, it would be a non-stop race. But it wasn't. Not for Alesi, who rejoined seventh (with Gerhard Berger out of the race on lap 37, due to loss of fuel pressure) and nor for Prost who, on lap 46, came in for a bodged 15.8s tyre stop that demoted him to seventh.

It wasn't one of Ferrari's better days, although the consistent Alain Prost popped up to claim six points for second place.

So on lap 47, six laps over half-distance and with two of the top men out, Senna was leading Patrese (what a fine drive by the veteran, in his 209th GP) by a commanding 32 seconds. More than enough for him to come in for a new set of Goodyears and to rejoin the race without losing his lead. Which is exactly what he did,

TEAM ANALYSIS

McLAREN

Numbers one and two again for the 1990 World Champion team, with virtually untested new Honda V12-powered MP4/6 car. Both drivers critical of ''lack of power'', but Senna still takes pole position (his 53rd) with a typically dominant lap (1m 21.434s, 102.208 mph) over a second faster than next best (Alain Prost). Then drives opposition into ground, leading from start to finish (including lap 48 stop for tyres) to take his 27th Grand Prix victory and equal Jackie Stewart's second-best-ever record. Berger, still troubled by lack of room for his feet, starts seventh for his 100th GP. Climbs to fifth by lap 35, but retires lap 37 with lack of fuel pressure. McLaren and Senna, looking as strong as ever, lead their respective championships by four points despite improved opposition.

TYRRELL

Strengthened team optimistically enters 1991 with Honda V10 engines, greatly increased sponsorship from Braun and Calbee, Shell fuel and Stefano Modena, who takes 11th place on grid. Stefano races ninth, laps 1-35, behind Piquet and Moreno. In points (sixth) on lap 43. Battles with Alesi until Jean's lap 70 retirement. Finishes excellent fourth (full distance). Nakajima starts 16th and climbs steadily to finish praiseworthy fifth (one lap down). Team takes third place in constructors' championship.

WILLIAMS

Very disappointing race after strong performance from both drivers. Mansell starts 150th GP fourth on grid, and races third to Senna and Prost until lap 36 retirement with new semi-automatic gearbox problem. Patrese superb in both practice and race. Starts third ahead of team leader Mansell. Down to fifth lap one but past Alesi to third, lap 43, after Mansell retirement. Second laps 47-49 (Prost tyre stop), but then spins to standstill due to faulty gearbox and is hit heavily by Moreno. So, in season where all points count, both drivers leave without any.

Aguri Suzuki was reminded of the perils of street circuits during practice. In the race, he salvaged a point for Gérard Larrousse's troubled team.

BRABHAM

Martin Brundle happily returns to Grand Prix racing 12th on grid. Mark Blundell starts first GP 24th. Brundle drops from tenth to last, lap nine, with long stop after brushing wall. Soldiers on with fuel pressure and differential problems to finish 11th (eight laps down). Blundell spins on oil, lap 33, when 18th. Hits wall and retires.

FOOTWORK

Ex-Arrows team start 1991 with revised A11C car and Porsche V12 motor. Caffi fails to qualify. Alboreto starts 25th. Stops with brake problem, lap 16. Rejoins but retires from last-but-two, lap 42, with broken gearbox. Badly needed new car scheduled to début at Imola.

LOTUS

Much-changed team delighted when very impressive Mika Häkkinen qualifies 13th for first GP. Mika pits with detached steering wheel, lap eight. Up to 12th lap 50, but retires lap 60 (broken oil union). Julian Bailey fails to qualify due to car problems.

FONDMETAL

Olivier Grouillard fails to pre-qualify old car (''no grip — spun twice!'').

LEYTON HOUSE

A fraught meeting for the new Ilmor-powered team. All three cars sabotaged (cut wiring looms and brake lines) on Friday night. After repairs, Capelli qualifies 18th and Gugelmin 23rd. Neither finishes. Mauricio retires from 15th, lap 35 (gearbox), Ivan from tenth, lap 41 (gearbox oil pump).

AGS

Race-rusty Stefan Johansson mars return by failing to qualify. Gabriele Tarquini does so (22nd), and races well to finish eighth (four laps down).

BENETTON

Using revised 1990 car, now on Pirelli tyres, Nelson Piquet starts fifth with team-mate Roberto Moreno eighth on grid. The two Brazilian friends then race seventh and eighth, chasing Patrese. Up to impressive third and fourth laps 46-50, when Roberto hits Patrese's stalled Williams and retires. Nelson finishes third, only 1.1s behind Prost.

DALLARA

In impressive new Judd V10-powered car, Emanuele Pirro and JJ Lehto pre-qualify first and second before qualifying even more impressive ninth and tenth. Then, sadly, both out of race with transmission problems. Emanuele from tenth, lap 17 (gearbox) and JJ from 18th, lap 13 (clutch).

MINARDI

The new Ferrari-powered, Goodyear-shod car ''is still

Fine start. Bertrand Gachot gave Jordan GP a promising début, challenging for a top six place until his engine blew.

very young'' says Pier-Luigi Martini, after qualifying 15th ahead of team-mate Gianni Morbidelli (26th). Gianni out lap 16 (gearbox) when 18th. Pier-Luigi races strongly up to creditable sixth by lap 73, but drops to ninth when engine blows with six laps to go.

LIGIER
Ponderous looking and overweight car. Comas fails to qualify for first GP, Boutsen only 20th. After damper problems and clutch failure, Thierry retires from distant 12th, lap 41 (engine).

FERRARI
After arriving at Phoenix full of confidence following successful winter testing, Ferrari dismayed by speed of virtually untested new McLaren. Prost qualifies second (but over a second slower than Senna), whilst Alesi (second in 1990, and fastest on Friday) starts sixth for first Ferrari race. Alain increasingly distant second to Senna until bodged 15.8s lap 46 tyre stop. Rejoins seventh. After Patrese/Moreno retirements, passes Modena and then, in one audacious move, Alesi and Piquet to regain second, lap 70. Finishes second for six valuable points. Alesi third by lap 35. Tyre stop lap 43. Second laps 53-68 but retires from fifth lap 73 (gearbox) after setting fastest lap of race (1m 26.758, 95.936 mph).

LARROUSSE-LOLA
Team severely downcast after FISA removes all hard-earned 1990 points, but spirits joyously uplifted when brand new and totally untested Hart-DFR powered car qualifies Eric Bernard 19th and Aguri Suzuki 21st. Bernard out lap five when engine blows but, after early stop to change damaged wheel, Suzuki drives superb race to finish sixth (two laps down), second Japanese driver in top six (Nakajima fifth). Team boss Gérard Larrousse deserves no less after losing Lamborghini engine, major sponsor and being unfairly penalised.

COLONI
At first GP meeting, Portugal's Pedro Chaves drives well in under-sponsored new C4 car with Ford DFR V8 engine. Unsurprisingly fails to pre-qualify after crashing.

JORDAN
Outstanding performance from new team with very impressive Gary Anderson-designed and Ford HB V8-powered car. Andrea de Cesaris distraught when fails to pre-qualify (''I selected second gear from sixth instead of fourth!'') but Bertrand Gachot pre-qualifies fourth and then qualifies 14th. Holds 11th from laps nine to 12 and up to eighth, lap 41. Hits Patrese debris when challenging for sixth, lap 56, and has to stop for tyres. Back to eighth when engine blows, lap 76, but both Bertrand and the team had made their mark...

LAMBORGHINI
All-new team with all-new car. Belgian Eric van de Poele fails to pre-qualify for first GP after suicidal madman lies on track in front of car and, later on, engine blows. But Nicola Larini pre-qualifies third and qualifies 17th. Drives steady race to finish seventh (three laps down), despite gearbox problem and appalling lap 39 tyre stop when right rear wheel jams on.

Thierry Boutsen heads fellow stragglers Gabriele Tarquini and Mauricio Gugelmin, all three about to be swallowed up by the approaching Senna.

Those high-rise blocks contain people who wouldn't recognise a Formula 1 car if it ran between their legs. Nelson Piquet heads for third place (right).

to exit the pit lane 15 seconds ahead of Riccardo's Williams. Would Patrese have lost his second place to Piquet if he'd had to stop for tyres? He certainly would, but that wasn't why Nelson took the place. Unknown to us Riccardo, like Mansell, had been having trouble with his new semi-automatic gearbox. Entering one of the right-angled left-handers on lap 50, it selected neutral — with no command from Riccardo — and then second to spin him to a standstill on the racing line exiting the bend. Piquet just missed the Williams but Moreno didn't. Riding over its nosecone, Roberto was more than lucky that he wasn't injured and Riccardo was even more fortunate, but they were both out of the race as Alesi, jinking left to avoid the debris, shot through into third place ahead of Modena and Prost. Only five cars were on the same lap now, with Senna nearly half a minute ahead of Piquet and a lapped Nakajima sixth in his Tyrrell followed by Bertrand Gachot's Jordan (well done Bert!) and Pier-Luigi Martini's Minardi-Ferrari.

With 31 laps still to go, if the race went the full distance (it didn't), and Senna pacing himself to victory, all eyes were now on the two Ferraris. Alesi, third, was catching Piquet, who was hampered by his choice of too hard a Pirelli compound, and Prost was doing his best to take fourth from Modena. Lap 53 saw Jean up to second with Nelson grimly hanging on; lap 57 saw Alain fourth. Eight laps later the three of them were together and then, on lap 70, we saw again how truly great a driver Alain Prost is. For as Piquet tried to get past a resisting Alesi, Prost opportunistically passed both of them to take second place with 11 laps of what turned out to be an 81-lap race still to go. There was no question of Alain catching Senna, who was nearly 40 seconds ahead, but he was as high as he could have hoped to be and on course for six vital points. Alesi was in trouble though. His previous efforts had gained him the fastest lap of the race (1m 26.758s, 95.936 mph) but now, with a sick and smoking engine, he retired on lap 73, leaving Stefano Modena to move up to fourth ahead of a lapped Nakajima. Martini lost sixth to Suzuki when his Ferrari engine blew.

ONE WAY
ICEBERG
ICEBERG
SANYO
SANYO
Mobil
20

So ended the Phoenix Grand Prix, Senna a magnificent winner in a car which hadn't turned a wheel until it got to Phoenix. Vindication for McLaren and its policy of patiently getting the car right, even if it meant delaying things until the very last moment. Vindication for Honda, who had always said that the new V12 was producing more power than its 1990 V10 and that, for the first race of the year, they always set the engine up for reliability rather than power. A disappointing race for Ferrari who had honestly felt that, at last, they were level with McLaren, and a very disappointing race for Williams, who clearly had work to do on their new gearbox. Benetton wasn't unhappy to have finished third with last year's car, and Tyrrell was naturally delighted to be the only constructor to get both its cars home in the top six. Two Japanese drivers in the points, and Gérard Larrousse was overjoyed to earn a point with his literally untested car — and to finish ahead of his arch-rival Guy Ligier! And hats off to Eddie Jordan's beautifully turned out team, who were on course for seventh and even challenging for sixth until Bertrand Gachot's engine let go with only five laps left.

With Senna winning, Prost second, Piquet third (only a second behind Alain and charging!) and every point to count, 1991 was starting as 1990 had finished. In two weeks' time it was the Brazilian Grand Prix, the race that Senna, who's home is in Sao Paulo, had yet to win and which Prost had won six times. Something to look forward to!

Nicola Larini gave the new Lamborghini team a good start, finishing seventh after surviving the rigours of pre-qualifying.

BRAZIL

March 23 1991 Circuit: Interlagos

At the start of a dramatic afternoon, Senna leads the Williams twins, team-mate Berger and the disappointing Ferraris into the first turn.

The city of Sao Paulo rejoined the Grand Prix scene last year — and the visitors didn't like it. In 1991, the second time around, they didn't like it any better. Whilst the financial chaos of 1990 had been largely eliminated, the city hadn't improved — and nor had the weather. There were strikes, there were power cuts. The ambiance of industrialised and crowded Sao Paulo, with its deprivation, shanty towns and solid traffic jams, was as depressing and unsettling as before, and now there were floods. But the superb, rebuilt circuit was just as impressive. Even in the rain, and there was more than enough of that. On Friday the track wasn't just wet — there were rivers across it.

Never were we allowed to forget that Sao Paulo is Ayrton Senna's patch. It's his home town, and he's even more of a mega-hero here than he is in the rest of Brazil. Each and every Paulista was as hungry for their idol to win his first home GP as Ayrton was himself. For, in seven years of trying — Toleman in 1984, Lotus from '85 to '87 and McLaren from '88 to '90 — victory in Brazil, the one he wanted to win more than all the rest, had escaped him. After his crushing win in Phoenix, Ayrton's confidence and resolve at Interlagos were total. Fastest on Friday's damp track for the provisional pole, fastest in the dry on Saturday for his 54th pole position (almost a second faster than his 1990 pole time), but only fourth fastest during Sunday morning's half-hour final practice. So what went wrong?

Nigel Mansell, Riccardo Patrese and Alain Prost were Ayrton's problems for what promised to be a close and exciting race. The two Williams drivers, after post-Phoenix testing to eliminate the semi-automatic gearbox gremlins, had been right on the pace in qualifying. Riccardo had again been faster than Nigel, and they were second and third on the grid with times very close to Senna's. Berger, Alesi and Prost were next up. On Sunday morning both the Williams men, first and third, and Prost were faster than Senna. So was Prost, six times a winner in Brazil, going to drive another of his tactical races to victory? Would his Phoenix belief, that the Ferrari would be much better at Interlagos, be justified in spite of the handling problems? Could Mansell and Patrese challenge Senna? Would the subdued Gerhard Berger rise to the occasion against his dominant team-mate? Those were the questions which surrounded the battle to come. No one else seemed to have a realistic chance of winning. Piquet's Benetton B190, seventh on the grid, was about to start its last race and Modena's Tyrrell-Honda, ninth behind Mauricio Gugelmin's vastly improved Leyton House-Ilmor, was 2.5 seconds slower than Senna. There was a final question though, one which could affect everyone. What was the weather going to do?

FISA chose Brazil to demonstrate its new warning flag signal.

It was dull and overcast when the green light started the 71-lap race. Rain had fallen, and was threatening to return, but the track was dry as Senna, willed on by the collective fervour of his ecstatic countrymen, made a perfect start to lead a close-running Mansell, Patrese, Alesi, Berger and Piquet (ahead of Prost). On lap eight, Ayrton headed Nigel by 2.8s and was 7.5s in front of Patrese. But even so it didn't look like another Senna benefit. Nigel was pressing incredibly hard (''I was having to drive much faster than I wanted to'' said Senna), and from then on the gap started to close. On lap 17 Mansell had halved it — down to 1.4s. On lap 20 he halved it again — 0.7s — looking calm, steady and supremely confident. His Williams-Renault was clearly every bit as good as Ayrton's McLaren. Patrese comfortably held third ahead of Alesi with Berger, whose McLaren had caught fire at the start and then extinguished itself, fifth and Piquet sixth. Alain Prost was still a frustrated seventh and on lap 17, unable to pass Nelson's Benetton, he decided to stop for new tyres, hoping to benefit from an early change. Rejoining 11th he didn't look much of a threat, but there was a long way to go. Alain was now on fresh rubber, and the others had still got to make the one stop that Goodyear had predicted.

It didn't work out that way though. Tyre stops were to shape the race. On lap 26, in came Mansell for his new Goodyears. The change

Nigel Mansell gave one of the tigering performances for which he is renowned, and might have profited from Senna's gearbox problems had he not had some of his own.

was good, but the stop was terrible. After 14.6 seconds, nearly half of which was spent fishing for first gear, Nigel was back in the race but down in fourth place, chasing Patrese and Alesi and followed by Berger, Piquet, Prost (still behind Nelson) and Moreno. Senna's wafer-thin lead of less than a second over Mansell had grown to over 20 ahead of Patrese. But where there's a will there's a way, and Nigel's never been short of will power! On lap 29, after both Senna and Patrese had stopped for tyres (Senna for a mere 6.93s, without losing his lead), Nigel was second once more — 7.2s behind the leading McLaren. And now he attacked again brilliantly.

On lap 34, the gap was 6.8s. On lap 37, 5.7s. On lap 42 it was down again — to just 2.9s. And things were humming behind Nigel too. Patrese was back to third, after losing the place to Piquet when he stopped for tyres. Nelson was fourth (without a stop), Berger fifth, Alesi sixth and Prost still only seventh after a second tyre stop. When Alesi stopped again too, it was clear that Brazil '91 was not going to see another Maranello win unless something very strange happened. But what chances of Williams being victorious? Ten of the 26 starters were out, but there seemed no doubt that Mansell would catch Senna. When he did though, would he be able to pass? At Interlagos, of all places, Senna wouldn't make it easy! But sadly Nigel never got the chance to try. On lap 50, with the gap now increased to 8.5s as Senna put the hammer down, in came the Williams again for a third set of tyres. Wear wasn't the problem this time. It was a puncture caused by debris; this second stop put Nigel a massive 35s behind the Brazilian. But, nothing daunted, he just put his head down and charged again.

TEAM ANALYSIS

McLAREN

A lucky race for the team and both its drivers. At his home circuit, where he had yet to win, Ayrton Senna again takes pole position (his 54th). Leads race, continually challenged by Nigel Mansell's Williams. Senna stops for tyres lap 26 without losing lead. After Mansell's lap 60 retirement, Patrese (Williams) closes on Ayrton, who is hobbled by inability to select third, fourth and fifth gears. Exhausted Senna hangs on to win his first Brazilian GP by only three seconds. With 28 wins, now second only to Prost in all-time success ranking and leads Alain in '91 championship by commanding 11 points. Berger qualifies third and races fifth after flash fire puts itself out following start. Passes Piquet to fourth, lap 46, and benefits from Mansell retirement to finish third only two seconds behind Patrese — despite sticking throttle. With three top-three finishes from four 1991 starts, McLaren already leads constructors' championship by a healthy 14 points to confirm Senna's Phoenix statement that "this year will be all about reliability."

TYRRELL

Brazil reverses team's Phoenix euphoria. Modena qualifies ninth, Nakajima 16th. Satoru spins out of race on lap 13 ("my fault"). Stefano up to seventh, lap 18, but retires, lap 20, with broken gear linkage (after destroying tub in practice).

WILLIAMS

Team fully competitive, after post-Phoenix testing by Damon Hill apparently nails semi-automatic gearbox's self-changing habit. Mansell third on grid, one place behind team-mate Patrese (again), but rockets past Riccardo at start to harry Senna until lap 25, when problematic stop (gearbox) drops him to fourth. Magnificently fights back to within three seconds of Ayrton but then, lap 51, has to stop again with cut tyre. Reduces 35s lead to 19s on lap 59, only to have gearbox lock up and force retirement — like Phoenix. Some consolation is fact that he sets fastest lap of race (1m 20.436s, 120.278 mph). Patrese, now second, thrillingly cuts gearbox-troubled Senna's 40s lead to 2.9s at end of race, but is unable to press hard enough to win due to sick gearbox missing downchanges. But superb Riccardo finishes second in his 210th GP, after he and Nigel show that Williams can live with McLaren — but need reliability.

BRABHAM

Demonstrating that their car is indeed "too old, too heavy, has too much drag and is under-powered", Mark Blundell qualifies 25th whilst Martin Brundle just scrapes in 26th. Mark retires from 15th, lap 37 (engine). With severe leg cramp, Martin is classified 12th, four laps down. Both eagerly look forward to new car at Imola.

FOOTWORK

In old car, with very disappointing, overweight Porsche V12, neither Alboreto nor Caffi ever look like qualifying — and don't.

LOTUS

Just like Phoenix, Häkkinen shines and Bailey has no luck. After impressing in Friday's wet practice, Julian has car problems on Saturday and, with no spare, fails to qualify in Mika's Lotus. Youngest driver (22) Häkkinen gets in 22nd, and then emphasises that he is a star in the making by driving intelligent and determined race to his first GP

Alex Caffi surveys the timing screens with an air of resignation. Neither Footwork-Porsche made the race.

European F3000 Champion Erik Comas made his F1 race début, though an oil fire put him out.

finish, taking ninth place (three laps down) and, incredibly, ninth fastest lap.

FONDMETAL

Olivier Grouillard pre-qualifying well in interim car until suspension breakage forces him into old chassis, in which he fails to make top four.

LEYTON HOUSE

In car which "is getting better and better as we build up the miles", Mauricio Gugelmin qualifies an excellent and heartening eighth. Capelli an even more impressive seventh on Friday but drops to 15th on Saturday with gearbox and set-up problems. Gugelmin receives chemical burns when cockpit fire extinguisher explodes in Sunday warm-up. Passed fit to race but, in severe pain, retires from home race in ninth place, lap eight. Ivan up to 13th, lap 12, but then retires, lap 18 (engine). But things getting better for team after awful 1989 and '90 seasons.

AGS

Financially hard-pressed team doubtful about its ability to carry on after Brazil. Tarquini qualifies 24th but Johansson, with excessive oversteer, again fails to make race. Disheartened team's depression increased when Gabriele locks rear brake and hits barrier on first lap.

BENETTON

Last race for Benetton's two Brazilians in reliable but outmoded B190. Piquet qualifies well in seventh as top V8 and top Pirelli driver. Moreno, unable to balance car properly, starts 14th. Nelson sixth laps 1-27. Then third laps 32-33. Down to fourth with clutch problem until too-late lap 47 tyre stop. Finishes satisfied fifth to remain third in championship. Roberto, inhibited by clutch problem and understeer, steadily improves to finish seventh (one lap down). New B191 to race at Imola.

DALLARA

Lehto and Pirro, first and fourth in pre-qualifying, start 19th and 12th. Emanuele, nerfed on to grass after start, pits for new nose before rejoining to finish 11th, three laps down. JJ gains five places on lap one before dropping to 16th; 13th laps 21-22 but retires lap 23 (alternator).

MINARDI

Both Martini and Morbidelli, using 1989 Ferrari V12 engine (not expected 1990 version), plagued by clutch and gearchange problems. Pier-Luigi qualifies unhappy 20th just ahead of Gianni. Martini spins over kerbing when tenth, lap 46, and cannot restart. Morbidelli finishes eighth, minus third and fourth gears and two laps. Team strapped for money.

LIGIER

Boutsen, unhappy with rotund car, 18th on grid. Comas qualifies 23rd for first GP. Miserable Thierry staggers round, mostly on ten cylinders, with "no clutch, low oil pressure, bad brakes and no grip" to finish tenth (three laps down). Comas retires from 11th, lap 51, with oil cooler fire after mounting kerb. Unlike several other teams, no new car for Imola.

FERRARI

"Phoenix doesn't suit the car but Brazil will," said Ferrari. It didn't. With the 642 failing to get best from qualifying tyres, Prost and Alesi fourth and fifth on grid. Jean runs fourth before lap 28 tyre stop. Down to fifth and then eighth after second tyre stop. Finishes sixth for first 1991 point. Alain makes first tyre stop, lap 17, after shadowing sixth-placed Piquet. Finishes fourth after second tyre stop, lap 39. With points in both first two races, still second in championship but now 11 points behind Senna. Ferrari second in constructors' contest, but 14 points behind McLaren. "We'll have a modified car with better engine and aerodynamics at Imola."

LARROUSSE-LOLA

Gérard Larrousse's team, like AGS, almost terminally short of money and fearful of future. But, heartened after Phoenix point, further delighted when both Bernard, 11th, and Suzuki, 17th, outqualify both arch-rival Ligiers. Nimble and fast car excellent, but luck terrible. Suzuki fails even to start when fuel pump breaks on starting grid. Eric Bernard retires from tenth, scrapping with Gachot, when clutch hydraulic pipe breaks on lap 34. Team now in desperate state.

COLONI

Pedro Chaves fails to pre-qualify.

JORDAN

Another excellent performance by most impressive new team fails to reap reward. After pre-qualifying second and third, Andrea de Cesaris and Bertrand Gachot 13th and excellent tenth on grid. Andrea retires from eighth, lap 21 (engine electronics). Bertrand up to seventh by lap 20 but down to 11th after lap 28 tyre stop. Retires from eighth, lap 64, with split exhaust pipe, fuel pick-up problem and excessive vibration.

LAMBORGHINI

Neither van de Poele (fifth) nor Larini (sixth) pre-qualifies.

With 21 laps to go, Senna was on target for his first win in Brazil. Mansell lay second, Patrese third (now only six seconds behind his team leader after that second stop), Berger fourth, Prost fifth and gaining, Piquet sixth and realising that he should have stopped for new Pirellis. Alesi was seventh and a lapped Moreno eighth. With a lead of 35 seconds, it seemed that Senna was safe even from a Mansell in such superb form, but how Nigel tried!

It was at this point in a truly gripping race that the mechanical emphasis turned from tyres to gearboxes. For, unknown to the onlookers, Senna had lost fourth gear and Mansell was about to suffer a repeat of his Phoenix débâcle. Having nearly halved Ayrton's 35-second lead on lap 59, and having set fastest lap of the race (1m 20.436s, 120.278 mph), Nigel would undoubtedly have won if he'd been able to keep going, because Senna's gearbox was now disintegrating. 'If' is a big word in motor racing though, and it was Mansell's 'box that gave up first — on lap 60. Capriciously, it went down to first instead of fourth, and round spun the Williams. Nigel got going again, but only for a few yards before it became clear that there was no transmission left. Bitter luck which, for the second race in succession, had denied him the chance of a podium finish.

So respite for Senna? Not at all! Ayrton was soon to be in real trouble. With Mansell out and 12 laps to go he led Patrese by a very reassuring 40 seconds — which rapidly declined. Because seven laps from the end of the race "my gearbox went completely crazy." Losing fourth may not have been all that much of a disadvantage, but when it started to rain heavily and fifth and third went missing too, Senna could see his Brazilian jinx striking again. "I changed my line and stayed in sixth, but in the medium and slow-speed corners it was a disaster. Several times I nearly stalled." And all the while a charging Patrese was getting closer, with visions of a fourth Grand Prix win from his record 210 World Championship starts. With four laps to go, Riccardo was within ten seconds of Ayrton and gaining at the rate of four seconds a lap. So why didn't he win? Because he too

Levity at Jordan. Gachot and de Cesaris were starting to make the 191 chassis look really good.

At last! It had taken a long time, but Ayrton Senna's first F1 win on home soil meant an awful lot (right).

had a dodgy gearbox! "I could see that Ayrton had got a problem, but changing down I was missing gears. I was thinking of what to do, but I really had no choice if I was to finish."

So an exhausted Ayrton Senna, racked with cramp and having to be lifted out of his car, finally won the Brazilian Grand Prix. He finished a mere 2.9 seconds ahead of Patrese, whilst Riccardo was only two seconds clear of Berger, struggling to cope with a sticking throttle. Five seconds thus covered the first three home with Prost fourth, Piquet fifth, Alesi sixth and a lapped Moreno seventh. McLaren, Ferrari and Benetton had got both their cars home, but although the two McLarens had been in poor shape, they were the ones who had the best combination of speed and reliability. And, as Senna had said, reliability was going to win the championship in 1991.

Brazil had seen a thrilling and ever-changing battle at the front, which had tended to distract attention from a lot of very worthy efforts behind. Bertrand Gachot, for instance, again drove an excellent race in his Jordan-Ford. After starting tenth, he had to retire from a certain eighth place with only six laps to go, suffering from fuel starvation. Mika Häkkinen again impressed enormously by bringing his Lotus-Judd home in ninth place, and posting ninth fastest lap. Emanuele Pirro finished 11th in his Dallara-Judd V10, despite having to stop for a new nosecone after he'd been punted off at the first corner. And Eric Bernard proved that the Lola-Hart DFR was a much better car than the 1990 Lola-Lamborghini V12, by battling with Gachot for ninth place until he had to retire.

Now the teams had five weeks to get themselves organised for the first of the European races, the San Marino Grand Prix at Imola. Senna and McLaren had commanding leads in the two championships, but everyone had got a lot to do. Williams and McLaren needed to bullet-proof their gearboxes; Ferrari had got to improve its car; Benetton, Footwork and Brabham had to race-ready their new cars. The competition would be hotter still in Italy.

Out of luck. Eric Bernard's stricken Lola gets a foam shower.

SAN MARINO

April 28 1991 Circuit: Imola

On a disastrous day for Italy, Jean Alesi was the most successful Ferrari driver. He didn't crash until lap three...

There are still people who maintain, contrary to the facts, that the World Championship season doesn't "really" start until the first European race at Imola. They say America and Brazil are, in effect, extensions of the previous season, that the teams can't test there, that some of them haven't got their new cars ready, that they're thousands of miles from their bases and that the long, five-week gap between Interlagos and Imola disrupts the championship.

They may have had some illogical justification for their view in the past, but not this year! The revised scoring system, with every points result counting, instead of the best 11 out of a possible 16, meant that Ayrton Senna's wins at both 1991's first two races had given him an immense advantage in the championship. And that was because McLaren had got its act together better than all its rivals — as usual. Williams had what was potentially the best car, but its unreliable semi-automatic gearbox had already caused three retirements from four starts. Ferrari, according to Alain Prost, had had a "crisis of confidence" over the winter and was in its usual state of internal warfare. Benetton was only introducing its new car at Imola, Tyrrell hadn't yet shown the form that was expected of them and the rest clearly weren't in it as far as World Championship success was concerned. There was a lot of catching up to be done.

When the first qualifying session began on Friday afternoon it was cold, overcast and rain was threatening. So, knowing dry track time could be limited and that it might be even worse on Saturday, everyone rushed out early to get a good time. Half an hour later it was the popular veteran Riccardo Patrese who held the provisional pole, with a searing lap in 1m 21.957s — the fastest ever at Imola. In the remaining 30 minutes only one man went faster. It was, inevitably, Ayrton Senna, but his time was only 0.08s quicker than Riccardo's. ''More to come tomorrow, with today's rubber on the track,'' said Ayrton — but he was so wrong!

On Saturday we were filled with gloom. It was wet for the morning's free practice (in which Mika Häkkinen was, sensationally, third fastest in his Lotus), and when final qualifying began the track was still wet. And that's the way it stayed, leaving Friday's times to decide the grid. So Senna was in his 55th pole position ahead of Patrese, Prost, Mansell (the Williams had thus gone very well), Berger, Modena, Alesi, Morbidelli and Martini (their Minardis benefiting from improved aerodynamics and Agip's 'rocket' fuel).

Riccardo Patrese became the first man other than Senna to have led a race in 1991.

To our delight, it was a different story on Sunday. Clear blue skies, bright sunshine and the temperature well up. There's always a four-hour gap between the end of the morning's final half-hour of practice and the start of the race, to allow any teams who may have a problem to put it right. And in those four hours the weather steadily deteriorated. At 13.30, with half an hour to go, we were back to the overcast gloom of the previous two days and then it began to rain. Rain? Deluge more like it — it bucketed down before it stopped with, quite clearly, better conditions on the way.

So what tyres to fit? Wets, to make the most of a track that was currently almost awash in places? Or slicks, in the hope that the track would dry out quickly? But everyone's mind was made up for them when another downpour made wets essential. Off they set for the parade lap, all on grooved rubber, and at the end of it there was uproar. Alain Prost slid off, lost control of his Ferrari on the wet grass and stalled his engine as the rest of the field were already forming up on the grid! Gerhard Berger did the same thing at the same place, but was lucky enough to get away with it.

So the San Marino Grand Prix started without the man who had won it twice, and at the end of the lap another past winner was out — Nigel Mansell! He had faltered at the start when, yet again, his gearbox let him down by refusing to select second. After getting going in ninth place, he was rammed by Martin Brundle's Brabham. ''His fault,'' said Nigel. ''No it wasn't — it was his,'' said Martin. Nothing changes!

But if there wasn't a Ferrari in the lead, the partisan crowd had got the next best thing to cheer. Their countryman Riccardo Patrese was not only in front, but pulling away from Senna — who had a big gap behind him to Modena,

Cruel luck. Belgian Eric van de Poele drove magnificently in his first GP, only for his fuel pump to expire on the last lap when he looked set to finish fifth.

Berger, Alesi, Morbidelli and Martini. Riccardo, who'd won in 1990, was in devastating form as, on lap two, out of the race slid Nelson Piquet. Then, to fill the *Tifosi's* cup of misery to overflowing, Jean Alesi did the same thing whilst trying a banzai passing move on Stefano Modena. "I knew my limitations," said Stefano "but he obviously didn't know his."

On, lap three, with four potential winners already missing, Patrese, driving swiftly, steadily and safely, led Senna by over three seconds — going away. It was the first time that Ayrton had been headed in 1991. Well done Riccardo! But he didn't stay there long. With Gerhard Berger up to third past Modena, and the track beginning to dry out, into the pits came Patrese and into the lead went Senna who, from over six seconds behind, had closed right up on the Italian. But what we thought was a courageously early stop to switch to slicks, even though the track was still very wet in places, turned out to be more than that. Riccardo had a misfire caused by a faulty camshaft sensor, and it took a long time to correct it. With his chances of a second successive win at Imola gone, he charged out again only to retire from last place nine laps later — but with the consolation of having set the fastest lap so far.

TEAM ANALYSIS

McLAREN

A crushing victory — greatly helped by their main rivals shooting themselves in the foot. Using new high-torque Honda V12 engine, Senna takes his 55th pole position during Friday's dry qualifying session and then, after running second to Patrese for the first nine laps, goes on to win his 29th Grand Prix, despite failing oil pressure. As first man ever to win all first three races, now leads championship by massive 20 points. Berger slides off course on parade lap, but recovers to start from correct fifth place on grid. Second by lap ten, after passing Modena and Patrese's retirement. Despite brake problems, catches slowing Senna in closing stages to finish second, only 1.7s adrift. Sets fastest lap of race (1m 26.531s, 130.29 mph) and moves up to second in championship. Both drivers lap everyone else; McLaren achieves first one-two since Belgium 1989 to lead constructors' championship by demoralising 30 points.

TYRRELL

Modena and Nakajima qualify well, sixth and tenth (top two on Pirelli tyres). Satoru gutsy fourth in Saturday's river-like conditions. Both in top four by lap ten — Modena third and Naka fourth. Nakajima out lap 16 (transmission). Stefano holds third until lap 42 retirement (transmission), after controversially blocking Senna's lap 35 attempt to lap him.

WILLIAMS

After encouraging Imola tests, team confident that semi-automatic gearbox problem has been nailed — but it returns in practice. Nevertheless, Patrese qualifies impressive second fastest only slower than Senna. Flu-stricken Nigel, baulked on fast lap, starts fourth. Mansell gearbox misses change at start and car falters. Nigel then hit by Brundle at end of lap and retires instantly with left rear puncture and suspension damage. Not best pleased with third successive failure to finish. Evergreen Riccardo storms into lead. Increases it to over six seconds, but pits on lap ten with misfire problem. Rejoins but retires from charging last (lap 18, camshaft sensor). Super car still marred by gearbox weakness.

BRABHAM

Début of all-new but almost completely untested B60Y. Brundle qualifies 18th and Blundell 23rd — both good efforts in difficult circumstances. Martin makes rocket start in deluge conditions and is up to tenth on lap one when he hits Mansell's Williams. Loses two laps in pits for new nosecone. Rejoins last but soldiers on to finish 11th, four laps down. Blundell drives excellent race to eighth place (three laps down) for his first Grand Prix finish, despite gearbox problem which necessitates holding lever in gear on corners.

FOOTWORK

After destroying all-new FA12 car in testing, a very part-worn Michele Alboreto (leg and rib injuries) understandably fails to qualify old A11C. Caffi fails to qualify second, just-finished new car, but team confident that post-Imola testing will get FA12 on the pace.

LOTUS

A marvellous race result gives hard-pressed team much needed boost, following the tragic death of mechanic David Jacques from a pre-race accident. After being sensationally quick in Saturday's slopping wet free practice — third fastest — Mika Häkkinen qualifies 25th whilst Julian Bailey gets in 26th for his first Lotus race. In much modified car (suspension, bodywork, airbox and brakes), both have superb race. Bailey in points at sixth lap 14, having gained 20 places. Makes second unplanned stop to remove brake duct tape and is caught and passed by Mika, after which the two duel together to end of race. Both finish in points, with Häkkinen fifth and

Stefan Johansson's place at AGS went to Italian F3000 graduate (and former Indycar racer) Fabrizio Barbazza. He couldn't qualify the JH25 either.

Bailey sixth (three laps down) less than a second apart. a magnificent achievement that gives team new heart.

FONDMETAL
Olivier Grouillard débuts Fomet 1 car but, with multitude of 'new car' problems, is unable to pre-qualify. ''I'm very happy with it though.''

LEYTON HOUSE
Following further management upheaval, Gugelmin and Capelli qualify revised car 15th and 22nd. Mauricio hits Gachot's Jordan debris on lap three and pits for repairs. Climbs to ninth on lap 55 but then retires (lap 56, engine). Capelli reaches fine fifth place on lap 16 after well-judged tyre stop. Still fifth on lap 25, has rear left puncture and spins out of race.

AGS
With new owners after financial collapse, team elbows Stefan Johansson (''not bothered'') and replaces him with ex-Indy racer Fabrizio Barbazza. Neither he nor Tarquini qualifies, but team now hopes to introduce new JH26 car.

BENETTON
New, but virtually untested, B191 introduced with further revised Ford V8. Several all-nighters for mechanics at Imola. Gear selection problems inhibit Moreno and Piquet, who qualify 13th and 14th. Nelson slides off on lap two and retires. Roberto races to fourth by lap 16. Up to third laps 42-51 (albeit lapped by Senna on lap 22) but, after losing three of his six gears, over-revs engine and finishes 13th (seven laps down). Team delighted with car which ''has enormous potential.''

DALLARA
Mixed fortunes in pre-qualifying. Emanuele Pirro fails and JJ Lehto just succeeds. Then things really look up! After shining in Saturday's wet conditions, JJ qualifies 16th and is sixth on lap 22. Driving ''steadily to make sure'' he moves to fifth, to fourth and then to an amazing third on lap 43. Stays there (only one lap down) for ''the happiest day of my life'' to give Dallara its first points since Canada 1989 and, almost certainly, to get them out of pre-qualifying after the British GP.

MINARDI
Revised aerodynamics and Agip 'rocket' fuel result in excellent eighth and ninth places on the grid for Gianni Morbidelli (highest yet) and Pier-Luigi Martini. Morbidelli out on lap 11 (gearbox), but Pier-Luigi in great form. Fifth by lap ten and again, lap 42, after tyre stop. Gives team first points since Australia 1989 by finishing fourth (two laps down), and hopefully enables it to avoid post-British GP pre-qualifying.

LIGIER
Enforced mass exodus of engineering staff after Brazil. In tubby car, Comas starts 19th and Boutsen 24th. Thierry finishes seventh, three laps down, after three stops for tyres. Eric tenth, minus four laps, after hastily switching to Boutsen's spare car when his own catches fire on parade lap.

The Benetton B191 made its début, but not for long in Nelson Piquet's case.

FERRARI
An unmitigated disaster for the Maranello team on its home ground, following excellent pre-race testing at Imola where Prost was fastest. Alain third on grid but loses car at end of wet parade lap and slides off track. With stalled engine, is out before the start! From an unimpressive (for him) seventh on the grid, Alesi then fails in gung-ho effort to take fourth from Modena on lap three and similarly slides out of contention. The atmosphere at Maranello was fraught enough already....

LARROUSSE-LOLA
A new sponsor (Orangina) and new Brian Hart narrow valve-angle cylinder heads for the Ford DFR engines. Bernard starts 17th and Suzuki 20th. Aguri out after only two laps after sliding off. Eric retires, lap 18, when 13th (engine). Hard pressed team hopes for better things at Monaco, where its nimble car is expected to go well.

COLONI
Pedro Chaves again fails to pre-qualify (broken gearbox).

JORDAN
De Cesaris and Gachot easily pre-qualify — first and third — and go on to qualify 11th and 12th. Andrea retires from fine sixth place after lap 14 tyre stop (broken gear linkage). After two damaging spins and three tyre stops, Gachot retires from 16th and last, lap 38.

LAMBORGHINI
Larini fails to pre-quality. Eric van de Poele not only does so, but qualifies 21st for his first GP. In brilliant drive, up to seventh by lap 14. Sixth on lap 42 after tyre stop. Then fifth laps 55-57 before sadly stopping with broken fuel pump. Classified ninth, four laps down.

The excitement was maintained though, for now Berger was catching Senna. Lapping one and a half seconds quicker than his McLaren team-mate, he cut the gap to less than five seconds with Modena third and Nakajima a superb fourth after passing the two Minardis. Behind them the two Lotus drivers were making their mark, with Bailey 11th and Häkkinen 15th — up from 26th and 25th. And then the tyre stops began, Berger on lap 14 and Senna a lap later. They were both typically slick and efficient McLaren stops (6.4 and 7.4 seconds), and Senna rejoined without losing his lead. But Berger was only five seconds behind the Brazilian — and gaining! On lap 15 he was within 1.4s of Ayrton, and it really looked as though we'd got a race on our hands. On lap 16 the gap was down to a second as Gerhard set a new fastest lap of the race. Great stuff! Then, with Senna disposing of the traffic in his usual masterly way, Gerhard was held up by a squabble between Gugelmin, Bailey and Boutsen. Not for long, but long enough.

Honda powered cars — McLaren and Tyrrell — held the first four places for six glorious laps and on lap 14 Julian Bailey, driving brilliantly in his first GP since Japan 1988, displaced Andrea de Cesaris's Jordan from sixth place. In the points! Nakajima retired from a fine drive on lap 16 (transmission), and by now the two McLarens were over a minute ahead of Stefano Modena. Time to look down the field a bit, for it was very different from usual. Moreno fourth, Capelli fifth and Boutsen sixth.

Poor Ivan Capelli, driving for Leyton House who desperately required a good finish, spun out of the race to be replaced by an inspired JJ Lehto, whose Dallara team needed points just as much. Then as a hapless Modena retired from third (transmission again) and a long-since lapped Roberto Moreno moved up, so too did Lehto — to fourth — with van de Poele's Lamborghini sixth in his first Grand Prix, behind Martini. This really was different!

The surprises weren't over yet though. Moreno retired on lap 52 (gearbox) which

Julian Bailey drove quite splendidly in the wet, and was still around when the track dried out to bag a point. He might have finished better than sixth but for a late unscheduled pit stop.

All pals together. Berger, Senna and first-time rostrum visitor JJ Lehto celebrate on the podium (right). At Imola, the Brazilian became the first man to win the opening three rounds of a World Championship season.

GOODYEAR
GOODYEAR
PIRELLI
Shell
BOSS
Marlboro
HONDA
Gerhard Berger
stand21
Shell
BOSS
MEN'S FASHION
Marlboro
McLAREN INTERNATIONAL
HONDA
NACIONAL
Ayrton
Senna
FINECO
Marlboro
WORLD CHAMPIONSHIP
PIRELLI
FINECO
stand21

advanced Lehto to third, Martini to fourth, the superb van de Poele to fifth and Bailey back to sixth — with Lotus team-mate Mika Häkkinen right behind him! And Berger was catching Senna. For just as we'd been ignorant of the fact that Ayrton had a major gearbox problem in Brazil, we were equally oblivious to the fact that, at Imola, the Brazilian's oil pressure light had been telling him for some time that his special high-torque Honda V12 wasn't feeling well. Closer and closer came Gerhard until, with a series of charging laps, one of which was the fastest of the race and a new Imola record (1m 26.531s, 130.29 mph), Senna's lead was down to 2.6 seconds as the last lap started.

Senna hung on to win though. His 29th Grand Prix victory, only 1.7s ahead of Gerhard, had been close, but it was enough. Only he and Berger went the full distance — a devastating achievement — with an overjoyed JJ Lehto, a lap adrift, achieving his first points with a place on the podium. Minardi, who like Dallara had failed to score a single point in 1990, was equally happy that Pier-Luigi Martini finished an excellent fourth. But neither of the Italian teams was as happy as Lotus, for whom Mika Häkkinen and Julian Bailey both finished in the points, fifth and sixth thanks to a charging last three laps by the Finn. Some consolation for a very sad team, one of whose mechanics, David Jacques, had tragically died after a fall in his hotel at Imola during the previous week's testing. Finally, in a meeting rich with emotion, the Lamborghini team went home in a state of frustrated gloom, after Eric van de Poele's fine drive to a certain fifth was terminated when his fuel pump broke on his very last lap.

Senna's victory made him the first driver in the history of the World Championship to win all of a season's first three races. With his dominance, allied to the superiority of his McLaren team which now had four times as many points as Ferrari in the constructors' championship, it was possible to see him winning the season's remaining 13 races on his way to a third World Championship.

Victory at Monaco in two weeks would be his third win in succession at the Principality, but maybe the opposition would be organised by then. Maybe...

The whole F1 paddock was delighted to see Alessandro Nannini doing the rounds. The former Benetton driver (centre) is making a good recovery from horrific arm injuries sustained in a helicopter accident, and hopes to return one day to the cockpit.

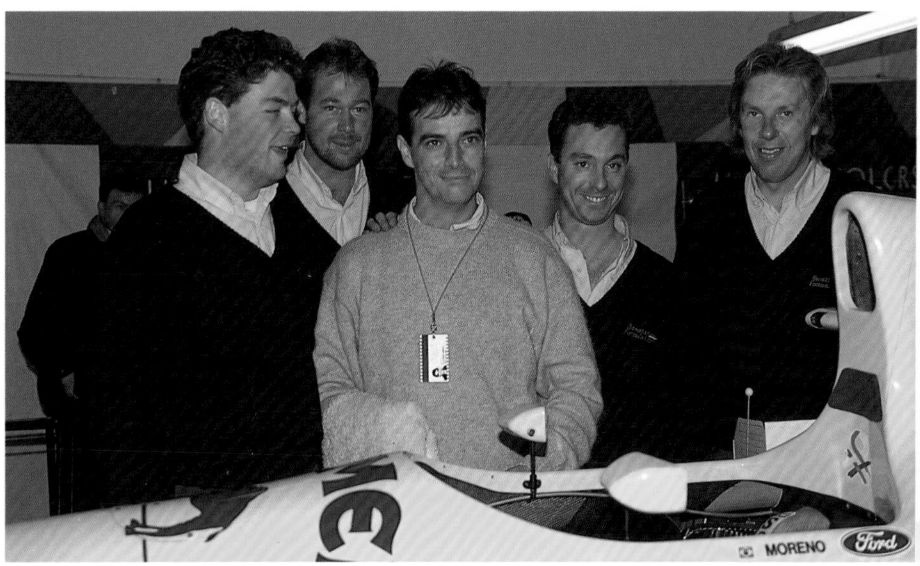

MONACO

May 12 1991 Circuit: Monte Carlo

Avoid the traffic queues: buy a yacht. On second thoughts, the roads are probably quieter than Monaco harbour at GP time.

There was something different about Monaco this year, but it wasn't the Principality. That was just the same as it had always been. The same squeaky clean streets and buildings, the same immaculate gardens, the same atmosphere of extreme wealth. The same casino, five-star hotels, mind-bendingly expensive shops and restaurants. The same fabulous yachts crowding every inch of the quays. The same profusion of Ferraris, Lamborghinis and other stunning cars. The same seductive girls who looked as though they'd stepped straight out of the pages of a fashion magazine. None of those were different. It was the sunshine. There wasn't any. Overhead, the sky was dull, leaden and threatening. There was a cold wind which made anoraks more than welcome and, during the first two days, there was rain. For the people who have to work there — the drivers, their teams and the media — Monaco, with its extreme congestion, totally inadequate pit and paddock facilities and its exhausting need to spend seemingly the whole day walking uphill, is demanding at the best of times. This year's gloomy conditions made it even more so than usual!

Four out of four. Another crushing display from Senna created a record that is unlikely to be matched for a long, long time.

But despite all that, Monaco's charismatic atmosphere overcame its drawbacks. For nowhere else can you get so close to the action. Nowhere else can you hear the sounds so loud. Nowhere else can you appreciate so well just what supermen the drivers are, as they rocket round the twisting, turning, rising and falling armco-lined 2.1-mile lap at an average of some 90 miles per hour. To watch the superstars exiting corners with the power hard on, brushing the barriers with their tyre sidewalls, knowing that to stray a fraction of an inch off line can lead to disaster, is truly awe-inspiring.

So never mind the weather. Enjoy the experience, because the weather forecast says Sunday is going to be OK and nowhere else is the Grand Prix social life so good!

At every Grand Prix, a good grid position is an enormous bonus. At Monaco it is absolutely essential. The track is so narrow and twisty that passing, without co-operation from the man in front, is well nigh impossible. So the pressure to be number one on the grid at Monte Carlo is greater than ever. Over the winter, some welcome improvements to the circuit had been made. Resurfacing of several sections, widening the exit from the tunnel down to the chicane (which was significantly to affect the race) and painting the tunnel walls and roof white were amongst them. As a result, everyone expected qualifying and race times to be quicker — and they were.

At Monaco, practice starts a day earlier than usual (so that the Principality gets extra

For the first time in 1991, Nigel Mansell reached the chequered flag, his daring outbraking manoeuvre on Prost earning him second place.

ncome!). On Thursday, expecting rain, everyone was out early. No surprises here, with Senna nearly a second faster than his 1990 pole time but, sadly, Martin Brundle was excluded from the whole meeting for failing to stop at a weight check. On Saturday, conditions were better and so was Senna. His 1m 20.334s lap, an incredible average of 92.658 mph, was the fastest ever at Monaco and it gave him his 56th pole position. Nothing strange about that, for we'd got so used to the Brazilian's dominance in qualifying that we'd have been surprised at anything else. But the next man on the front row certainly was an eye-opener ... for it was Stefano Modena! At last the introspective Italian's alliance with the nimble, Honda V10-powered Tyrrell had come good, and it was also the first time that a Pirelli-shod car had been on the front row since the Milan concern had re-entered Grand Prix racing in 1989. A welcome fillip for them, especially as another of their drivers, Nelson Piquet in the new Benetton-Ford B191, was in fourth place. With Riccardo Patrese third, sandwiched between the Pirelli men and ahead of Mansell and Berger, the grid had a different look about it — especially as the Ferraris of Alain Prost, four times a winner at Monaco, and Jean Alesi, a brilliant second last year in his Tyrrell, were down in seventh and ninth. At Monaco, that was very bad news indeed for Maranello.

Whilst it certainly wasn't bikini weather on Sunday, it was dry, warm and much brighter.

TEAM ANALYSIS

McLAREN

A curate's egg Monaco for McLaren. By failing to improve on his Thursday time, Gerhard Berger qualified only sixth. Collides with Piquet on lap one. To pits for new nose. Rejoins last and retires on tenth lap when hits armco due to oil-smeared visor. Senna totally destroys and demoralises opposition. Takes 56th pole position with new track record (1m 20.344s, 92.658 mph). Then leads commandingly from start to finish to win his fourth successive 1991 GP, his fourth Monaco in five years and to extend his World Championship lead to 29 points — after four races! McLaren now leads constructors' championship by 34 points. Gloomy rivals wonder if this is going to be another 1988.

TYRRELL

Team succeeds brilliantly in qualifying. Nakajima 11th on grid at a circuit he hates, Modena a sensational second for his first-ever front row GP start. On his 28th birthday, Stefano magnificent in race. Stays within striking distance of Senna for 37 laps until consistently blocked whilst trying to lap Pirro (who mistook him for Nakajima). With gap increased to over 20 seconds, fighting for second wi Patrese on lap 43 when Honda V10 disintegrates to en his best GP yet. Nakajima spins from ninth place int retirement at chicane on lap 35.

WILLIAMS

What should have been team's best race to date marre by bad luck. Patrese again outqualifies Mansell (third an fifth, despite both being baulked). Riccardo fights f second with Modena from lap 37, but smashes int retirement on Stefano's oil on lap 43. Mansell holds fourt for 29 laps until faulty throttle sensor causes engine to sto twice. Drops to fifth but, with Modena/Patrese out, make magnificent recovery and passes Prost for second on la 64. Finishes second (best ever Monaco result) for his firs points of 1991, having reduced a cautiously-slowin Senna's lead from over 40 seconds to 18.3. Mansell an Patrese set second and third fastest laps of race. A ver heartening event for Williams, who appear to hav overcome gearbox problem.

BRABHAM

Meeting starts badly when Martin Brundle is disqualifie on Thursday, for failing to stop at a weight check. Mar Blundell does well to qualify 22nd for his first Monaco G In 14th place on lap 42, hits Modena oil and smashes int retirement — fortunately unhurt.

Stefano Modena drove brilliantly all weekend, only for a blown Honda to rob him of second place. Alain Prost follows, the Ferraris again unable to match the leading pace.

FOOTWORK

1991 continues to dismay as team grapples with new car problems. Having failed to set qualifying time on Thursday, Alex Caffi has colossal accident in swimming pool section on Saturday. Destroys car but is uninjured. Alboreto, still not fit after pre-Imola accident, qualifies 25th in inadequately tested FA12. Retires from lapped 19th and last, lap 40, when engine cuts out. ''But at least we got 39 laps of experience with the car.''

LOTUS

Spirits high following Imola, until Julian Bailey fails to qualify after hitting barrier on Saturday. Mika Häkkinen just gets in 26th. With another impressive drive, advances to 11th by lap 49, challenging Gachot and Bernard, but retires lap 65 with oil fire.

FONDMETAL

Olivier Grouillard fails to pre-qualify with slowest time.

LEYTON HOUSE

With major handling problem (''the car is bouncing uncontrollably''), Mauricio Gugelmin and Ivan Capelli only qualify 15th and 18th. Both discover metal-fatigue radiator leaks on dummy grid. Gugelmin's fixed. Capelli takes spare car. Ivan pits from 15th, lap eight, with brake problem. Rejoins last but retires lap 13 (brakes). In evil-handling car, Mauricio soldiers round until retiring from eighth place, lap 44. Things not looking good for Leyton House, who just don't seem to be able to get it together at the moment.

AGS

Fabrizio Barbazza fails to qualify (28th). Tarquini 20th, but retires from 19th, lap ten (gearbox).

BENETTON

A rewarding but disappointing meeting for Benetton. Hard work since Imola to remedy dodgy gearchange mechanism improves reliability, with resultant development benefits. Nelson Piquet, who loathes Monaco, qualifies excellent fourth. Moreno eighth after switching to spare car. Nelson, savaged by Berger after start, retires at Mirabeau (broken rear suspension). Roberto races seventh and then fifth after lap 43 Modena/Patrese débâcle. On ''too hard'' Pirellis settles for fourth place and first three points of year (one lap down). Overall, team delighted with confirmation of new car's potential, and looks forward to real progress after further testing.

DALLARA

What a contrast to 1990, with team's second successive points finish. Lehto and Pirro sail through pre-qualification, first and third. Then qualify well, 12th and 13th. With another stunning drive, JJ gains four places on first lap and is in points (sixth) on lap 43. Then drops back with gearbox stuck in sixth, but still finishes 11th (three laps down). Pirro chases JJ all the way. Up to sixth, lap 67, and finishes there (one lap down) for his first point since Australia 1989 (Benetton), although highly unpopular with Modena for holding him up in the mistaken belief that he was Nakajima — who Emanuele had just passed! Much of credit for team's improved performance due to John Judd's excellent V10 engine.

MINARDI

Martini and Morbidelli start 14th and 17th. Piero down from 12th, lap nine, to 22nd and last with gearbox problem. Rejoins race but, with return of problem, repeatedly blocks lapping leaders and incurs Formula One's first-ever ten seconds time penalty after being black-and-white flagged. Staggers on to be classified 12th and last, six laps down. Gianni Morbidelli tenth out of 14 by lap 44, but retires lap 49 (gearbox).

LIGIER

Boutsen complains about car being ''very difficult to drive'', but qualifies 16th. Comas complains about traffic but qualifies 23rd. Thierry then drives good race in far from suitable car to finish seventh, two laps down, for second successive race. Eric has tyre stop and drives at rear of field to finish tenth (two laps down).

FERRARI

Not at all happy Monaco for Maranello. Unable to find a good set-up, Prost and Alesi qualify demoralising seventh and ninth. Alain fastest (on half tanks) in Sunday warm-up. Passes Mansell to fourth, lap 30, when Nigel's engine stops. Then to second, 44s behind Senna (Modena/Patrese out), which he loses when Mansell stupefyingly passes him on lap 63. With steering upright fouling front rim, dives into pits, lap 72. Rejoins on new tyres to post record last lap and fastest of race (1m 24.368s, 88.239 mph). Finishes fifth, lapped by Senna. Alesi, using different differential to Prost, complains of massive understeer and heavy tyre wear. ''I just did my best to finish.'' Which he did — third (full distance).

LARROUSSE-LOLA

Despite car-smashing spin, Suzuki qualifies 19th with Bernard 21st. Aguri retires from 15th, lap 25, after going off at Ste Devote (brakes), whilst Bernard finishes a contented ninth (two laps down) 0.3s behind Gachot.

COLONI

Chaves pre-qualifies faster than Grouillard — but not fast enough.

JORDAN

Another ''almost but not quite'' race for Jordan. Andrea de Cesaris and Bertrand Gachot delight team boss Eddie J by pre-qualifying for the team's first Monaco — second and fourth. Both then qualify, Andrea extremely well in tenth and Bert 24th. De Cesaris has excellent race, running strong seventh behind Alesi until lap 22 retirement (broken throttle cable). Gachot consoles team by giving it its first Grand Prix finish in eighth place (two laps down), despite collision with Boutsen which causes steering and suspension damage.

LAMBORGHINI

Fifth and sixth, both Larini and van de Poele fail to pre-qualify.

Prost was fastest in the half-hour warm-up (on half tanks), and Patrese and Mansell were third and fourth behind Senna. But with Ayrton, three times a winner in the last four years and in pole position for the fifth time in seven, confidently sitting at the front of the grid with a clear road in front of him, the general feeling was that only a mechanical problem or a collision would deny him another victory in Monte Carlo.

When the lights turn to green at Monaco, you hold your breath. The first corner, Ste Devote, is only about 300 metres from the start, and everyone tries to get round it first — which often results in a race-stopping pile-up. No stoppage this year, but a charging Gerhard Berger drove into the back of Piquet's Benetton, effectively to remove them both. Nelson retired at Mirabeau with broken rear suspension whilst Gerhard, having stopped for a new nose, was out nine laps later when, hindered by an oil-smeared visor, he drove into the barrier at the swimming pool. Two potential winners out of contention before the end of the first lap.

But there was no lack of interest at the front. Stefano Modena, third in a Brabham in 1989, was making the most of his grid position and was hanging on magnificently to Ayrton Senna, the master of Monaco. For lap after lap he stayed just out of the buffeting slipstream of Ayrton's McLaren, and ahead of 1982 winner Riccardo Patrese who, in turn, led his team-mate Nigel Mansell with Prost fifth, Alesi sixth and an inspired Andrea de Cesaris in his Jordan-Ford right behind the young Frenchman.

By lap 13 of 78, Senna and Modena were both lapping the tail-enders and Ayrton had eased out a 2.5s lead. Nine laps later, the unfortunate de Cesaris retired with a broken throttle cable after a storming drive which could well have give the Jordan team its first World Championship points. Of greater interest to the enthralled crowd was the fact that Alain Prost

After team-mate Caffi's awful practice crash, Michele Alboreto hauled the recalcitrant Footwork FA12 into the race. Gianni Morbidelli and a charging Mansell are in pursuit.

was catching Nigel Mansell. Closer and closer to the Williams-Renault he got for, unbeknown to us at the time, Mansell had got a major problem, a faulty throttle sensor making his engine cut out. Twice it stopped altogether, and Nigel had to bump-start the Renault V10 on the clutch. As if Monaco wasn't difficult enough!

On lap 30 the inevitable happened — Prost moved up to fourth past Mansell, with the outstanding Modena still fighting at the front as he and Senna carved their way through the traffic. As Senna lapped Pier-Luigi Martini's Minardi-Ferrari for the second time, Stefano was only 2.6 seconds behind — but that was the closest he got, for now his race fell apart. Ahead of him, JJ Lehto, Satoru Nakajima and Emanuele Pirro were fighting for eighth place. As they bore down to lap Martini, who was suffering from gearbox trouble, Naka lost the Tyrrell and spun out of the race. This meant that Modena was now behind Pirro, trying to lap him, but the Roman, thinking that Stefano's Tyrrell was that of a recovering Nakajima, refused to let him through. So now we had Pirro stuck behind Martini, who was refusing to move over, and an increasingly frustrated Modena stuck behind Pirro. By the time it was all sorted out, and Stefano had got past both of them on lap 42, Senna was long gone — over 20 seconds ahead of the Tyrrell. What was even worse from Modena's point of view was the fact that Riccardo Patrese, who had been over ten seconds behind him, was now virtually attached to his gearbox.

On lap 43, Stefano and Riccardo swept into the tunnel. As they exited it at over 160 mph, an oily plume of grey smoke belched out of the Tyrrell. Stefano's Honda V10 had grenaded itself! As Modena shot into the escape road at the chicane, a helpless Patrese smashed into retirement. "I was flat in sixth and suddenly driving through hot oil and metal. I could do nothing." Of course he couldn't, and he was very lucky that, after cannoning off the armco, he was able to roll to a standstill and get out of his Williams unharmed.

So now Senna was untouchable. Admittedly 35 laps still remained but, with a lead of more than 40 seconds over Prost's Ferrari, he had only to pace himself to victory — taking care not

Martin Brundle's Monaco GP came to an early end, when he was excluded for failing to stop at a qualifying weight check.

Erik Comas leads the unlucky Lehto. JJ was set for points until his car jammed... in sixth gear!

to lose concentration and crash out of the lead as he had in 1988. But the rest of the 1991 Monaco GP was far from boring. For Mansell's errant throttle sensor had cleared itself, and Nigel was on one of his inspired charges. Carving over a second a lap out of Prost's advantage, he steadily closed on the Ferrari until, on lap 63, after a series of fastest laps, he was alongside Alain as they exited the tunnel. Taking full advantage of the fact that the pavement was no longer there, Nigel dived inside the Ferrari and, with his brakes locked up, sneaked past into second place. Fantastic!

Now only the first four were on the same lap, for the brilliant Senna had passed everyone up to an unhappy Jean Alesi, struggling with a Ferrari not set up to his liking. So, on lap 71, Senna led with Mansell gaining steadily as the Brazilian, warned on his pit-to-car radio to take things easy as his oil pressure was suspect, eased up. Prost was an increasingly distant third with a handling problem, Alesi fourth, Roberto Moreno a lapped fifth and Emanuele Pirro sixth, after his team-mate JJ Lehto was forced to drop back with his gearbox jammed in sixth (at Monaco!).

All over bar the shouting? Not a bit of it! Into a dozing Ferrari pit shot Alain Prost, with a front suspension upright machining its way through the wheel rim. In an absolute shambles of a stop, his mechanics slapped on a new set of wheels and then let the car down on to the air wrench! After he'd been jacked up a second time to free it, Alain left the pit lane down in fifth place — an unhappy man with two points at the end of the race instead of four. That he set the fastest lap of the race — a record — on his new Goodyears (1m 24.368s, 88.239 mph) was probably of scant consolation.

Ayrton Senna, having lapped everybody up to the third-placed Alesi, won the 49th Monaco Grand Prix from Nigel Mansell by 18.34s, and in so doing he became the first man in the history of the World Championship to win all of a year's first four races. That he had won every one of them with a car problem was another indication of his driving genius, and as they packed up to return to their bases his rivals in the Williams, Ferrari, Benetton and Tyrrell teams reflected on the fact that, if they were to win races in 1991, they'd need to make a *massive* improvement.

Unwanted record: drastic under-utilisation of his Minardi's mirrors earned Pier-Luigi Martini F1's first 'naughty boy' time penalty.

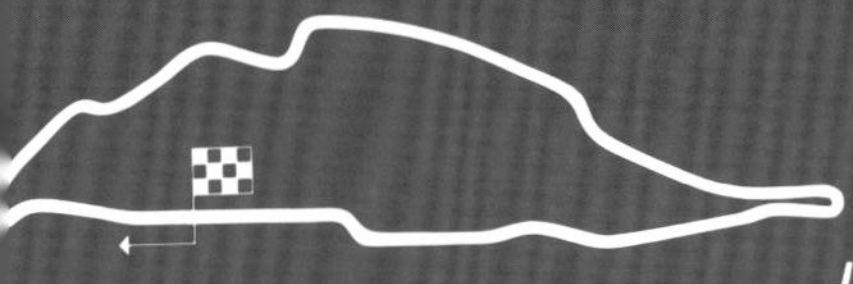

CANADA

June 2 1991 Circuit: Gilles Villeneuve, Montreal

Rivals had the rare sight of seeing Senna's McLaren stricken at trackside on Friday, the Honda V12 having gone bang in comprehensive fashion. Ayrton practises begging Ron Dennis for forgiveness.

After Ayrton Senna's run of four successive victories, people were getting bored. "I know he's a genius. I know the team Ron Dennis has built, with Honda power, is so good that it richly deserves all its success. And, yes, I know that it's up to the others to catch up. But I'm still bored!" Well Canada certainly got their attention, with a race so full of drama that if it had been scripted it would have been rejected as over the top.

There was plenty to talk about when the teams got to the beautiful city of Montreal. Ferrari had resolved the long-standing political battle between team manager Cesare Fiorio and Alain Prost by firing Fiorio — and appointing a management triumvirate which seemed likely to make things worse rather than better. Johnny Herbert was to return to Grand Prix racing to replace the cashless Julian Bailey in the financially strapped Lotus team. Stefan Johansson was to drive for his tenth Grand Prix team — Footwork — by substituting for Alex Caffi, injured in a road accident. Brabham's manager Dave Price had left. Disgruntled Group C team owner Walter Brun was threatening to disrupt the meeting, to protest

''Coooee! I'm back!'' Stefan Johansson was recalled to F1 yet again, this time as substitute for Footwork's Alex Caffi, injured in a road accident. Mauricio Gugelmin gives chase.

After qualifying an impressive fifth, Roberto Moreno (right) spun out of contention early on. At the time, he was running with team-mate — and eventual winner — Piquet...

about damage caused to his cars by track deficiencies in the 1990 sports car race. The island circuit in the St Lawrence Seaway had been partly resurfaced and modified at the dangerous pits approach, and there had been a great deal of progress by the teams in post-Monaco testing.

The 2.75-mile Gilles Villeneuve circuit has long, fast sections followed by hairpin bends, which make it very hard on brakes and fuel consumption. The harsh winters in Montreal make the track bumpy and slippery, but the drivers like it. With no pre-race testing, the teams who have been there before are at an advantage, but everybody's problems are compounded by the fact that the weather is notoriously changeable.

Friday morning was reasonable, but in the afternoon it was wet and the qualifying times were over 12 seconds slower. So, in a situation where Senna seemed to have made pole position his personal province and where his wet-track prowess is legendary, it created a small sensation when Ayrton went back to his hotel on Friday in third place on the provisional grid. Partly because his Honda engine had blown in the morning, but far more because at last the opposition seemed to be closing the gap. Nigel Mansell had said earlier in the season that there were going to be circuits where the Williams cars would just disappear, and it looked as though Montreal was going to be one of them. But if Nigel was fastest ahead of Alesi, it was hardly surprising that his team-mate Riccardo Patrese was only eighth. Riccardo had gone off very hard indeed on Senna's oil in the morning and, with whiplash pain and very sore chest muscles, it was surprising that he'd been able to go out at all. On Saturday then there was a real buzz. Would Senna do the usual, and decimate the opposition? He would not!

Saturday saw a reversal of the weather. Dry, and very hot indeed. An amazing reversal of the grid situation, too, with Patrese in pole position by almost a second! The popular Italian had only three poles in his 212 races, and to be top man on the grid in Canada — in his physical

COLORS OF BENETTON.

TEAM ANALYSIS

McLAREN

Senna's contention that he had been pushed hard in first four races proved right in Canada. After his engine blew on Friday he qualified third (first time not on pole for eight races), with Berger sixth. Both McLarens fail to finish. Gerhard into pits from eighth, lap four, with electrical problem. Rejoins briefly but retires, lap five. Senna third, increasingly distant from Mansell/Patrese, until lap 26 when retires with failed alternator. No McLaren points indicates that 1991 may not repeat 1988's total domination.

TYRRELL

A good race for Modena compensates for Monaco disappointment. From ninth on grid, Stefano up to strong fourth at half-distance. To third, lap 41, when Patrese pits. Down to fifth after lap 47 tyre stop. Charges hard to pass Lehto and flagging Patrese and finishes second. Best Grand Prix result yet lifts him to sixth in championship. Nakajima starts 12th after going off in warm-up. Races 14th/15th until side-swiping wall, lap 11. To pits for inspection and tyres. Finishes tenth, two laps down, after steady race.

WILLIAMS

A bitter-sweet meeting for Williams. Mansell and Patrese sensational in practice. Riccardo hits wall very hard on Friday morning after going off on Senna's oil, but brilliantly and bravely takes fourth career pole position on Saturday — again outqualifying Nigel. Mansell has to switch to spare car, but qualifies second to form all-Williams front row. Nigel and Riccardo then dominate race, consistently pulling away from Senna. Patrese pits with right rear puncture, lap 41, and rejoins sixth. Third by lap 47 but, with recurrence of gearbox problems, steadily loses time. Mansell storms on and makes fastest lap (1m 22.358s, 120.286 mph). With a lead of over 50 seconds, sensationally stops half way round last lap when "it just went into neutral and the engine cut out." Patrese, passed by Modena with two laps to go, finishes third, Mansell sixth (one lap down). Yet again, lack of reliability denies success to what is currently the best car.

BRABHAM

Team manager Dave Price leaves. Martin Brundle qualifies 20th ("not fast enough") and Mark Blundell fails to get in for the first time. Brundle pits with broken gearshift, lap 11, and loses four laps. Retires, lap 26, with engine failure. Team sadly failing to progress.

FOOTWORK

After Alex Caffi breaks jaw in road accident, Stefan Johansson joins his tenth Grand Prix team and reports that Porsche engine is "gutless." Nevertheless, both he and Alboreto qualify — 25th and 21st. Michele smartly advances to 15th, lap one, but retires, lap three, with jammed throttle. Stefan has same problem but carries on until loss of gears and engine failure causes lap 48 retirement. Despite lack of success, team boss Jackie Oliver contends that progress is being made.

LOTUS

Johnny Herbert replaces Julian Bailey, who has run out of money. Johnny impresses on his return to GP racing — but fails to qualify after having to switch to spare when race car fails. Mika Häkkinen starts 24th and is up to 16th, lap 21, when he ploughs across sand trap, stalls and retires.

FONDMETAL

Grouillard, still a second off the pace despite improved car and Hart-DFR engine, fails to pre-qualify for the fifth time in five races.

LEYTON HOUSE

Team continues frustrating season of misery and under-achievement. Ivan Capelli qualifies 13th and Mauricio Gugelmin 26th (clutch and fuel leak). Ivan, battling with JJ Lehto, sixth by lap 28 and then to excellent fourth on lap 42 — only to retire, lap 44, when Ilmor engine blows. Gugelmin, battling against poor handling, retires from 11th, lap 62.

AGS

Further, potentially terminal, lack of success for the hard-pressed French team, neither of whose drivers qualifies. Barbazza fails to get in by only 0.3s whilst Tarquini misses out by a mere 0.4s.

BENETTON

Victory! A lucky one but to win you've got to finish — and Mansell didn't. Team makes substantial progress with new car in post-Monaco testing. Moreno, fastest on Friday morning, qualifies fifth (highest ever) with Piquet eighth. On lap two Nelson passes Roberto who spins out of seventh, lap ten. Piquet runs fifth laps 11-25. Third laps 30-41 (having passed both Ferraris). Then second, over 50 seconds behind Mansell, until the Williams expires on last lap to hand Piquet his 23rd GP victory. Nelson's third win from seven races is also Pirelli's first since Mexico 1986 (Berger/Benetton). Piquet and Benetton move up to second in championships.

DALLARA

A disappointing but encouraging race for the Brescia-based team. Pirro and Lehto again sail through pre-qualifying first and second, after which they qualify tenth and 17th. Emanuele hits de Cesaris, lap one, and pits for tyres suspecting puncture, which turns out to be handling problem caused by collision. Nevertheless finishes ninth (one lap down). JJ drives superbly to enhance his growing reputation. In points at half-distance, enjoying long battle with Capelli. Up to superb fourth, laps 49-50, only to retire, lap 51, when his Judd V10 lets go.

MINARDI

Not much to shout about despite Ferrari engines. Martini qualifies 18th and starts from pit lane in spare car, after having brake problem on parade lap. Races to espondent seventh place (one lap down) with same rake problem. Gianni Morbidelli starts 15th and bandons stalled car on track after spinning out of 11th lace, lap 21.

.IGIER

No points again in situation where things getting esperate, with likelihood of once-great team having to re-qualify after Britain. 1989 winner Thierry Boutsen (in Villiams) 16th on grid whilst Comas gets in by 0.03s. hierry staggering fifth fastest in spare car during Sunday varm-up. Up to commendable ninth by lap 26, but out ap 27 when Lamborghini engine blows. Comas, owever, has another reliable non-stop race and does vell to finish eighth (one lap down) for his highest GP lacing.

FERRARI

Cesare Fiorio, contentious manager of divided team, fired t culmination of long political battle with Prost. riumvirate comprising Piero Ferrari (Enzo's son), ex-manager Marco Piccinini and ex-Lancia rally manager Claudio Lombardi takes over. With revised front uspension, Prost and Alesi qualify fourth and seventh. Alain chases, and keeps up with, third-placed Senna for en laps before letting close-following Alesi and Piquet hrough whilst struggling for gears. Repasses Alesi for ourth as Senna pulls off, lap 26, but retires, lap 28, with ransmission problem. With Senna out Alesi, now third, pits for tyres but retires from fourth, lap 35, when engine blows. Alain down to third in drivers' championship and Ferrari to fourth in constructors'. Can new management take team to top? Only time will tell.

LARROUSSE-LOLA

Bernard and Suzuki qualify 19th and 22nd. Aguri hastily evacuates when car incinerates itself, lap three. Bernard also fails to finish by retiring from praiseworthy ninth place, lap 30 (gearbox).

COLONI

Despite now having Hart-DFR engine, Chaves again fails to pre-qualify.

JORDAN

A joyful occasion for Eddie Jordan's very impressive new team — now using higher-spec Ford HB engine previously confined to Benetton. After pre-qualifying third and fourth, de Cesaris and Gachot start 11th and 14th. Andrea and Bert ninth and 11th lap 30, eventually to finish a superb fourth and fifth. With both cars in the points in only their fifth race, Jordan will almost certainly avoid pre-qualifying after the British GP.

LAMBORGHINI

With grave money problems, things looking dire for the team — especially as both Larini and van de Poele fail to pre-qualify for the third time.

Johnny Herbert returned to Lotus after Julian Bailey's piggy bank ran dry. Quick in the wet, the Briton failed to qualify after car trouble in Saturday's dry session. Here, he leads Emanuele Pirro.

state — was a superb achievement which also saw him outqualifying Mansell for the fifth time in five races. Not bad for someone who had been regarded as a compliant number two when the season began! Senna was third (not even on the front row) ahead of Prost, a very impressive Roberto Moreno in the new Benetton, a forlorn Gerhard Berger, Jean Alesi and Nelson Piquet, with Monaco hero Stefano Modena in ninth place.

So it was an all-Williams front row for the first time since Hungary 1990 (Boutsen and Patrese). When the lights turned to green, Mansell took the lead and started to disappear with Riccardo settling in behind. Hardly able to believe what it was seeing, the world watched the two Williams-Renaults increasingly distance themselves from Senna's McLaren, which had the Ferraris of Prost and Alesi tucked up tight behind it, with Piquet's Benetton rapidly closing in sixth. The unfortunate Berger didn't last long — out on lap five with electrical problems. On lap 11 Mansell, driving with all the forceful brio which makes him such a joy to watch, was over five seconds ahead of Patrese, whilst Riccardo led a hard-chasing Senna by nearly four seconds. Amazing! But Prost was no longer fourth. Fishing for gears, he'd moved over to let Alesi and Piquet through and now Nelson started to attack Jean for fourth place. "The new car is good," he said after the race "but w still don't know it yet. There's a lot to come whe we do." But already the John Barnard-inspire Benetton was clearly a match for the Ferraris Piquet had caught and passed Prost, and on la 26 he got by Alesi to take third place.

Third place? Yes third, because Senna wa out! Suddenly the McLaren slowed, and u went the Brazilian's arm as he pulled on to th verge with a failed alternator. But this time wasn't from a commanding lead. It was from distant third. He'd repeatedly said that his fou previous victories hadn't been as easy as they' seemed, and it looked as though he had bee right. As Ayrton stopped, his countryma Nelson Piquet shot past Alesi in a brilliantl opportunistic move, to be followed by Prost Piquet third, Prost fourth, Alesi fifth and Moden up to sixth, with Mansell now seven second ahead of Patrese, who led Nelson by nearl 17. Williams, Williams, Benetton, Ferrari Ferrari, Tyrrell. This was a bit different!

Sadly though the Ferrari placings didn't sta that way for long. Everyone likes to see th Maranello cars going well, for they hav charisma like no other team. But on lap 28 whilst we were still agog at Senna's departure Prost retired (gearbox) — to be followed seve laps later by Alesi with a broken engine. Not good start for the new Ferrari management

Disbelieving victor: over 50 seconds behind Mansell as he started his last lap, a win was not exactly foremost in Nelson Piquet's mind, though he wasn't complaining afterwards.

vho'd now be taken apart by the whole of Italy. \lesi had actually got back into third place ahead of Piquet for three laps, but now Nelson vas the man chasing the two Williams, 33 econds behind Patrese.

At half-distance, lap 35, there was no change to the top three, but Stefano Modena vas fourth, pursued by a colossal battle for fifth between Ivan Capelli's Leyton House and JJ ehto's Dallara (and JJ had had to pre-qualify!). With Nigel and Riccardo blasting round at the ront, that battle continued. On lap 42 it was for ourth place behind Modena, as Patrese's Williams slowly motored into the pits. "Jolly vell done Riccardo," we thought, in the belief hat he was understandably having to give up exhausted after his Friday crash. Not a bit of it. He had a puncture, and soon rejoined in sixth place on a new set of Goodyears to drive faster han ever. On lap 44 he was fifth as Capelli's Ilmor engine gave up, once more to deny the talian a finish. On lap 46 he took fourth from ehto, and on lap 49 he was third as Modena stopped for tyres. A superb recovery.

The Jordans were flying too. In the previous Grands Prix they'd shown that they had points potential, and now they were proving it. The oft-criticised Andrea de Cesaris, driving beautifully, was sixth ahead of team-mate Bertrand Gachot. But the drama at the 1991 Canadian Grand Prix hadn't finished. Not by a long chalk. Out went the talented and very mpressive Lehto from what had seemed like another certain points finish, when his Judd V10 "just went bang!" Up to fourth, fifth and sixth went Modena, de Cesaris and Gachot. Both Jordans in the points!

Mansell, securely on his way to his 17th very well-deserved Grand Prix victory, which would make him the most successful Englishman in the history of the sport, now led by over 50 seconds and had lapped everyone except Piquet, who was driving conservatively in the knowledge hat Patrese couldn't possibly catch him. Riccardo unlapped himself in his efforts to catch Nelson but, on lap 66 with only three to go, Mansell was back in front of his team-mate with the fastest lap of the race (1m 22.385s, 120.286 mph). "Steady on Nigel," was our eaction. "No need to push it. Riccardo may have outqualified you, but you've got nothing to prove." This was not a fair judgement for, unbeknown to us, Patrese's gearbox was up to its old tricks again, refusing to change down. It wasn't so much that Nigel was going a lot quicker, rather Riccardo was going slower. Because of that, the charging Modena took third from Patrese on the 67th lap out of 69. So now Williams was going to be first and fourth instead of first and third. Never mind, it would still be a very considerable achievement.

Down to the hairpin, waving to the crowd with nearly a minute's lead and only a few hundred yards to go, came Mansell – and suddenly he slowed down. And then, beating the steering wheel in sheer frustration, he stopped! Modena and Patrese passed him to

Nigel Mansell utterly dominated the Canadian GP, for all but the final couple of hundred yards.

unlap themselves and then Piquet did so — to lead! ''It's almost unbelievable. I went in to the hairpin and changed down from fifth to fourth like I always had, and then it went into neutral and the engine stopped,'' said Nigel, who'd had certain victory snatched from him in literally the closing yards. He'd had some bad luck in his career, but this topped everything.

Victory in Canada for Nelson Piquet then (his third from the last seven races), with Stefano Modena second, Patrese third, the Jordans of de Cesaris and Gachot fourth and fifth (no more pre-qualifying after Britain!) and poor Mansell a lapped sixth. Great for Benetton, Jordan, Tyrrell, the TV viewers and the spectators, but bitter gall for Williams — and no justice for poor Nigel, who'd driven faultlessly. To add to his misery the car, with ten litres of fuel still left, started and the gearbox worked perfectly when his mechanics collected it.

But was McLaren really now just *one* of the top teams and not *the* top team? It was going to be exciting to find out when the teams met again in Mexico in two weeks' time!

In the points. Jordan twins de Cesaris and Gachot took fourth and fifth, to boost their chances of escaping pre-qualifying later in the season.

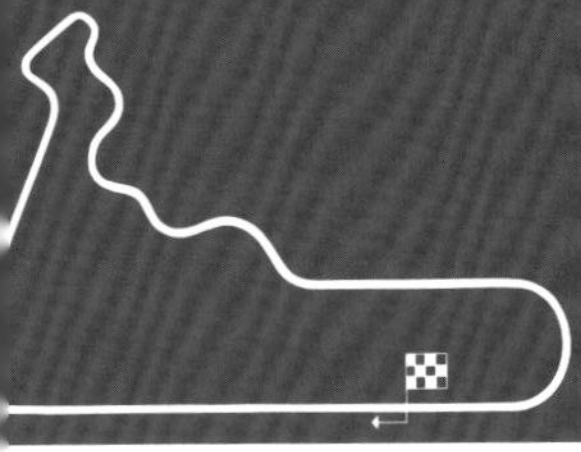

MEXICO

June 16 1991 Circuit: Hermanos Rodriguez, Mexico City

Despite an overheating Renault V10, Nigel Mansell was able to hold off the persistent challenge of Ayrton Senna for many laps. When normal service was resumed, the Englishman pulled away to challenge his team-mate.

"Nothing to say. Riccardo was dominant during the race and he deserved the victory. Nigel was quick in the late stages, so they were dominant all through the weekend. Although they didn't win in Montreal, I think here they finally established their true performance and they were one-two!" So said Ayrton Senna in Mexico, as he graciously acknowledged the crushing defeat by Williams of the McLaren team which had seemed likely to sweep all before it in 1991.

Piquet's Benetton may have won in Canada, and the unreliable Williams-Renault may have repeatedly shown itself to be superior to the McLaren-Honda when it was going, but deep down most people felt that this was going to be another McLaren year. Senna may have had problems in all five races so far, but he had won four of them. When the team really got the car sorted he'd surely be unbeatable, wouldn't he? Mexico, by far the best race of the year to date, showed the answer to be no.

The writing was on the wall after Friday's qualifying session, with Riccardo Patrese holding the provisional pole position ahead of

The Grand Prix rumour silly season is usually in full flow by June. French actress Beatrice Dalle was a visitor to Mexico; would she take Berger's place at McLaren in 1992?

his team-mate Nigel Mansell. Senna was only third after a violent shunt at the dreaded Peraltada bend. Mexico City — with its high altitude, thin air, smog, violence, corruption and extreme poverty — is the least-liked GP venue of them all, and the low-grip track is appallingly bumpy. But a saving grace of the Hermanos Rodriguez circuit is the Peraltada, the 180-degree right-hander which leads into the main straight ... and which is taken at a mind-boggling 165 mph. It is one of the most demanding and spectacular corners in Grand Prix racing. Bertrand Gachot had already gone off there in a big way when Senna, anxiously trying to displace one of the two Williams from the front row of the grid, decided to take it in sixth gear for the first time. He didn't succeed and finished upside-down in the sand trap, more than lucky not to add to the ten stitches he already had in his head from a jet-ski accident in Brazil. The World Champion was under considerable pressure.

Saturday was wet for most of the qualifying session and none of the top seven improved their times, so it was the two Williams men heading the list again. And for the sixth time in 1991 Riccardo Patrese, in spite of two days' gut-wrenching misery from the Mexican trots, had outqualified his number one in the team's second successive front row monopoly. And just like Canada, Senna was third on the grid. A mere 0.3s covered the next seven — Alesi, Berger, Piquet, Prost (who'd started 13th and won in 1990), Modena, Moreno and Grouillard, so there was every prospect of a cracking race. Olivier Grouillard's achievement in the Fondmetal-Hart DFR was outstanding. He'd failed even to pre-qualify at the previous five meetings, but lots of testing and hard work by the team, especially new engineer Richard Divila, had transformed the situation.

So far so good for Williams, but would they last the race? With only three finishes from the last ten starts, there was no guarantee that they would. And if the cars *could* finish, could the weakened Patrese? Like Canada — after his blameless practice crash — he doubted it, but hoped the adrenalin of the race would take his mind off his insides. It did indeed!

Fastest again in the Sunday morning warm-up, Riccardo had to sit through two aborted starts which reduced the race length from 69 to 67 laps. The first came when JJ Lehto's Dallara overheated, the second when Grouillard switched off his engine in response to waved yellow flags — for which he was put to the back of the grid, thus negating his superb qualifying achievement. It was third time lucky and, in a repeat of Canada, Nigel Mansell led at the first corner ahead of Jean Alesi, as the Frenchman catapulted his Ferrari into second place past Senna and a slow-starting Patrese. Ayrton didn't appreciate that one little bit. On the next lap he showed his anger with an equally forceful move, almost banging wheels with the Ferrari as he took second place behind Mansell.

We'd thought that Montezuma's Revenge was already affecting Patrese, but he proved us wrong on lap three by surging past Alesi to take third and he started to close on Senna. Ayrton was finding the going tough, and so was his team-mate Gerhard Berger. In fifth place and holding up the writhing snake that contained Modena, Piquet, de Cesaris and Moreno, he suddenly had his Honda V12 explode as the consequence of a split radiator. Out he went and so, too, did the unfortunate Pier-Luigi Martini as he hit Berger's oil slick.

Seven laps later, McLaren's fortunes took another nosedive as Patrese got past Senna, who was just plain outperformed by the tremendously impressive Williams-Renault. So now it was Mansell first, Riccardo second, Senna third, Alesi fourth, Modena fifth and de Cesaris a superb sixth having passed Piquet. On lap 15 Patrese was in the lead! Nigel certainly didn't make it easy for him as they drove through the right-left-right after the main straight, but ''there was nothing I could do. For some reason my engine was running tight and I just hadn't got the straight-line speed to hold him back.'' From that moment on Riccardo, driving faultlessly in a car he later said was perfect, raced away from the field until, on lap 45, he led Mansell by over 25 seconds.

It was all action behind Nigel though, as Alesi caught and passed Senna to take third place. Ayrton was only fourth in a healthy McLaren! But not for long because Jean, troubled by a faulty clutch, rotated down to ninth behind Prost on lap 15 — and now Piquet was on a charge. Past Modena to fourth (and that was the end of Stefano's hopes, as he made a series of stops with tyre problems), he started to catch Senna. This was definitely the race of the year so far, for there was entertainment all down the field. De Cesaris,

Olivier Grouillard was one of the stars of qualifying, heading the times for 15 minutes on Friday afternoon and winding up 10th. A misunderstanding at the start saw him relegated to the back of the grid, however ...

TEAM ANALYSIS

McLAREN
Beaten fair and square for the second successive race. Berger qualifies fifth. Races fifth until lap five, when retires with split radiator and resultant engine blow-up for fourth retirement from six races. Senna arrives in Montreal with ten head stitches from jet-ski accident. Crashes heavily at Peraltada on Friday trying to get on front row of grid. Starts third. Second laps 2-10. Down to third, lap 15, behind both Williams-Renaults. Repeatedly tries to pass Mansell but fails and settles for third, 57 seconds behind Patrese. "The Williams were dominant. Now we must work very hard to improve both the chassis and the engine." What a turn-up!

TYRRELL
Team shattered by departure of designer Harvey Postlethwaite to Mercedes-Benz. George Ryton takes his place. Modena eighth and Nakajima 13th on the grid. Stefano advances to fifth by lap five but thereafter, like Satoru, plagued by tyre problems. Makes four stops (one caused by spin and another by flat-spotting tyres) before finishing 11th (two laps down). Nakajima stops twice but finishes 12th, also two laps down.

WILLIAMS
At last the total victory that team, car, Renault and drivers deserve. For second race running an all-Williams front row, with Patrese in fourth career pole (again out-qualifying Mansell, despite two days of suffering and dehydration from Mexican trots). Racing spare car Nigel leads laps 1-14 but, with "tight" engine, yields to Riccardo on lap 16. Steadily drops back, resisting determined efforts to pass by Senna, until lap 46 when, having richened mixture, speeds up and dramatically catches Patrese. With a series of record laps (the best a 1m 16.788s, 128.793 mph) finishes 1.3 seconds behind Riccardo and a staggering 56s ahead of Senna. Superb drives by both men give Williams its first one-two since Canada 1989 and lifts Patrese and team up to second in the two championships.

BRABHAM
John Macdonald to replace Dave Price as team manager. Increased Yamaha power and gearbox improvements, but Brundle only 17th on grid. Blundell an excellent 12th for first Mexico race. Martin to pits from 16th, lap 20 (tyres). Retires next lap when right rear wheel comes off (!). Blundell up to impressive seventh, laps 52-54, but retires lap 55 (engine). With no points, team faces prospect of having to pre-qualify after British GP.

FOOTWORK
Oil-surge problem returns at demanding Peraltada corner in practice. Johansson fails to qualify. Flu-stricken Alboreto just gets in 26th. Starts from pit lane as unable to fire up engine after race start aborted. Races at rear of field until lap 26, when retires with lack of oil pressure. "We will have a new oil system in France." Footwork will have to pre-qualify after Britain on present form, despite much-vaunted Porsche engine and massive expenditure by Japanese sponsor. A very sorry state of affairs.

LOTUS
Both drivers qualify — Häkkinen 24th and Herbert 25th (for his first GP since Australia '90). Both then race reliably, together for whole race, to finish two laps down, ninth (Häkkinen) and tenth.

FONDMETAL
What a turnabout! Following hard work by engineer Richard Divila and much testing, Olivier Grouillard pre-qualifies (second) for the first time in 1991. Then, using latest Brian Hart Ford DFR engine, sensationally qualifies tenth having headed Friday morning's times for 15 minutes! Sadly demoted to last on grid, for causing second start to be aborted after switching off engine having seen yellow flag signal. Storms through field to 19th by lap seven, but retires lap 14 (broken oil line).

LEYTON HOUSE
Gugelmin and Capelli, still unable to set car up properly, qualify 21st and 22nd. Mauricio races last until lap 16 when he over-revs engine and retires. Ivan out from 17th, lap 21 (engine).

AGS
Team now even more hard-pressed after failure of Tarquini (28th) and Barbazza (30th) to qualify.

BENETTON
Just-victorious team (Canada) struck potentially grievous blow by resignation of illustrious designer John Barnard. "Inability of principals to agree on policy and development of team." Barnard's place taken by Gordon Kimball. Piquet (top Pirelli) and Moreno sixth and ninth on grid. Nelson charges to strong fourth place on lap 16 and harasses Senna for third until retiring, lap 30, with clutch problem and failed left rear wheel bearing. Roberto finishes fifth (one lap down) after lap 49 tyre stop. Piquet and team down to third in drivers' and constructors' championships.

DALLARA
Emanuele Pirro fails to pre-qualify. JJ Lehto does so — fastest — and then qualifies 16th. Minor car fire causes first start to be aborted. Runs 11th laps 2-15. Eighth laps 19-22 but retires lap 31 (engine).

MINARDI
Neither driver qualifies well — Martini 15th (but sixth fastest in warm-up) and Morbidelli 23rd. Pier-Luigi spectacularly spins off at Peraltada on Berger's oil and water (lap five), but 23 year-old Morbidelli drives excellent race to highest-yet seventh place (one lap down).

LIGIER
Only 27th, Erik Comas misses qualifying by 0.05s. Thierry Boutsen gets in 14th and then drives his usual capable race to finish eighth (two laps down), with engine cutting out as he crosses line.

Mark Blundell qualified an excellent 12th, but was denied a top seven finish — which Brabham needed to avert the threat of pre-qualifying — by a late engine failure.

FERRARI

Things still no better under new management. Prost, a brilliant first from 13th on the grid in 1990, qualifies seventh, three places behind Alesi. Alain, in trouble from the start with poor handling, races ninth laps 5-13 but retires in pits, lap 17, when alternator fails. With heavily bruised foot from practice crash, Alesi thrusts through to inspired second at first corner but soon passed by Senna and Patrese. Races fourth, laps 4-13. With dodgy clutch spins down to ninth lap 15. Recovers to fourth, lap 32, and stays there until retiring, lap 43, when engine blows. Team plans to have new car at French GP, with new chassis and greatly revised aerodynamics.

LARROUSSE-LOLA

Team in dire money trouble. Gérard Larrousse in Japan trying to drum up funds. Bernard and Suzuki start 18th and 19th. Suzuki up to ninth out of 15 runners, lap 45. Retires lap 50 (gearbox). Eric Bernard does much better. Climbs up through field, battling with Morbidelli, and finishes fine sixth (one lap down) for his first point of 1991. Good news for Gérard!

COLONI

Team almost certain to withdraw from championship, due to lack of funding, after Pedro Chaves fails to pre-qualify for the sixth time.

JORDAN

Another excellent race for Eddie's very impressive new team. Both de Cesaris and Gachot pre-qualify (third and fourth), although Bert only does so thanks to Larini's exclusion. Gachot has major shunt at Peraltada on Friday but both qualify — Andrea 11th and Bertrand 20th. De Cesaris, inspired in the Jordan team, drives great race. Eighth on lap one. Then passes Moreno and Modena to run fifth, laps 17-42, battling with Piquet and Alesi. To fourth when Alesi retires and finishes there for the second race running. But is lucky to do so as throttle problem stops him on last lap. Disqualified for pushing car but reinstated after protest accepted. Gachot drives excellent race to fifth, lap 49, but misses gear and spins out, lap 52. Pre-qualification team now sixth in constructors' championship!

LAMBORGHINI

Really tough luck for the struggling Italian team. Eric van de Poele fails to pre-qualify by only 0.06s. Larini (third) pre-qualifies for the first time since Phoenix, only to be disqualified for having rear wing too high.

derided so often in the past as a rich no-hoper, was magnificent. He moved to fourth on lap 29, as Piquet stopped for tyres, but now Senna was swarming all over Mansell's gearbox! For lap after thrilling lap the Brazilian, with Alesi and de Cesaris right behind him, tried every way except over the top to get past the Williams — but he never succeeded. Nigel's Renault V10 may have been a bit short of puff, but it still had enough to out-grunt Senna's Honda V12. But, everyone asked themselves as this riveting race progressed, would the two Williams last the distance?

On lap 45 the tension rose. With Alesi out (lap 43, broken clutch) after a brilliant charge which had taken him back to fourth following his spin, a lucklustre Prost, who'd never been higher than seventh, long since gone with a misfire (lap 17) and Piquet out with a seized rear wheel bearing (lap 31), it was time to take stock. Patrese now led Mansell by a seemingly race-winning 25 seconds. Nigel and Senna were still gearbox-to-nosecone. De Cesaris was fourth with Moreno right behind him and Gachot was sixth. Both Jordans in the top six again! But the people with stopwatches (and how can you truly follow a Grand Prix without one?) now spotted something very significant; Mansell was starting to catch Patrese!

It wasn't that Riccardo was going slower. Nigel had really got the hammer down and, in the process, he was leaving Senna well behind. "I richened the mixture and that made all the difference," explained Nigel. It sure did, for down came his lap times and down too went Riccardo's lead. Prost's lap record went on lap 51 as Mansell closed the gap to 17 seconds.

Disqualified for pushing his car across the line, Andrea de Cesaris was eventually reinstated, taking his Jordan to its second consecutive fourth place finish.

Mexico marked the fourth victory of Riccardo Patrese's long career, and it was thoroughly deserved. Not even the ill-effects of Mexican cuisine could deny him (right).

GOODYEAR
Labatt's
RENAULT
elf
FRED PERRY
Labatt's
Labatt's
Riccardo Patrese

Eric Bernard prepares to score a valuable point for the hard-pressed Larrousse team.

With an incredible string of seven successive lap records, Nigel held us spellbound. Our attention was only distracted by the unfortunate Bertrand Gachot, now a praiseworthy fifth, missing a gear at the Peraltada (of all places!) and departing the race. With Moreno thus now fifth, Eric Bernard up to sixth and Senna slipping steadily backwards, settling for third place and four points, Mansell got closer and closer to Patrese. Lap 56 — ten seconds. Lap 61, the fastest of the race in 1m 16.788s (128.789 mph) and only 0.1s slower than Riccardo's pole time, saw the gap down to six. As the two flying Williams-Renaults started the 67th and last lap, Nigel was only 1.1s adrift. As has been said so many times though, catching is one thing, passing quite another.

Young Italian Gianni Morbidelli scored his best result to date, taking his Minardi to seventh.

Passing never came into it. Riccardo knew the score and had something in reserve. His last lap was his fastest and brought him home for a magnificent fourth victory of his career, 1.3 seconds ahead of Mansell for the first Williams one-two since Canada 1989. Senna finished third in his outclassed McLaren-Honda, a demoralising 57 seconds later, but the drama still wasn't over. As Andrea de Cesaris came round the Peraltada for the last time, to take his second successive fourth place for Jordan, he stopped — within sight of the chequered flag. Even worse than Mansell in Canada! Out got Andrea and, to the horror of the cognoscenti, started to push. He obviously didn't know, as they did, that there's a penalty for pushing. He should have. It is a disqualification offence and excluded he duly was. But he was reinstated after a protest by the astute Eddie Jordan, who pointed out that the race had finished before Andrea had got out of the car and started to shove. A lucky man, but it had been a fine drive which was more than worthy of the place.

With Roberto Moreno fifth and Eric Bernard taking a single point for sixth that might well enable the poverty-stricken Larrousse-Lola team to raise the money it needed to continue racing, so finished an exciting and memorable Mexican Grand Prix. Senna hadn't had trouble (except some overheating, which had also affected Mansell). He hadn't retired from a commanding lead to leave everyone feeling he was the moral victor. He had been well and truly beaten. ''The main thing was to finish on the podium to take four points for the championship and, in the meantime, to give Honda and McLaren the chance to make some modifications to both the chassis and the engine.'' You could bet your boots they'd be doing so!

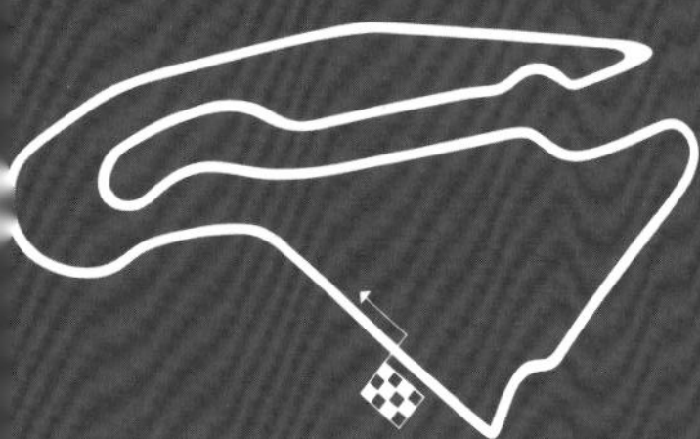

FRANCE

July 7 1991 Circuit: Nevers Magny-Cours

No expense had been spared preparing Magny-Cours for its first GP. This is the impressive pits complex.

Since the World Championship began in 1950, the French Grand Prix had been held at six different circuits. In 1991, for reasons not obvious to the uninitiated, it moved to a seventh — the totally rebuilt, 2.65 mile Magny-Cours track near Nevers. It all seemed to be about money and politics, because the Paul Ricard circuit near Marseille had been well liked for its layout and location — and had just had a great deal spent on it. There was a lot of opposition to the move, but Magny-Cours it was to be for the next five years. The track is about three hours' hard driving south of Paris, in the very attractive Nièvre region between the Loire and Allier rivers. The area is heavily populated by sheep and magnificent Charolais cattle, but there aren't many hotels! Leastways, not nearly enough for the sophisticated needs of the Grand Prix entourage; stories of horrifically inadequate accommodation were legion. On Saturday, for instance, having left their hotel in disgust, Martin Brundle and Mark Blundell, due to drive in the race the next day, didn't know where they were going to spend the night!

Having abandoned the unsuccessful Porsche V12 for the time being, Footwork converted the FA12 to take Cosworth power. Alboreto made the race ... just.

Prost gets the jump on Mansell, Senna, Berger and Alesi at the start, as poleman Patrese is swamped by the pack, his gearbox playing tricks on him again (right).

But if the hotel situation left a lot to be desired, the Magny-Cours complex itself most certainly did not. After the expenditure of a stupefying £35 million, it was a model of how it should be done with super garages, paddock, media facilities and grandstands. The track was super-smooth and, from the spectators' point of view, absolutely terrific, with fast, spectacular sections and enough gradients and corner variety to make it interesting. The drivers weren't so enthusiastic. Most of them complained that there were too many chicanes and that there weren't enough overtaking places. But all in all it was regarded as being a good effort — if only there had been somewhere decent to stay!

No complaints about the weather though. It was warm, dry and sunny. On Friday, the temperature was 33 degrees when the cars blasted out of the pit lane for the first qualifying session — amidst speculation about prospects for the race. After being beaten in Canada and Mexico, McLaren was far from optimistic about its chances in France. ''We're under no illusion that we've got the best car at the moment,'' said supremo Ron Dennis. ''Part of the problem is in the engine area, but we're not going to panic. Both Honda and ourselves know what needs to be done and we're doing it, but it all takes time.'' So there were poor odds on another Senna win, especially as the Williams-Renault was getting more impressive by the race — and Renault was obviously all-out to repeat its Mexican win on home soil. But there was more to McLaren's opposition than Williams, for Ferrari produced its new 643 and very impressive it was too. Now with the fashionable upswept nose, as a result of Jean-François Migeot's move from Tyrrell to Ferrari, and with new front suspension, it was on the pace straight away.

On Friday it seemed as though Ron Dennis had been too pessimistic, for Ayrton Senna scorched round in 1m 16.557s — half a second faster than Nigel Mansell. If there was rain tomorrow that would be his 57th pole position and, with overtaking being so difficult, probably his 31st win. But it didn't rain on Saturday and the oppressive heat had gone, so conditions were very much faster. Two seconds faster in fact, with Riccardo Patrese, the man we had misjudged for so long, taking his third successive pole position in 1m 14.669s! He was

TEAM ANALYSIS

McLAREN
Team arrives in France expecting to be outclassed — and is. With engine and chassis deficiencies compared with Williams and Ferrari, Senna and Berger third and fifth on grid (Senna after blowing an engine on Saturday). Gerhard retires from fourth place, lap seven, with broken Honda V12 — his fifth retirement from seven races. Senna has trouble-free run, staving off Alesi's Ferrari to finish third, 35 seconds behind Mansell. Ayrton still leads championship by 25 points but McLaren lead over Williams down to 13. High pressure work in hand at Woking and Wako to regain initiative.

TYRRELL
Hampered by Pirelli tyres unsuited to track, Modena and Nakajima start 11th and 18th. Stefano side-swiped by Martini on lap eight but car undamaged. Retires from 13th place, lap 58, with gearbox problem. Satoru slides into sand trap when 13th, lap 13, and retires.

WILLIAMS
A dream meeting for Frank's team on Renault's home ground. With revised aerodynamics and Elf 'rocket' fuel, the sensational Riccardo Patrese takes his third successive pole position — once again to outqualify Mansell who starts fourth. Experiencing gear selection problems, Riccardo has appalling start and drops to ninth. Mansell, closely chasing Prost, outdistances everyone else. Brilliantly passes Alain on lap 22 and builds 17s lead, which he loses after overdue tyre stop, lap 32. Fights back in typical fashion to retake lead on lap 55 and win his 17th GP, beating Stirling Moss's record to become the English Grand Prix driver with the most victories. Also sets fastest and record lap (1m 19.168s, 120.679 mph) and moves up to second in the championship. Riccardo makes excellent recovery to finish fifth (one lap down) despite gearbox problems. Renault overjoyed with its first French GP victory since 1983 — and Williams now within 13 points of McLaren in constructors' championship.

BRABHAM
Not a happy meeting, despite more Yamaha power and revised aerodynamics. Blundell starts 17th but Brundle only 24th. Martin up to 16th but loses gears and retires, lap 22. Mark 11th laps 33-36 but crashes into pit wall, lap 37, after impressive drive.

FOOTWORK
After three weeks non-stop work, team appears with Hart-DFR engines in revised FA12 chassis, having decided to abandon Porsche V12 until it can be made competitive. Team's problems compounded when Alex Caffi tries, unsuccessfully, to obtain an injunction to regain his lost drive. Stefan Johansson fails to qualify but Alboreto does well to make the grid in 25th. Retires from 15th, lap 32, when hastily designed, built and untested new drive-transfer gearbox fails.

Failed again: Berger added to his seasonal tally of exploding Honda V12s.

LOTUS
Mika Häkkinen misses qualifying by 0.23s due to oil on track from Grouillard's Fomet. Le Mans winner Johnny Herbert starts 20th. Loses half a lap at start after stalling and having to be push-started due to gear selection problem, then drives excellent non-stop race to finish tenth (two laps down).

FONDMETAL
Grouillard again pre-qualifies easily and qualifies 21st — in bad odour for laying oil on track which causes Senna to spin and destroys Häkkinen's fast qualifying lap. Hits kerb on lap one avoiding Gachot's spinning Jordan. Resultant damage inhibits performance. Olivier retires from last-but-one, lap 48, with radiator leak.

LEYTON HOUSE
'Bouncing' handling problem cured after substantial mods to suspension, wings and floor. Gugelmin qualifies well in ninth place with Capelli starting 15th. Mauricio up to seventh, lap 17, and stays there (two laps down) for team's best 1991 result to date, despite being penalised ten seconds (and fined $10,000) for allegedly blocking Mansell on lap 70. Ivan retires from 16th, lap seven, after spinning and stalling in avoiding Morbidelli/Piquet collision — his seventh failure to finish in seven races.

AGS
Both Tarquini and Barbazza fail to qualify again.

BENETTON
Team unsettled by ramifications of Barnard resignation. Piquet and Moreno qualify seventh and eighth. Nelson races spare car and is fifth, after Berger retirement, when hit by over-ambitious Morbidelli. Runs sixth, laps 10-58, in now unbalanced car which obliges him to make late tyre stop. Finishes eighth (two laps down). Moreno loses first and second gears early in race. Drops to 11th and retires, lap 64, feeling ill and unable to continue.

ALLARA

manuele Pirro does not pre-qualify. JJ Lehto does so econd) and then qualifies 26th. Gains seven places on st lap. Retires, lap 40, racing strongly with Modena and omas in 14th place, when left rear tyre disintegrates.

AINARDI

fter qualifying tenth and 12th both Morbidelli and Aartini involved in race collisions. Pier-Luigi side-swipes Aodena on lap eight and Gianni hits Piquet whilst hallenging for fifth on lap nine. Morbidelli retires after esultant stall. Martini continues and finishes ninth (two aps down).

IGIER

leavily revised aerodynamics and new Elf fuel improve erformance. Erik Comas qualifies 14th, two places head of Boutsen. Thierry improves to ninth, lap 11, but as to stop twice to fix broken body-retaining bracket. inishes 12th, three laps down. Comas does better to nish 11th, two laps down, despite understeer, gearbox roblems and two tyre stops.

ERRARI

lappy days are here again with introduction of new 643. rost qualifies second fastest (and is quickest in Sunday arm-up) whilst Alesi starts sixth. Five times French GP vinner Prost scorches into lead at start but is caught and assed by inspired Mansell, lap 22. Regains lead, lap 2, when Nigel stops for tyres. Is again caught and assed, so finishes second five seconds adrift. Alesi pends whole race about two seconds behind Senna, nsuccessfully trying to get by. Nearly does so on harging last lap but just fails. Very encouraging race for ew team management.

LARROUSSE-LOLA

Financially beleaguered team able to continue racing thanks to new sponsorship and favourable legal moves. With all their worries and inadequate testing (no funds), Suzuki and Bernard do well to qualify 22nd and 23rd. In an excellent eighth place on lap 44, Bernard retires with transmission problems. A fine race for Suzuki similarly marred when, in 11th place on lap 33, his clutch breaks with "a big bang!"

COLONI

Yet again, for the seventh time in seven races, the hard-trying Pedro Chaves is unable to pre-qualify his Coloni-Ford. In such a small, underfunded organisation it seems unlikely that he ever will, but the team's determination and dedication has to be admired.

JORDAN

Yet another great race for the enormously impressive and enthusiastic Jordan team. Andrea de Cesaris and Le Mans winner Bertrand Gachot pre-qualify fastest and fourth before qualifying 13th and 19th. Bert's race lasts only until the first corner where he spins off, stalls and cannot continue. But de Cesaris compensates for Gachot's misfortune. Up to 11th on lap seven but 23rd and last on lap eight, after suffering from the Modena/Martini collision. After passing 13 people, sixth by lap 60 and stays there for his third successive points finish (one lap down). Team Jordan sixth in constructors' championship, only two points behind Tyrrell.

LAMBORGHINI

Eric van de Poele crashes at end of pre-qualifying in unsuccessful effort to beat the cut (driver OK). Larini also fails to go any further.

AGS spent what little budget it had on a fresh coat of paint, but neither Barbazza (pictured) nor Tarquini could drag themselves into the race.

Alain Prost served notice of the brand new Ferrari 643's potential, with a sterling drive to second place.

three places ahead of his number one, Nigel Mansell, whom Riccardo had now outqualified seven times in seven races. For Nigel the pressure was really on. And, for the third race running, Senna wasn't on the front row, let alone in pole position. He was third fastest, next to Mansell, whilst alongside Riccardo was Alain Prost, well pleased with his 643 and even optimistic about his chances for a sixth Grand Prix win in his homeland. With Berger fifth, Alesi sixth and the two Benettons of Piquet and Moreno occupying row four, expectations were high — and higher still after Sunday's warm-up, in which Prost was comfortably quickest.

Patrese had squandered his pole position in Canada and Mexico with poor starts — and he did exactly the same thing in France. "I went from first to neutral instead of second." Then the semi-automatic gearbox brain selected third and, by the time the hapless Riccardo had got it all sorted, he was down in ninth place. Meantime, Alain Prost led a Grand Prix for the first time in 1991. He was followed closely by Mansell, these two well ahead of their pursuers — Senna, Berger, Alesi, Piquet, Moreno, Martini and Patrese. By the sixth lap Prost was nearly 2.5 seconds ahead of Mansell, who led the closely-packed trio of Senna, Berger, and Alesi by nearly nine seconds. But poor Gerhard's race was over on lap seven when, for the fifth time in seven events, he retired his McLaren from the fray — with a very broken Honda V12 to blame. Senna might well prove to be right about reliability deciding the championship, for it certainly wasn't going to be Berger's title!

On lap nine out of 72, Patrese was up to fifth thanks to a superb bit of opportunism. Ahead of him Minardi's Gianni Morbidelli, an excellent sixth after starting tenth, had tried to take Nelson Piquet at the Adelaide hairpin. But the Italian got it all wrong and clouted the Benetton. Quick as a flash, Riccardo darted inside both his rivals to gain two places. Piquet's Benetton, which had been going so well, was never the same again and Morbidelli was out. In fact you hardly knew where to look in the early stages because, on lap seven, Gianni's team-mate Pier-Luigi Martini had biffed Stefano Modena's Tyrrell at the same place and demoted the following Andrea de Cesaris from 11th to last.

This was turning out to be a great race. Even this early it was obvious that Senna had decided to settle for third place and four points in the championship. His McLaren was clearly no match for Prost's Ferrari and Mansell's Williams. On lap 20 the Brazilian was an incredible 20 seconds behind the battle for the lead — and just two seconds ahead of Alesi's Ferrari. How times change! But it was last year's Ferrari team-mates that everyone was watching. Race leader Prost, with Mansell right behind him, got closer and closer to Andrea de Cesaris and Martin Brundle, fighting for 13th place and about to be lapped. As Andrea braked from 175 to 30 mph for the Adelaide hairpin on lap 22, Prost pulled out to pass the Jordan — and as he did so Mansell sliced inside both of them to lead! It was a brilliant passing manoeuvre, and, once he'd got by, Nigel pulled away from Prost to build a comfortable cushion.

As ever, it seemed likely that tyre changes would affect the race order. They began on lap 26, when Patrese was the first to stop. Some

Having a GP a few yards from the factory gates inspired Ligier to the dizzy heights of midfield; but for a couple of unscheduled stops, Boutsen would have fared better than 12th.

12.2 seconds later he left, still fifth. Then it was Senna, who took only an amazing 5.5 seconds to change all four wheels and tyres. Even so, he lost third place to Alesi. One lap later Prost was in for 6.2 seconds, and he was still second when he left. But Mansell stayed out and while he did so Prost, on his new rubber, started to carve chunks out of his lead. Alesi was in on lap 31 (7.2 seconds), promoting Senna back to third, and it wasn't until lap 32 — four laps after Prost's stop — that Mansell came in. Like Patrese's it was a slower stop, due to Williams' suspension modifications. It took 10.5 seconds and cost Nigel the lead. Prost was now 5.5 seconds ahead, the Ferrari sounding terrific and looking good to the delight of the partisan French crowd, who were roaring encouragement to their hero. But Mansell didn't hear and didn't care!

Alain was in amongst the traffic again, chasing a fast-moving snake comprising Roberto Moreno, Pier-Luigi Martini, Eric Bernard and Aguri Suzuki in eighth to 11th places. One by one he picked them off and so, behind him, did Mansell. But they soon found themselves with yet more cars to pass. On lap 48 the gap, which had fluctuated up and down, was 2.2 seconds — but next time round both Alain and Nigel had got a clear track in front of them, to which the Englishman responded with a record lap in 1m 19.168s (120.679 mph). The battle was reaching its climax, for now the Williams was only 1.5s behind the Ferrari. On lap 55 it was in front!

As the two of them swept up to the hairpin where Mansell had passed before, Nigel calmly outbraked the Ferrari and retook the lead on the *outside*. Tremendous! Now there was yet more traffic ahead, but this time it helped Nigel for amongst it was his team-mate Patrese, still lying fifth albeit nearly a lap behind. Soon he *was* a lap down as Nigel went by and Riccardo didn't exactly fall over himself to make it as easy for Prost to follow suit. By the time Alain had done so Mansell was long gone, five seconds ahead and showing every sign of staying there.

Magny-Cours marked the first win of the season for Mansell and the 17th of his career — a new record for an Englishman.

Which he did, to win his 17th Grand Prix, smash the jinx which had been dogging him all year, give Renault the home win it richly deserved and become the 'winningest' English Grand Prix driver of all time by breaking Stirling Moss's long-standing record of 16 victories. It was a very emotional moment.

Alain Prost never put a wheel wrong either and was delighted with the performance of the new car which had gone so well. Ayrton Senna finished third, 35 seconds behind Mansell and a mere second ahead of Alesi after staving off a terrific challenge from the Frenchman on the last lap. Patrese took a fine fifth place despite the fact that, unbeknown to us at the time, his gearbox had again been playing up for muc of the race. And to round things off nicely it wa Andrea de Cesaris who took the final point having moved up from last on lap 12 to sixth a the end — passing 13 people to do so for hi third successive points finish. And Jordan wa a pre-qualifying team!

What a marvellous preface to the Britis Grand Prix the very next weekend! Manse was back at the top of his very considerabl form and now second only to Senna in th championship (admittedly a massive 25 point adrift), with Williams eight points closer t McLaren in the constructors' contest. It wa going to be a sell-out at Silverstone!

GREAT BRITAIN

July 14 1991 Circuit: Silverstone

Last year they waved Ferrari flags, this year Union Jacks. A record crowd turned up to cheer Mansell home, and they weren't to be disappointed.

've never sat down to work out how many Grands Prix — car and motor cycle — I've been to, ut it's an awful lot. My first was when I was two-and-a-half years old (a long time ago!), but know that never before have I been to such a Grand Prix *occasion* as Silverstone 1991. It was abulous. A great new track, based on the old one we knew so well but very different in its haracteristics, was thronged from early on Friday until late on Sunday by a bubblingly nthusiastic, good-natured and knowledgeable crowd. The weather was ideal, the result remendous. It was Mansell-mania!

Nigel was fastest in both sessions on Friday, oth sessions on Saturday and Sunday norning's warm-up. He set fastest lap in the ace (a record, of course, on the new circuit), von his third British GP and his 18th overall. In loing so he gave his thousands of adoring fans xactly what they wanted, and they justifiably went wild in celebration of his dominance.

Not that McLaren took it lying down. Stung by defeats in Canada, Mexico and France and pressed by Senna to improve (although it needed no pushing), the team arrived with five cars to test different set-ups, assorted Honda V12 engines and various Shell fuels. But the five practice sessions showed that none of them were going to be good enough to beat the Williams-Renaults of Mansell and Patrese. McLaren was under pressure, but so were others. The British GP was the halfway point of the championship. Team performances over the previous two half-seasons would be assessed to decide who was going to take part in the dreaded pre-qualification sessions from Germany onwards. To avoid them, AGS, Brabham and Footwork needed to finish seventh or better at Silverstone. Sadly for them none did.

The revised Silverstone, with major changes to the Becketts, Stowe and Club corner areas and an entirely new complex of bends after Abbey, was much-liked by the drivers. "I think it is the most fantastic circuit in the world today," said Nigel Mansell, and it was great for television and the spectators too. TV coverage of Saturday's final qualifying session was superb. It showed Ayrton Senna doing a spellbinding lap, taking his McLaren by th scruff of its neck and hurling it round to displac Mansell from pole position. But not for long Nigel was sitting in his Williams ready for jus such an eventuality. Out he shot to circulate i 1m 20.939s — an amazing 0.7s faster tha Senna's incredible lap! With Patrese third o the grid ahead of Berger, Prost, Alesi, Moren and Piquet, anyone wavering about whether t get in the car and go to Silverstone on Sunda needed no further motivation. They went!

From first light the skies over the circuit wer thick with helicopters and the roads wer choked with traffic. It was a record crowd an half of them seemed to be carrying a Unio Jack. They made the Monza *tifosi* look like bunch of part-time enthusiasts. At two o'cloc though, as the lights turned from red to green there was a collective gasp of dismay a Mansell momentarily sat on the line with a excess of wheelspin, letting Senna surg

Senna and Mansell already have a fair lead at the start, the rest of the field being delayed by the spinning Patrese. Alesi's Ferrari also ran off the track, narrowly avoiding the stricken Williams.

A rear suspension failure pitched Andrea de Cesaris into the wall on the way into Bridge; happily, the Italian escaped from his wrecked Jordan with nothing worse than a shaking.

ahead. But as Nigel pulled out of the McLaren's slipstream before Stowe and took the lead, there was a concerted roar of approval and encouragement that never stopped. From then on Mansell led all the way, with Senna obviously settling for second place and six points just as he'd settled for third place and four in France. And it looked as though second would be no problem for the Brazilian, because Riccardo Patrese was already out after he and Berger had both tried to occupy the same piece of track at Copse. Exit Riccardo and past Berger went Roberto Moreno's Benetton, as Gerhard came to terms with bent front suspension and a skewiff steering wheel.

With Mauricio Gugelmin an excellent sixth in his Leyton House, Moreno held that third position for just three laps before giving way first to Berger, then to Prost and then to Alesi, who began a three-cornered fight that was to last for 18 closely contested laps. Alain was pushing the McLaren in front of him very hard indeed but, in spite of Gerhard's problem, which was to blister the Austrian's hands badly, he just couldn't get by. On lap 14 Prost was caught out himself when Alesi blasted past on the exit from the new, and tremendously spectacular, 160 mph Bridge corner. So now it was Mansell leading Senna by over 16 seconds, with Ayrton four ahead of the Berger/Alesi/Prost confrontation. With Moreno, Piquet and Modena sixth, seventh and eighth, that's the way it stayed until lap 22, when Roberto's gearbox called it a day — and Berger made the

TEAM ANALYSIS

McLAREN

In effort to regain lost dominance, team takes five cars to Silverstone to test various Honda V12s, Shell fuels and new front wing and front suspension. None of them good enough to beat Williams. Senna briefly holds pole position after searing Saturday lap but starts second to Mansell. Races increasingly distant second in non-stop race until running out of fuel on last lap. Classified fourth (one lap down). Championship lead reduced to 18 points. Berger fourth on grid after blowing two engines. Collides with Patrese at first corner but continues, with damaged front suspension, to take praiseworthy second before running dry after crossing finish line. Team's championship lead now down to 12 points.

TYRRELL

After starting tenth and 15th, Modena and Nakajima come home seventh and eighth (both one lap down). Naka lucky to finish at all, after having to stand on everything to avoid de Cesaris's crash on lap 42.

WILLIAMS

A race of very mixed team fortunes. Nigel Mansell dominates whole meeting with fastest times in all five practice sessions (his 16th pole position) and leads race from Stowe on lap one until chequered flag. Sets fastest (and record) lap in 1m 26.379s (135.325 mph) but is fortunate to win his third British and 18th career GP with semi-automatic gearbox malfunctions for last ten laps of race. Now within 18 points of Senna's championship lead. Patrese third on grid but collides with Berger at first corner and spins out of race. After three consecutive wins team closes championship gap behind McLaren to 12 points, but nagging doubts about gearbox remain.

BRABHAM

New stiffer underbody, better Pirellis, high-revving Yamaha V12 and improved fuel raise hopes for the seventh place needed to avoid pre-qualification from Germany onwards. Blundell's 12th and Brundle's 14th on grid best yet for team, and both drivers well pleased with improvements. But Martin starts in spare after blowing engine during parade laps. Improves to ninth by lap 22, but retires lap 29 with broken throttle cable. Mark Blundell works up to excellent eighth place by lap 32 before retiring when 11th, lap 53 (engine). So, sadly, hard-trying team faces early call for rest of season.

FOOTWORK

Team's ghastly 1991 continues with repeated failures of new transfer gearbox, hastily produced to allow use of Hart DFR in place of disgraced Porsche V12. Johansson fails to qualify after various engine and transmission problems. Alboreto qualifies 26th. Starts from pit lane in spare due to transmission oil leak in race car. Retires from 19th, lap 25 (transfer gears again). Team must now pre-qualify for rest of season.

LOTUS

A good race for Lotus, especially in view of its low-funds situation. In need of more power, Herbert and Häkkinen start only 24th and 25th. Johnny has superb drive, running ninth laps 47-55, until engine loses oil pressure two laps from end. Still finishes 14th (four laps down). Mika has straightforward race to finish 12th (two laps down).

FONDMETAL

The Fomet-Ford is a good car, but for the sixth time in eight meetings problems prevent the competent Olivier Grouillard from pre-qualifying it.

LEYTON HOUSE

Mauricio Gugelmin, happy with ninth on the grid, up to excellent sixth, laps 1-5. Lap ten tyre stop (blisters) drops him to 24th before retiring from rear of field, lap 25, when vibrations from broken floor cause leg numbness. Ivan Capelli starts 16th amidst rumours of a move in 1992. Ninth laps 11-16 but then selects wrong gear, spins, stalls and retires. Team just avoids need to pre-qualify during second half of season.

AGS

Current car not good enough to enable Tarquini and Barbazza to qualify. Pre-qualification beckons from Hockenheim onwards.

BENETTON

Grand Prix world electrified and delighted by news that Tom Walkinshaw's TWR organisation has bought 35 per cent shareholding of Benetton — a move that will greatly strengthen team in terms of leadership, structure and administration. Roberto Moreno and Nelson Piquet qualify seventh and eighth. Roberto has superb start, benefits from Patrese/Berger collision and moves to third. Down to sixth, laps 7-21, before retiring, lap 22, with broken gearbox. Nelson makes bad start and is down to eighth after lap 30 tyre change. Gets head down and recovers to finish fifth (one lap down). But team needs TWR touch to match front-runners.

DALLARA

Team pre-qualifies easily for last time — Lehto fastest and Pirro third. Both then qualify with JJ 11th and Emanuele 18th. Pirro clipped by Gachot at start but, despite being "too slow on straights", finishes tenth (two laps down). Lehto drops from tenth to last with lap seven pit stop (electrics). Restarts last after long delay and does well to finish 13th (three laps down), setting excellent eighth fastest lap in process.

MINARDI

Team suffers from failure to attend Silverstone tyre tests. Morbidelli only 20th on grid and Martini 23rd. Despite miserable repetition of familiar clutch problem, Pier-Luigi finishes well in ninth (one lap down). Gianni has massive oversteer in race but comes home 11th (two laps down).

LIGIER

Comas fails to qualify and Boutsen only 19th on grid,

disappointed after good progress made at French race. Thierry retires from 12th place, lap 27 (engine). Massively funded French team only 12th in pecking order after last 16 races in sad contrast to rival Gérard Larrousse's impoverished Lola-Hart organisation, which lies tenth.

FERRARI
Prost and Alesi have to set up new 643 for Silverstone's revised layout, having used 642 for tyre tests. "The car is only good on full tanks," says Alain, who qualifies fifth (just 0.002s slower than Berger!) with Alesi sixth. Jean on to grass at first corner to avoid Patrese/Berger squabble. Breathtakingly takes fourth from Prost on lap 15. Then to third when Gerhard tyre-stops, lap 24. Retires, lap 32, after colliding with Suzuki. Alain spins on Alesi oil, lap 30. Obliged to stop for tyres, lap 43, after puncturing on de Cesaris's crash debris, losing any chance of passing Berger. Finishes third and sets second fastest lap of race. Team, Prost and Alesi now well out of touch in respective championships.

LARROUSSE-LOLA
After qualifying 21st, Eric Bernard starts in spare Lola when race car runs onto seven cylinders on assembly lap. Improves to 17th, lap 17, but retires lap 22 when crown wheel and pinion give up. Aguri Suzuki starts 22nd and is comparatively contented 14th in oversteering car on lap 30 when collides with overtaking Alesi. Aguri carries the can in stewards' enquiry and is fined $10,000. But impoverished team still proudly in top ten (and ahead of bitter Ligier rivals).

COLONI
Poor Pedro Chaves achieves his eighth successive pre-qualification failure.

JORDAN
No more pre-qualifying! Eddie's outstanding new team says goodbye to eight o'clock practice with final second and fourth for de Cesaris and Gachot, who then qualify 13th and 17th (after Andrea had been an incredible fifth on Friday — faster than both Ferraris!). Bertrand spins to 23rd after colliding with Pirro at start, but up to astounding fifth on lap 32 after superb comeback charge. In non-stop run, concedes the place to Piquet on lap 56 as tyres deteriorate, but finishes sixth to give team its fourth successive helping of points. Disastrous race for Andrea though. After lap 12 tyre stop, recovers from 23rd to a fine eighth, lap 41, but has colossal crash, lap 42, when suspension component fails. Fortunately driver OK.

LAMBORGHINI
Larini and van de Poele fail to pre-qualify for the seventh time each, but team joyously celebrates fact that Larini's seventh place in Phoenix enables them to avoid the eight o'clock session from Germany onwards.

Mark Blundell qualified well once again for Brabham, but neither he nor Martin Brundle could obtain the seventh place necessary to escape relegation into the pre-qualifying ranks.

FISA's pit lane access credentials are to change in '92. The existing credit card will be replaced by colour-coded tights (above).

first tyre stop.

Goodyear had predicted that, even though nearly all their runners were using the soft C compound, there'd be no need for them to stop. That obviously didn't apply to Berger, whose bent suspension was giving his tyres a very hard time indeed. Gerhard's stop lasted for only 6.9s, but it was enough to put him down to sixth place behind Piquet and ahead of Gachot, who'd spun down to 23rd place at the start but had recovered magnificently. Then Alain Prost spun: "I'd got some oil from Alesi's engine on my visor and I just made a mistake and hit the kerb." He kept his place but was now out of touch with the battle for third — until Alesi hit Suzuki. Jean was coming up to lap the Lola when they collided and, as usual, each said it was the other's fault. The stewards later agreed with Alesi and fined Aguri a massive $10,000. That was no consolation to Alesi though, because he was out of the race with irreparable damage to the front of his car.

So on lap 32 Prost was third, Berger fourth, Gachot a superb fifth and Modena sixth, with Piquet down to seventh having stopped for tyres. But what about Mansell and Senna? They were still there, first and second, and both were looking very secure indeed, although now the Williams headed the McLaren by 20 seconds after a succession of ever-faster laps from

Johnny Herbert gave a good account of himself in the Lotus, climbing as high as ninth before fading oil pressure dropped him to an eventual 14th.

Nigel and Leo Mansell celebrate dad's French GP victory on the eve of his 18th F1 success.

Nigel. With 27 laps to go, the crowd still roared every time Mansell passed by. ''The support I was getting was fantastic. I salute them and dedicate this race to the fans.''

But then, just as we'd decided that all was well with the Williams, in came Mansell for new tyres on lap 37. Why so late? What was wrong? Why did he need them against all predictions? The answer was that he'd lost balance weights from two wheels and the resultant vibration was more than even Nigel could take. Thanks to new wheel nuts, which had been designed and fabricated after slow pit stops in France the previous week had shown that the car's new front suspension was creating a problem, Nigel was out of the pits in 8.4s — just ahead of Senna, who was trying valiantly to get past Andrea de Cesaris's Jordan and receiving no help from the Italian. Which was just what Nigel needed! By lap 40, with 19 to go, he was ten seconds ahead of Ayrton and lapping consistently faster. But nine laps later he'd got a major problem. The dreaded Williams semi-automatic gearbox was being its unpredictable self again. ''I kept getting the wrong gear or, even worse, no gear at all. If that happens everything can stop like it did in Canada. My heart was in my mouth and for the last two laps I stayed in the same gear all the way from the start of the lap until I got to Club.'' Thank heavens the crowd didn't know!

Alain Prost was very lucky too, because on lap 42 de Cesaris had a colossal accident right in front of the Ferrari as, approaching the daunting Bridge corner absolutely flat out, he lost control of his Jordan when his suspension failed. Alain miraculously avoided him (as did Satoru Nakajima, who was right behind Andrea fighting for eighth place), but in the process he ran over some debris and collected a puncture. By the time he was out of the pits with a new set of Goodyears, Alain looked set for fourth place behind Mansell, Senna and Berger. But, on the very last lap, a sensation changed the order. As the wildly cheering crowd welcomed Mansell home for his third British Grand Prix victory, Ayrton Senna was rolling to a standstill at Club — out of petrol!

Only three men went the full 59 laps at Silverstone on July 14 — Mansell, Berger and

"I had that Ayrton Senna in the back of my cab once." The dominant Mansell offered Senna a taxi ride home after the Brazilian's McLaren ran out of fuel on the final lap.

Prost. Nigel won by a clear 42 seconds and his 43rd lap was the fastest of the race, to create a record for the new circuit in 1m 26.379s (135.325 mph). His second successive victory closed the championship gap between himself and Senna to 18 points — but he had been a bit lucky to finish, just as Senna had in each of his four 1991 winning drives. But never mind that, the crowd went home euphoric at having seen what they'd come for — Nigel had won!

Their attention had been almost entirely devoted to Mansell's brilliant drive, but there'd been others that were more than worthy of note. Gachot's sixth place in the Jordan, for instance. He'd been caught and passed by Nelson Piquet's Benetton-Ford with only three laps to go but, with his fighting recovery, he'd still put a Jordan in the points for the fourth race in succession, solidly to underline the superb new team's right to leave the ranks of the pre-qualifiers. Johnny Herbert too was magnificent, thrusting his underpowered Lotus-Judd up to ninth before losing time and places through lack of oil pressure with just three laps left.

But the best was yet to come. As Mansell completed his cooling-off lap after taking the chequered flag amidst scenes of jubilation, he saw Senna standing by the side of the track. "I thought of running over his foot," he joked, "but as a good RAC man I gave him a lift home instead!" As the TV pictures showed Senna climbing aboard the Williams and patting Nigel on the helmet, a warm gesture of thanks and a sign to go, I felt a lump in my throat. And when Mansell, Berger and Prost joined hands on the podium, wreathed in smiles, it got a lot bigger. After all the talk about bad blood between the top drivers, it was a very happy way indeed to finish what had been a truly memorable day of Grand Prix racing.

And there were still eight races to go. Marvellous!

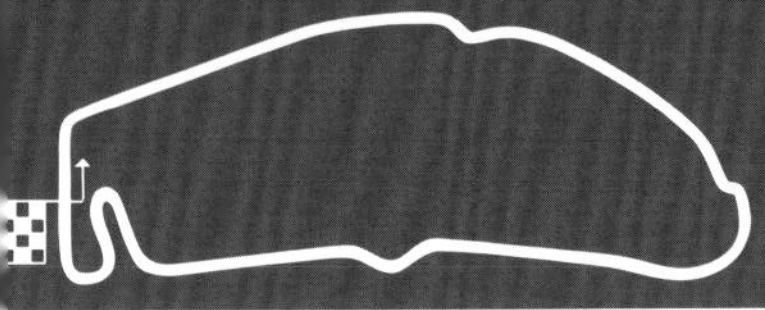

GERMANY

July 28 1991 Circuit: Hockenheim

Hat-trick hero: Mansell speeds past the packed stadium grandstands on his way to a third consecutive victory.

Britain was aglow after Nigel Mansell's fine win at Silverstone. His optimistic fans expected him to narrow the 18-point World Championship gap between Ayrton Senna and himself when they met at Hockenheim (near Heidelberg), for the German Grand Prix. But although the Williams-Renault was now very clearly the car to beat, it seemed a pretty tall order to hope that the gap would shrink by much. With every point counting in 1991, Senna could stay ahead for several races if he finished consistently in the top three — even if Nigel kept winning. McLaren and Honda had spent another two weeks trying to overcome their handling and engine problems, and neither concern hangs about when it comes to getting things done! So we could expect the contest to be much closer in Germany, and maybe even to see McLaren winning again — because Hockenheim had got something that was going to tax every car to its limit.

Or, to be exact, two things — the long, semi-parallel curved legs which join the 4.3-mile circuit's twisty stadium section and which, with their three chicanes, are engine and gearbox killers. The Renault V10 in the Williams, allied with its Elf fuel, might well be the most powerful engine, but what about that semi-automatic gearbox which had given so much trouble? Mansell had been fastest in the pre-race tyre tests but, faced with Hockenheim's demands, would his (and Patrese's) transmission go a full race distance? And if it was hot everybody's tyres would take a pounding, because the need to maximise speed on the straights by running as little wing as possible meant there wasn't much downforce to keep them on the tarmac. The wear rate would therefore be high. So the German GP result was by no means a foregone conclusion. Indeed, if you finish at Hockenheim you've done well!

The Germans like their motor racing (although with their superb automotive industry, it is a mystery that they don't support Formula One more) and on race day they turn out in their thousands in shiny new Porsches, Mercedes, BMWs and Audis (I even saw a few Trabants this year!) to fill the vast concrete grandstands that surround the stadium. There's no point in going anywhere else, except the top chicane, because the long connecting curves simply slice their way through huge and gloomy pine forests and you see little. They all got value for money in 1991.

After the reshuffled pre-qualifying (which relieved the Jordan, Dallara and Lamborghini teams of the need to get up early, but demoted Brabham, Footwork and AGS), the Friday and Saturday practice sessions saw the usual six at the front of the grid for Sunday's 45-lap race. But the times for the first two rows were really close! Less than 0.4s covered Nigel Mansell, in his second consecutive pole position, and fourth-placed Riccardo Patrese. The two Williams-Renaults sandwiched the McLarens of Senna and Berger. As at Silverstone, if Ayrton could get the drop on Nigel at the start he'd have the enormous advantage of being in front with a clear track ahead. The Ferraris of Prost and Alesi were next, but two seconds slower than Mansell (although Prost was second fastest in Sunday's final half-hour warm-up and optimistic about his chances in the race). Senna was to be angrily frustrated and disappointed though!

''I'll swap you 10 per cent of your salary for a reliable fuel gauge.'' Ron Dennis and Ayrton Senna discuss McLaren's rare lean spell.

"So where's the baseline?" Steffi Graf turned up at Hockenheim to support brother Michael, who was taking part in the GM Lotus Euroseries race that formed part of the supporting programme.

The Brabhams (below) faced up to pre-qualifying for the first time, and sailed through. Brundle (11th) and Blundell (12th) both made the finish, despite the latter's first corner spin.

This time Senna's departure failed to match Mansell's — or Berger's. Despite getting a bit sideways, Nigel set off like a missile to lead Gerhard out of the stadium followed by Senna, Prost, Alesi and Patrese. Berger had outdragged Senna and, once again, Riccardo had bodged his getaway. On lap two Patrese surged past Alesi into fifth and Piquet took seventh from de Cesaris's Jordan, but already Mansell was looking as though only a mechanical problem was going to deny him his third consecutive win. Nigel was out on his own and obviously pacing himself, but behind him there was action, action, action! Berger held on to his second place but there was a furious struggle going on for third between Senna and Prost, with the Ferrari almost glued to the McLaren's gearbox and Patrese closing on both of them. This was real racing — at speeds of over 200mph!

The interesting thing to those in the know, though, was that Jean Alesi, who was sixth but well in touch with the battle ahead, had fitted Goodyear's harder B compound tyre in the hope that racing non-stop would see him ahead at the end. He'd have no worries with

TEAM ANALYSIS

McLAREN

A depressing meeting for McLaren, who lose leadership of constructors' championship for first time in last 40 Grands Prix. After being lucky to survive 200 mph accident at Hockenheim during tyre testing, Senna second on grid to Mansell. Using latest spec Honda V12 engine, races third resisting constant Prost pressure for 13 laps but down to fourth, still with Prost, after lap 16 tyre stop. "Loses" Alain after controversial lap 38 incident but, as at Silverstone, runs out of fuel on last lap. Finishes very unhappy seventh, a lap down and out of points. Coolly dismisses Prost's post-race allegations that "dirty" driving by Senna caused him to slide off at chicane. Ayrton's championship lead over Mansell reduced to eight points. Berger starts third after suffering engine failure during Sunday warm-up. Second to Mansell until 16-second tyre stop (lap 13), caused by cross-threaded wheel nut. Recovers from tenth place to finish fourth and runs out of petrol on slowing-down lap — just like Silverstone.

TYRRELL

Satoru Nakajima starts 13th, one place ahead of team-mate Stefano Modena, after announcing his retirement at end of season. Both men unhappy with Pirelli tyres in race. Satoru stops twice for replacements before retiring, lap 27, with gearbox failure. Stefano stops three times for tyres and for battery change to correct misfire. Finishes 13th (four laps down).

WILLIAMS

Another perfect race for Williams, whose fourth successive victory moves team ahead of McLaren in constructors' championship for the first time since commencing 1989 partnership with Renault. Nigel Mansell takes 17th pole position and, as at Silverstone, is fastest in all five practice sessions. Leads all the way excepting laps 19-20 (tyre stop) and easily wins his 19th Grand Prix (first hat-trick) to close within eight points of Senna in championship. Patrese fourth on grid, only 0.4s slower than Mansell. Makes another poor start and drops to sixth. Third after 6.6s tyre stop (lap 20), but catches and passes Alesi to second, lap 38. Remains there to give team its second one-two of 1991. Also posts fastest (record) lap on lap 35 (1m 43.569s, 146.913 mph). "But now I must learn how to start!"

BRABHAM

Like all Pirelli teams at Hockenheim, Brabham very unhappy with tyres. But both drivers get through pre-qualifying — Brundle fastest and Blundell fourth. Both

Michael Bartels made his F1 début on home soil, but Johnny Herbert's temporary replacement failed to qualify his Lotus.

qualify (Martin 15th, Mark 21st) and happy to finish 11th (Martin) and 12th, two laps down. Mark lucky to finish after spinning at start without being hit.

FOOTWORK

Now faced with need to pre-qualify, team's awful 1991 gets even worse. Alex Caffi, returning after missing four races, unsurprisingly fails to pre-qualify. Alboreto deserves praise for doing so, in spite of repeated transfer gearbox breakages, but then fails to qualify.

LOTUS

Strongly-recovering team announces purchase of Williams wind tunnel. Mika Häkkinen crashes heavily on Friday but qualifies well (23rd). Collects chicane marker cone, lap two, and pits for removal. Retires from last place, lap 20, when valve spring breaks. German driver Michael Bartels, replacing Johnny Herbert whilst he fulfils F3000 obligations in Japan, impresses during his first F1 efforts but fails to qualify.

FONDMETAL

Grouillard blows engine in pre-qualifying and fails to get through.

LEYTON HOUSE

Still chasing first points of 1991, Ivan Capelli and Mauricio Gugelmin qualify 12th and 16th (after Mauricio's better Friday time disallowed — because his camera ballast weight was the wrong shape!). Ivan misses Sunday morning warm-up with upset stomach and has to transfer hastily to spare car after Ilmor engine fails on parade lap. Nevertheless races very well to lie eighth by lap 18. Into pits with misfire, laps 37 and 38, and retires, lap 40, when engine blows. Poor Ivan yet to finish in 1991. Gugelmin races to 12th, lap 18, despite gearbox and steering problems, but retires lap 22 (gearbox).

AGS

Team now demoted to pre-qualifying. Barbazza fails. Tarquini gets through well in second but, with 29th fastest qualifying time, goes no further.

BENETTON

In presence of new part-owner, Tom Walkinshaw, Piquet and Moreno qualify eighth and ninth. Nelson races eighth, immediately followed by Roberto until lap 13 tyre stop. Retires from eighth, lap 28, with gearbox problem. Moans bitterly about car sliding "each time I pushed hard." Moreno finishes eighth (one lap down; he is also very unhappy with Pirelli tyres.

DALLARA

Emanuele Pirro qualifies 18th with Friday time and races well to finish tenth (one lap down). JJ Lehto, having shared his team-mate's Judd V10 engine problems on Saturday, qualifies 20th with Friday time. Races up to 12th, lap 32, but retires lap 36 (engine).

MINARDI

Not a happy Hockenheim for Minardi. Pier-Luigi Martini qualifies well (tenth) but spins out of action on his own oil, from tenth place on lap 12, when Ferrari V12 expires. Gianni Morbidelli starts 19th and works way up to 13th before his engine also gives up.

LIGIER

Thierry Boutsen qualifies 17th with Friday time. Stops for tyres when 11th, lap 17. Thereafter has clutch and brake problems but finishes ninth (one lap down). "Before complaining about their car, every other driver ought to be made to drive a Ligier!" Erik Comas has gigantic crash at Ostkurve chicane on Saturday morning, but ignores hospital advice and returns to track to qualify 26th. Using spare car, flat-spots tyres twice on first lap but races on, only to retire from 18th on lap 22 (oil pressure).

FERRARI

Prost and Alesi start fifth and sixth, 0.01s apart but two seconds slower than Mansell. Alain races third, right behind Senna until both stop for tyres, lap 16. They leave pits together, fourth and fifth. Nose-to-tail battle continues, with Senna refusing to give way. On lap 38 Alain, trying to pass at first chicane, locks up, slides into slip road and stalls. Unable to restart, retires and angrily denounces Senna. "He had me on the grass twice, weaved, braked dangerously and would not let me by although I was faster. I accept that I cannot win the championship but I will do by best to help Mansell. If I come across Senna in the same situation again, I will push him off. He should be fined like Gugelmin and Suzuki were in previous races." Jean Alesi takes gamble by fitting hard-compound Goodyear B tyres for non-stop run. Holds sixth place but takes lead, laps 19-20, when others stop. Down to third, lap 38, and finishes there.

LARROUSSE-LOLA

Relieved team announces new sponsor — DOI of Japan. Suzuki and Bernard qualify 22nd and 25th. Aguri starts from pit lane in spare car after engine breaks on parade lap and then retires from 19th, lap 16 (engine). Eric retires from 22nd, lap ten (crown wheel and pinion).

COLONI

With no prior testing, Chaves again unable to pre-qualify.

JORDAN

Another great race for Jordan. Team celebrates release from pre-qualifying with best grid achievement so far — de Cesaris seventh and Gachot 11th. Andrea drives fine race to finish fifth and so does Bert, sixth despite stalling during tyre stop. Team's fifth successive points finish lifts them past Tyrrell to fifth in constructors' championship — a superb achievement. Top drivers now very anxious to drive for Jordan in 1992!

LAMBORGHINI

Team now out of pre-qualifying but still unimpressive. Van de Poele 26th on Friday but fails to qualify after blowing engine in final session. Nicola Larini starts 24th for first race since Phoenix, but spins on to grass whilst avoiding rotating Blundell at first corner. Stalls and cannot restart.

the Pirelli users (Brabham, Benetton, Dallara and Tyrrell), because most of them had been moaning about their tyres all weekend. His Goodyear rivals were all on the softer Cs. To prove the point, de Cesaris (Goodyear) passed Piquet (Pirelli) to take seventh on lap seven, whilst the glorious scrap behind Mansell and Berger raged on. Senna, Prost and Patrese were nose to tail for lap after lap.

Berger was the first to come in for new tyres (lap 13), and his stop ruined his race. It took 16 seconds for the McLaren men to get him out, because his right front wheel nut cross-threaded as they airgunned it on. When the Austrian left the pit lane, amidst great excitement, he was down in tenth place. But it was nothing like the buzz that was caused when Senna and Prost, second and third, came in to the pits as one on lap 16. Their stops might have been choreographed because they shot out together, with Senna still ahead, to rejoin the race fourth and fifth behind Mansell, Patrese and Alesi. On lap 18 Mansell came in with a 17-second lead. After 8.3 seconds at rest he rejoined third, behind Patrese and Alesi. Riccardo was going to stop, Jean wasn't. This was getting interesting, because it looked as though the Frenchman just might have made the right decision about racing on harder tyres.

On lap 19 a Ferrari was ahead as Patrese peeled off into the pit lane for tyres and Alesi took the lead with Mansell now second. But just two laps later Nigel was back in front with a record lap on his new Goodyears. So we had Mansell first and looking invincible, Alesi second, no reduction of Prost's pressure on Senna for third and Patrese fifth, catching the Ferrari and McLaren ahead. But now it was all eyes on Prost and Senna. Alain was continually trying everything in his considerable book of experience to pass his former team-mate. Braking late. Diving to the left and the right. Forcing up the outside and the inside. Whatever he did, Senna just sat on (or nearly on!) the racing line, increasing his rival's frustration by leaving him no room to get by. But, amazingly, Patrese took both of them on lap 22. He did for Prost with a demon bit of late braking at the third chicane, and nabbed Senna a few hundred yards later at the entrance to the stadium. In his 217th Grand Prix, Riccardo was driving as well as ever.

At two-thirds distance, lap 30, Mansell was over ten seconds ahead of Alesi, driving smoothly, consistently and taking great care not to overstress anything. But Patrese was thrashing the daylights out of his Williams as he squeezed every last ounce of power out of his Renault V10 to close the gap on Alesi. On lap 32 he set the fastest lap of the race (a new record) — 1m 43.659s (146.913 mph). This reduced Jean's advantage to just 2.1 seconds. On lap 37, after trying initially to keep Riccardo back, Alesi gave way — so now it was Williams-Renaults first and second!

With Alesi third and seemingly uncatchable, the difference between three points for fourth and two for fifth meant a lot to Ayrton Senna, and there was no way he was going to let the persistently challenging Prost take him. Not even when, with eight laps to go, the Ferrari's nose aggressively appeared alongside him at the approach to the first chicane. Moving marginally to his left, Senna not only made it impossible for Prost to pass but prevented him from taking his 140 mph line for the two rapid changes of direction. With tyres smoking, Alain slid to a standstill up the slip road and then stalled his engine as he waited for a marshal, in compliance with a new ruling, to move cones from the exit line and let him proceed.

Alain, who'd already had two major collisions with Senna in his career (Japan '89 and '90), was livid. "That was the only place where I could overtake him. I was much quicker than him on the straight and I was trying left and right with him weaving and braking in a strange way. Yet when Patrese was behind him he let him go very easily! I have nothing to lose now. I can't win the championship but I will do my best to help Mansell — and if I come across Senna again in the same situation I'll push him off!" Harsh words, but Senna was unimpressed. He'd got something else to bother about because, with a certain fourth place and three points in the bag, he'd once again run out of fuel on the last lap when his computer said he'd got sufficient left. It was an exact repeat of Silverstone!

Hockenheim 1991 was Nigel Mansell's race

Jean Alesi's decision to run Goodyear's harder B compound tyres paid off, the Frenchman taking an excellent third place behind the flying Williams duo.

Erik Comas crawls from he wreckage of his upturned Ligier on Saturday morning. He bravely returned from a hospital check-up to qualify 26th in the afternoon.

from start to finish. For the first time in his career he had won three Grands Prix in succession. This victory, allied to Senna's failure to score, took him to within eight points of the Brazilian's championship total. A rueful Senna admitted after the race that he was now well and truly up against it, with no sign that the performance gap between the McLaren-Honda and the Williams-Renault had been reduced. Williams, with its second one-two in five races, had ripped past McLaren to lead the constructors' championship for the first time since joining forces with Renault in 1989.

Frank's men weren't the only ones to go home rejoicing. Eddie Jordan's amazing team, in its first season of Grand Prix racing, had finished fifth and sixth with Andrea de Cesaris and Bertrand Gachot and had impudently moved ahead of the long-established Tyrrell organisation, with its Honda V10 engines, to take fifth in the teams' championship. With Alesi a well-deserved third after his non-stop drive and Berger fourth after a fine recovery from his long tyre stop, four different constructors, ranging from the oldest to the newest, were amongst the points scorers.

The next Grand Prix was in Hungary, where Mansell had won for Ferrari in 1989 and Williams had finished first and second in 1990. Nigel in a Williams at the Hungaroring, on a charge to lead the World Championship, would be something to see!

If you're president of FISA, you don't need to bother winning races to enjoy the spoils of victory.

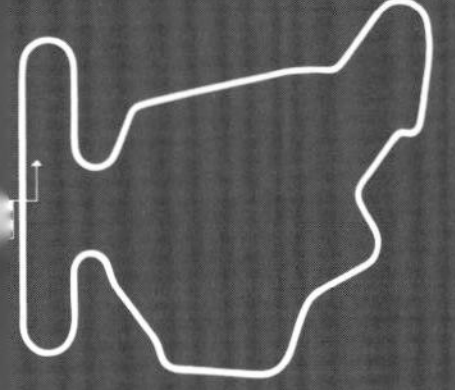

HUNGARY

August 11 1991 Circuit: Hungaroring

Ivan Capelli hadn't seen a chequered flag waved under his nose for quite some time. His first finish of the season netted a welcome point for the beleaguered Leyton House team.

Just as there was talk in Mexico last year about the 1990 Grand Prix being the last, so there was talk in Hungary this year that we would not be returning. Just why this might be wasn't clear. Not many people would fight to keep Mexico on the fixture list — but Hungary is a different matter. Budapest, whose twin cities straddle the majestic River Danube, is a truly beautiful capital with its boulevards, palaces, parliamentary buildings, St Stephens cathedral, opera house, museums and other magnificent historic architecture. The weather is invariably superb during Grand Prix week and, now that the country has shaken off the depression and suffocating control of its former communist masters, there is an altogether cheerful atmosphere. The shops may not be jammed with merchandise, but the restaurants are superb and Hungarian wines are excellent. I for one hope that we keep going there!

If there is a problem, it concerns the Hungaroring itself. The 2.5-mile track rises and falls as it makes its way round a valley, and the result is a superb viewing circuit for the thousands of eager spectators from Hungary, Germany, nearby Austria and Czechoslovakia, all of whom throng there to see the only F1 event held in a former Iron Curtain country. It has good facilities (bar the grossly overcrowded media office!) and an excellent surface, but it also has a major snag. It is virtually impossible to pass. The result is that nose-to-tail crocodiles of cars form high-speed processions, increasingly frustrated drivers looking in vain for a way to get by the men in front. That, in turn, can lead to over-ambitious passing attempts, like those of Senna and Berger in 1990 which controversially bundled Nannini and Mansel out of the race. So getting pole position at the Hungaroring is vital. In 1990 Thierry Boutsen started at the front and won his third Grand Prix for Williams because no one could force a way past him. 1991 was to see more of the same.

When the proceedings began there was a strangely bitter-sweet atmosphere of acrimony and harmony. FISA, the governing body of the

Fault-free zone. Despite incessant pressure from the Williams-Renaults, Senna never put a foot wrong as McLaren ended its unusually long barren period.

sport, had issued a warning to both Senna and Prost about their driving conduct in the German Grand Prix and had also given Prost a one-race suspended ban for speaking out after the race. That was the acrimonious bit. The harmony came when Ayrton and Alain talked out their differences for two hours. They emerged smiling, saying that they were reconciled and, if not chums, at least no longer enemies. Which was, of course, exactly what they'd said after their famous handshake at Monza the year before. We could only hope that this time it would stick.

In the paddock, everyone was mourning the death of the great Soichiro Honda, founder of the company which had made such a massive contribution to automotive sport and technology. Of late, Honda had been suffering defeat in Grand Prix racing and it was sad that Mr Honda did not live to see his company's return to the top of the tree with the Hungarian victory that came its way.

After its downfall in Canada, McLaren had greatly accelerated its development programme. As a result, there was a 15kg lighter car at the Hungaroring for Senna (''and there'll be another for Berger in Belgium''). Weight had been saved on the bodywork, chassis and, especially, the Honda V12. The latter had also been developed, in association with new fuels from Shell, to produce yet more power. Ayrton Senna, determined to take the pole position that mattered so much, used the revised car to do just that (his 57th), with another of the spectacular laps which are his speciality. It was nearly two seconds faster than Boutsen's 1990 pole and, more importantly, a staggering 1.2 seconds faster than Riccardo Patrese's second quickest time. Strangely enough Williams, who'd won three of the five Hungarian Grands Prix held so far, were neither surprised nor disheartened. ''This is a high downforce circuit,'' said designer Adrian Newey. ''Our car is built to go best at medium downforce tracks. Our characteristics aren't precisely right for here — but we'll go well everywhere after this!''

So the team wasn't unhappy with Patrese's second place on the grid. Nigel Mansell, who was third, was actually pleased because he would be starting from the cleaner, grippier side

Reasons not to be cheerful, part one. Roberto Moreno waits for team-mate Nelson Piquet to return the surviving Benetton to the pits during Saturday qualifying. Sharing one car, both qualified well down the field.

of the track. With Prost fourth, Berger fifth and Alesi sixth it was business as usual at the front, but there were some surprises behind them with Emanuele Pirro a fine seventh in his Dallara, Ivan Capelli ninth in his Leyton House and Martin Brundle an excellent tenth in the highest-yet Brabham-Yamaha starting position.

TEAM ANALYSIS

McLAREN

Endeavour rewarded! Mourning the death of the great Soichiro Honda, McLaren arrives at Hungaroring with much revised lightweight car for Senna following intensive development initiated after Canadian GP. Some 15kg saved through body, chassis and engine weight reductions. At circuit where front row grid position is as important as Monaco, Senna (using new Shell qualifying fuel for the first time) takes 57th career pole position with yet another electrifying lap, 1.2s faster than Patrese. Then drives inspired race to 31st victory, holding non-stop lead from start to finish, resisting continuous pressure from Patrese then Mansell. Championship lead over Nigel extended to 12 points. Ayrton cautioned by FISA stewards for conduct during battle with Prost in German GP. Berger takes provisional pole position on Friday but drops to fifth on Saturday and races to finish fourth. Senna briefly drives new semi-automatic gearbox car on Friday. Team retakes constructors' championship lead from Williams by two points but ''we're not there yet!'' says Ron Dennis about car development.

TYRRELL

Modena qualifies well in eighth. Nakajima 14th. Stefano blots copy book with two spins in race (in the first of which, at the start, he collides with Pirro) and finishes 12th (two laps down). Naka races to 15th (three laps down). Not an impressive result for the Honda-engined team.

WILLIAMS

Despite winning three out of five races at Hungaroring, team pessimistic for '91 because of FW14 car/Renault RS3 engine characteristics. So well pleased with second and third on grid for Patrese (after hitting barrier on Friday when brake seal failed) and Mansell. Riccardo makes superb start (for a change!) and is incensed at being squeezed off inside line by Senna at first corner. Maintains continuous pressure on Ayrton for 44 out of 77 laps until brakes deteriorate. Waves Mansell through and finishes third. Nigel increases pressure on Senna but has to back off from lap 57 when his brakes also fade. Finishes second, now 12 points behind Ayrton in championship. Team back to second in constructors' contest, two points behind McLaren. ''But we're going to be back at the front from here on!''

BRABHAM

Amidst rumours that it is to lose its Yamaha engines in 1992, team encouraged by Martin Brundle's tenth place on grid, his highest-yet in '91, after pre-qualifying second to team-mate Mark Blundell. Delighted with car's set-up, Martin drives excellent race to get team in points for first time with sixth place on lap 30. Down to tenth after tyre change and then has to retire, lap 59, with foot cramp. Blundell, an excellent ninth fastest on Friday, qualifies unhappy 20th after engine blows on Saturday. Up to 11th, lap 61, after tyre change, but spins into retirement, lap 63. Despite disappointing race, team feels real progress being made.

FOOTWORK

After repeated failures of transfer gearbox required to use 1991 rear suspension with interim Hart V8 engine, team produces ''cocktail'' car comprising FA12 front and A11 rear with previous transverse gearbox — but still fails. Caffi does not pre-qualify and Alboreto only does so 2.7s off the pace — before failing to qualify. Team understandably despondent and in bad shape.

LOTUS

Designer Enrique Scalabroni leaves team. Michael Bartels fails to qualify. Mika Häkkinen, just in at 26th, drives commendably in reliable car, after initial handling problems, to finish 14th (three laps down) in gruelling first Hungarian GP:

FONDMETAL

This time Olivier Grouillard pre-qualifies (third), but fails to qualify by 0.1s. ''But we fight on and will persevere with the car's development.''

LEYTON HOUSE

A point at last! After intensive testing at Silverstone and modification of front suspension, team pleased with Capelli's ninth place on grid (fourth and fifth in the two morning sessions). Ivan up to excellent fifth laps 29-45. Makes ''safety'' tyre stop, lap 46, and is passed by Alesi but finishes for first time in '91, taking sixth place (one lap down) for team's first point in 15 races. Gugelmin starts 13th after problems but drops to 20th, lap one, delayed by Modena/Pirro collision. Stops for tyres lap seven, suspecting puncture, but finishes 11th (two laps down). First 'double' finish in 1991 delights team and Ilmor engine supplier.

AGS

Both Tarquini and Barbazza (first time in Hungary) fail to pre-qualify.

BENETTON

Team in doldrums, off the pace despite tyre and aerodynamic experiments. Piquet qualifies 11th and Moreno 15th, both with gearbox problems. Roberto satisfied with eighth place (one lap down) in what was still only his 20th Grand Prix. Disenchanted previous winner Nelson Piquet ('86 and '87 with Williams) retires from ninth, lap 39, after being delayed by Modena/Pirro first corner fracas and then struggling with defective gearbox. Nelson reportedly anxious to move to another team in 1992.

DALLARA

Excellent best-yet seventh place on grid for Emanuele Pirro — partly thanks to using ''go-faster'' (extra 200 rpm) button. Then spoils it all by colliding with Modena at start and bending suspension. Drops to rear of field and retires with oil pressure loss, lap 38. Lehto starts 12th. Runs excellent seventh, laps 30-37 but with clutch, gearbox, brake and oil pressure problems (not much left!) retires from 16th, lap 50.

MINARDI

Ferrari-engined Martini and Morbidelli only 18th and 23rd on grid. Pier-Luigi 11th, lap 59, but retires lap 65 (engine). Gianni into pits lap two to remove grass collected avoiding Modena/Pirro collision. Runs last until lap 28 but improves to finish 13th (out of 17), two laps down.

LIGIER

Designer Gérard Ducarouge rejoins team from Larrousse-Lola after ten-year absence. Thierry Boutsen, 1990 winner in Williams, qualifies 19th with Erik Comas starting 25th. Comas drives excellent non-stop race to finish tenth (two laps down), exhausted by vibration from flat-spotted tyres. Boutsen up to tenth, lap 67, despite clutch problem and tyre stop. Acts as mobile smokescreen before stopping on circuit, lap 72, but is classified 17th (six laps down). Very creditably sets sixth fastest lap of race.

FERRARI

Alain Prost given harsh, much criticised, suspended one-race ban for criticising FISA governing body after his near-collision with Senna in Germany. Qualifies a useful fourth using special engine and fuel and is fastest in Sunday's warm-up session. Races strongly behind Senna, Patrese and Mansell until retiring, lap 28 (engine). Drops to fifth in championship. Jean Alesi qualifies sixth and gambles by fitting hard C-compound Goodyears. Gamble fails. Stops for softer Ds when holding sixth place, lap 25. Rejoins eighth. Finishes fifth. Still waiting for a Ferrari win after ten races.

LARROUSSE-LOLA

Designer Gérard Ducarouge amicably leaves for Ligier and is replaced by Michel Tetu. New "green top-flash" livery to mark start of Central Park sponsorship. Bernard and Suzuki start 21st and 22nd and race at rear of field. Both retire on lap 39 (engines).

COLONI

"The car should go better here," says persistent Pedro Chaves. But sadly it doesn't go well enough and, for the tenth time, Pedro fails to pre-qualify.

JORDAN

"It's our first time here. We don't know the track well enough," says Gary Anderson. So Gachot qualifies 16th and de Cesaris 17th. Startling improvement to second (Gachot) and tenth on Sunday morning. Both drive fine races to finish, one lap down, seventh (Andrea, non-stop) and ninth, with Bertrand posting his first-ever fastest (record) lap in 1m 21.547s (108.847 mph) after late, lap 69, tyre stop in unsuccessful effort to take eighth from Moreno.

LAMBORGHINI

Basically disorganised team finding it hard to get it all together. Eric van de Poele fails to qualify through trying too hard. Larini in at 24th and runs steady race with two tyre stops to finish 16th (three laps down).

Emanuele Pirro qualified a superb seventh... then spoilt it all by clobbering Modena at the start.

How to fail your geography O-level. Contrary to what the sign might suggest, the last Austrian Grand Prix took place in 1987. Obviously, the Austrian GP was closer to reality than we realised in 1991. But where did the Hungarians get that sign?

Significantly, seven of the nine cars in rows four to eight of the grid were Pirelli-shod; their drivers were expected to hold up the Goodyear runners amongst and behind them (especially the Leyton House chassis of Capelli and Gugelmin and the two Jordans), because their race tyres were thought to be inferior to those of their American rivals. We would see!

The race, in 30-degree heat, was long and exhausting for the drivers and was, frankly, of interest to Formula One connoisseurs rather than casual television viewers. For, as expected, it was a high-speed procession. If you understood and appreciated the tactics and the skill required to keep a slower car in front, as Senna did so brilliantly, it was great. If you didn't, it was no spectacle. Since I count myself amongst the former group, I thought it was terrific. After the race Nigel Mansell said ''it was decided at the first corner'', and he was right. Riccardo Patrese had practised starting in Friday's qualifying session and he made an absolute blinder, which brought him right up alongside Senna into the right-hander at the end of the pit straight. On the inside line he tried valiantly to take the lead, but Senna would have nothing of it and ruthlessly chopped across Riccardo's Williams to head the field into lap one. Patrese was incensed about it after the race but, on reflection, admitted that he'd have done the same thing himself!

For the first 27 of the 77 laps there was no change at the front. Senna was first with Patrese tight up behind him, trying to provoke the Brazilian into the mistake he never made. Mansell was as close to Riccardo as Patrese was to Senna, and Alain Prost lurked just behind the second Williams, looking as calm and

Last respects. Following the death of Honda's founder, Ron Dennis and his McLaren colleagues sported black armbands all weekend.

Murray says he hopes the rumours of the Hungarian GP's demise aren't true. He alleges it has something to do with the architecture, but we have our doubts...

relaxed as ever and apparently just waiting his moment. Every lap it looked as though the positions could change, but they never did! Senna's reworked Honda V12 had got so much grunt coming out of the corner onto the main straight that he was always able to get enough distance between himself and the pursuing Williams to make it impossible for Riccardo to close and outbrake him into the first turn. With team orders now on his side, Mansell was happy to let Patrese try to wear Senna down, but surely Prost would have to go for it? We never found out, for on lap 28 Alain peeled off into the pit lane with a blown engine — the first retirement.

That let Berger up to fourth, Capelli (who'd shot up two places at the start when Pirro and Modena drove into each other!) to fifth and Alesi, recovering fast after a tyre stop, to sixth. Senna started lapping the tail-enders as early as lap 12, but slicing his way through the field is one of his many strong points and he never put a wheel wrong, thereby denying Patrese a passing chance. Immediately behind the top six, Martin Brundle was driving a superb race and fleetingly got the Brabham-Yamaha into the points for the first time before stopping for tyres on lap 30 — real encouragement for the hard-trying team which was sadly to be spoilt when Martin later had to retire with, of all things, foot cramp.

On lap 45 Riccardo had had enough. ''I had a brake problem and Nigel was coming very quickly so I waved him through.'' Nice one Riccardo! Could a charged-up Mansell now succeed where his team-mate hadn't, and might Senna run out of fuel again as he had in the two previous races? The short answer to both questions was "no". Nigel was soon as close to Senna as Patrese had been, and for three whole laps there was less than half a second between them. But from lap 57, with 20 still to go, Nigel began to drop away. He too had got a brake problem and decided to settle for second and the six points that went with it. So ended what may have been the last Hungarian Grand Prix. Senna, able to conserve his fuel in the closing laps, was a magnificent winner just as Boutsen had been the year before, refusing to give way to non-stop pressure, never getting rattled, never letting the traffic ahead delay his progress and exploiting the power of his Honda engine where it mattered most.

His 31st Grand Prix win extended his championship lead over Nigel Mansell to 12 points whilst Berger's fourth place enabled McLaren to regain the constructors' championship lead that they had lost to Williams in Germany. But there were other noteworthy achievements. Like Bertrand Gachot's superb fastest (record) lap in 1m 21.547s (108.85 mph), when he was on a mighty charge after a late tyre stop (lap 69) in an effort to take eighth place from Roberto Moreno's Benetton — an effort which failed by only four seconds after he had been over 30 behind. And Ivan Capelli's sixth place — his first finish in 1991's ten races, his team's first point in 15 and the first ever for an Ilmor engine.

McLaren's superb recovery may have put it back at the top but we all remembered what Adrian Newey had said before the race, and looked forward with relish to the Belgian Grand Prix at Spa, on the world's finest circuit, in two weeks' time!

At this point in the 1990 championship, McLaren had led the constructors' contest by 26 points. Now they led by two and the outcome of the drivers' championship was far from resolved.

1991 was turning out to be a gripping season.

"It's great to be a racing driver." Häkkinen and Bartels celebrate the prospect of trying to qualify a Lotus in Hungary.

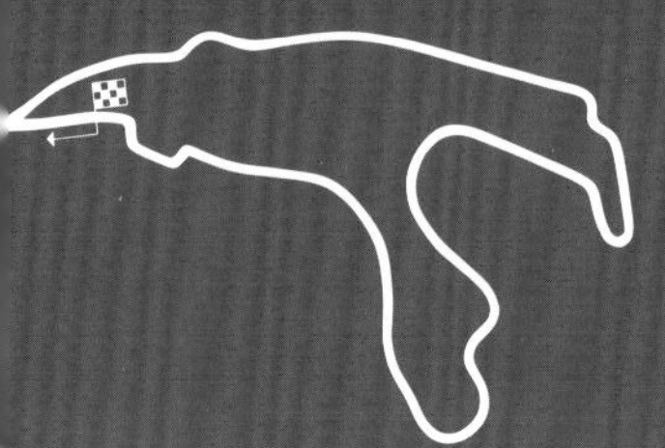

BELGIUM

August 25 1991 Circuit: Spa-Francorchamps

The start of the 1991 Belgian GP was highly unusual. For the first time in several seasons, there was no destruction derby at La Source.

Every once in a while there is a Grand Prix meeting where momentous things happen that you remember forever. This year at Spa was such an occasion, for we had four days in glorious surroundings packed with excitement, drama, controversy and action — together with the outstanding debut of a potential superstar.

So where to begin? We'll start with Bertrand Gachot. Bert claims to be 'European', but holds a Belgian licence, so the Grand Prix at Spa is of supreme importance to him. This year it was especially so, because he was to drive for the Jordan team as one of the three men who had jointly won the Le Mans 24 Hours and was also having his most successful Grand Prix season.

FUJIFILM
7UP
DEKRA
DEKRA
Philips CarStereo
Philips CarStereo
Philips CarStereo
Philips CarStereo
BP
Philips Car Stereo
Philips Car Stereo
M. SCHUMACHER

With four championship points he was on a high — until he appeared at a London court the week before his home race, charged with assaulting a taxi driver with CS gas. Bertrand was found guilty and sentenced to 18 months in prison. Belgium was outraged. The British were vilified, ''Gachot — Why?'' T-shirts were everywhere, there were demonstrations, slogans were painted on the track and there was a rumour that Nigel Mansell was going to be kidnapped.

But Gachot stayed where he was — in Brixton. Which meant that Eddie Jordan had to find a replacement driver. From a long list of eager hopefuls, 22 year-old Mercedes-Benz sportscar driver Michael Schumacher was chosen. If it was regarded as a risky decision, Eddie's talent-spotting genius was soon shown to have worked again for the German was not only sensationally impressive but an obvious future superstar. It was bitter gall and salt in the wound for the distraught Gachot.

It was sad indeed that there had to be an atmosphere of outrage at Spa, for it is, without doubt, the finest Grand Prix circuit in the world. Some 4.3 miles long, it carves its way through the glorious Ardennes countryside by way of specially-closed public roads which swoop round the sides of a valley. So there are gradients aplenty, super-fast straights and every kind of corner. Spa is a driver's circuit. And with plenty of room to pass, it enables the racers fully to exploit their talents. It is also tough on cars, which need lots of power, perfect balance, strong brakes and reliability to go the distance. The one real snag can be the rapidly-changing weather, which can be dry one minute and soaking wet the next. But there was no such problem this year — it was hot, dry and sunny the whole time. Perfect conditions.

Drafted in to the Jordan team to replace the incarcerated Bertrand Gachot, Michael Schumacher was sensational in qualifying. The young German's race didn't last long, but he made his mark (left).

Eau Rouge remains one of the most daunting obstacles on the Grand Prix calendar, and that's just to spectators...Johnny Herbert jinks through en route to seventh place.

TEAM ANALYSIS

McLAREN
McLaren goes home beaming after lucky but well deserved one-two finish. Further aerodynamic, suspension, Shell fuel and Honda engine developments (including variable-height trumpets) help Senna achieve 58th pole position. Leads race for 15 laps with Mansell attached to gearbox. Fifth after 9.9s tyre stop, lap 15, but benefits from tyre stops/problems and retirements of Mansell, Berger, Piquet and Alesi to win his 32nd GP (fourth successive Belgian), despite major gearbox glitch from lap 26. Increases championship lead over Mansell to 22 points. In new lightweight car, Berger starts fourth with Friday time after losing two engines on Saturday. Down to ninth, lap 18, after 17.8s tyre stop and spin exiting pits. Like Senna, benefits from rivals' misfortunes to finish second, complaining about down-on-power engine. Team says still much to do but delighted with increased constructors' championship lead over Williams — now 16 points.

TYRRELL
Modena qualifies tenth. Up to sixth on lap three. Nearly hits spinning Berger, lap 18. Retires from sixth with oil fire, lap 34. Lacklustre meeting for Nakajima. Only 22nd on grid. Spins out of 19th into retirement, lap eight. (''My fault. Sorry!'')

WILLIAMS
Heartbreaking race after confident expectations. Bad Friday for Patrese (sixth fastest), inconvenienced by back problem. Qualifies superb second only to be demoted to 17th with Friday time after scrutineers find defective reverse gear. Mansell benefits to start third. Races second shadowing Senna and takes lead, lap 15, when Ayrton stops for new tyres. Has own tyre stop next lap, 2.5s faster than Senna's, and leads confidently until lap 23 when electrical problem forces retirement. Now 22 points behind in championship. Riccardo has brilliant race. From 17th on grid up to incredible fifth on lap 18. Passes Piquet to take third, lap 30, but immediately takes to grass at Kemmel with long brake pedal. Amazing second and challenging for lead, lap 42 out of 44, but passed by Berger, Piquet and Moreno to finish frustrated fifth with only fifth gear still operational. Williams now 16 points behind McLaren in championship. Both Nigel and Riccardo re-sign for 1992 — to irritation of Senna, who was negotiating to join!

BRABHAM
Brundle and Blundell pre-qualify first and second. Mark starts 13th, Martin 16th. After poor start Blundell drives determined race to take his and Brabham-Yamaha's first point with fine sixth place (full distance). Brundle stops twice for Pirellis but finishes ninth (one lap down), giving team its best result so far. But joyful prospect of avoiding '92 pre-qualification blunted by news that Yamaha engines will go elsewhere in 1992.

FOOTWORK
Another disastrous meeting. Alboreto does not pre-qualify. Caffi does so (fourth) but fails to qualify (29th).

LOTUS
Johnny Herbert returns from Japanese F3000 commitments and qualifies 21st — three places ahead of Häkkinen. Mika, delighted with his car's handling, up to excellent tenth, lap 23, only to retire with blown engine, lap 26. Herbert drives magnificent race to finish seventh (full distance).

FONDMETAL
In new chassis with '91 spec Hart engine, Grouillard pre-qualifies third and qualifies 23rd. Then races to tenth (one lap down) — his first 1991 finish.

LEYTON HOUSE
Another depressing showing after success in Hungary. Gugelmin starts 15th with new engine after Sunday warm-up failure, but it blows at La Source on second lap. Capelli starts 12th and lasts until lap 14 when same thing happens whilst ninth. Gloom all round (four finishes from last 22 starts).

AGS
Two more failures to pre-qualify by Tarquini (massive accident at Blanchimont — driver OK) and Barbazza (who also crashes without injury).

BENETTON
Team unhappy about gearbox and Pirelli problems, but pleased with sixth and eighth grid places for Piquet and Moreno. Nelson starts well. Third laps 3-15 and actually leads, lap 17, after Senna and Mansell tyre-stops. Down

Jean Alesi was all set to score his maiden GP victory — and Ferrari's first of the season — when the Italian V12's legendary unreliability set in.

Mark Blundell did a splendid job to haul his Brabham-Yamaha into the points, albeit several races too late to have escaped pre-qualifying.

ɔ sixth after lap 18 tyre change. Climbs to third but, roubled by lack of grip, passed by de Cesaris and atrese. Benefits from their problems to finish third. oberto has similar race to finish fourth, with first-ever astest lap (1m 55.161s, 134.806 mph).

DALLARA

irro and Lehto blow three Judd V10 engines during ualifying and start 14th (Lehto) and 25th. JJ advances ɔ ninth, laps 31-33, but retires, lap 34 (engine again). manuele does much better by racing strongly to finish ighth (one lap down), after long and fierce struggle with Aartin Brundle.

MINARDI

ar much better after Monza tests but team desperately hort of money. Belgian first-timer Gianni Morbidelli has wo major crashes on Friday and Saturday but still ualifies 19th. Retires from tenth, lap 30 (clutch). Pier-Luigi Aartini qualifies well, as usual, in ninth. Races strongly ɔ seventh, laps 34-38, but then loses gears. Finishes 12th two laps down) with only fourth left.

LIGIER

After pronouncing car "undriveable" on Friday, Thierry Boutsen starts 18th for his home race. Comas scrapes in 26th. Both improve significantly in Sunday warm-up to 10th (Thierry) and 15th. Boutsen 11th, laps 4-11, but then as puncture, lap 12. Does well to finish 11th (one lap down) with clutch and brake problems. Comas has ouncture on lap eight. Then crankshaft breaks when unning last, lap 26. No points for team in last 36 races.

FERRARI

Things going from bad to worse. Prost third fastest in ualifying but starts next to Senna thanks to Patrese demotion. Passed by Mansell lap two. Out lap three with engine fire caused by broken oil pipe. Down to sixth in championship. Alesi starts on Goodyear's harder Bs, hoping for non-stop run. Looks good for his first win and Ferrari's first in '91 when leading race by 11 seconds on lap 31. Senna closes and waits for Jean's tyres to lose grip, but Ferrari engine blows first.

LARROUSSE-LOLA

Suzuki fails to qualify for the first time in a Lola. Bernard qualifies 20th and starts on Goodyear Bs, intending to run non-stop. Nearly rams Nakajima when Satoru goes off, lap seven, but races on until lap 22 retirement when 16th.

COLONI

For the 11th time in as many meetings, poor Pedro Chaves never even looks as though he is going to pre-qualify.

JORDAN

Jordan's Belgian GP would make a book of its own! Bertrand Gachot, jailed in London for assaulting a taxi-driver with CS gas, is replaced by 22 year-old Michael Schumacher, Mercedes-Benz's Sportscar World Championship driver, who is sensation of meeting. With only 36 laps of Silverstone's south circuit in the Jordan under his belt (his first Formula One drive), and never having even seen Spa before, he is fastest for much of Saturday morning's practice session, qualifies a staggering seventh and is fourth fastest in Sunday's race-trim warm-up! Rockets away from start and passes Piquet and Alesi before first corner, but immediately retires with failed clutch caused by standing-start inexperience. Eddie is rumoured to have him signed for 1992 already! De Cesaris almost as impressive. Starts 11th, but fifth in warm-up. Magnificently races to second on lap 31, harrying Senna for lead until has to retire only two laps from end of race, when rubber-blocked radiator causes engine to overheat and blow. Classified 13th, three laps down. No points but mega-glory for Jordan.

LAMBORGHINI

Trying too hard to qualify for his home race, Eric van de Poele has gigantic shunt on Friday and unsurprisingly fails to make cut on Saturday. Nor does Larini.

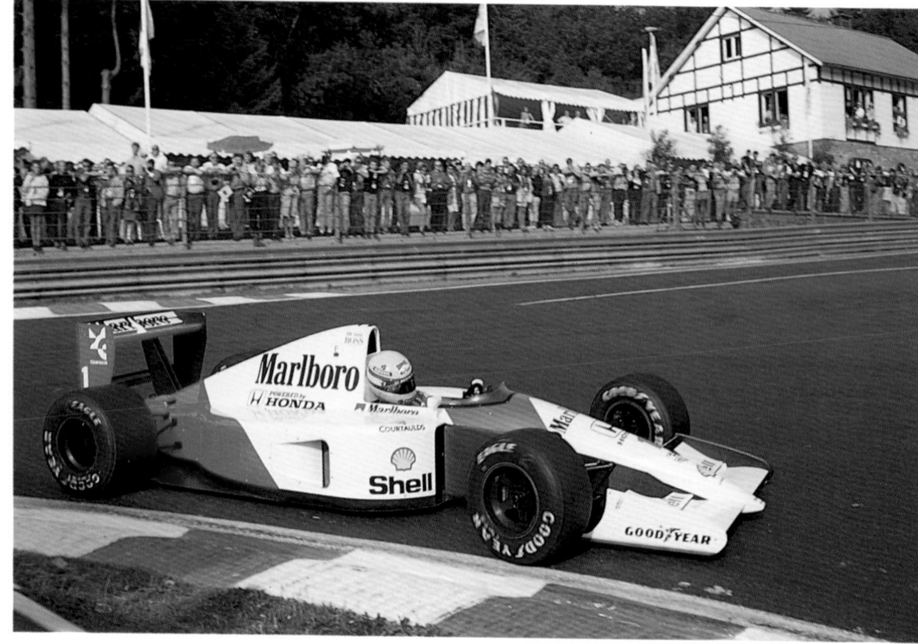

Ayrton Senna rounds La Source on his way to a victory that owed as much to his rivals' misfortunes as it did to his own speed.

''Senna may have won in Hungary by virtue of getting to the first corner first and staying there on a circuit where passing is well-nigh impossible, but it's going to be different here.'' That was the general opinion. McLaren's intensive development campaign had yielded real benefits and the revised, lightweight MP4/6, thanks to its faster-spinning (by 1,000 rpm) Honda V12 and Shell's potent new fuel, seemed to have caught up a little. But the Williams-Renault FW14 was thought still to have the edge, albeit slightly.

We were wrong though! Senna and Berger were fastest in Friday's qualifying session and Ayrton took his 58th pole position on Saturday with a lap that was 0.8s faster than the next best — Riccardo Patrese's. But official scrutineering established that Riccardo's reverse gear did not work, due to a broken electrical connection. That led to his Saturday time being annulled, and the unfortunate Italian went down to 17th on the grid. Up to second went Alain Prost's Ferrari, followed by Mansell, Berger, Alesi, Piquet and Schumacher. Schumacher? Yes indeed! For Michael, who'd never driven a Formula One car on a full GP circuit before and who'd never driven at Spa was, almost unbelievably, eighth fastest on Friday and *quickest* for much of Saturday morning. He qualified seventh and was fourth in Sunday morning's half-hour practice session. And his speed wasn't the result of driving recklessly. He was cool, smooth, safe, consistent and the source of delighted amazement for his race engineer, the experienced Trevor Foster. We could hardly wait for Sunday, with its prospect of Mansell challenging Senna for the championship points they both needed, Prost vying with them for the lead, the possibility that Schumacher could be up there too and the knowledge that Riccardo Patrese (fastest in the warm-up, 1.5s quicker than Senna) would be charging up from row nine of the grid. And what a race it turned out to be!

Apart from the weather there is another snag about Spa — the hairpin at La Source, which immediately follows the very short pit straight and which, for year after year, has caused a race-stopping pile-up after the start as 26 drivers try to get round it together. Not this year though. Everyone made it safely and, at the front, Schumacher was past Piquet and Alesi and up to fifth! But as he chased Senna, Prost, Mansell and Berger down towards the breathtakingly fast Eau Rouge, his clutch packed up. A pity, but he'd done enough already to put his name on everyone's lips.

Alain Prost didn't last long. Passed by Mansell on lap two, he rounded La Source with flames belching out of the back of his Ferrari from a broken oil pipe. Exit Alain, but we still had plenty to enthuse about. For 14 laps Senna led with Mansell's Williams attached to his gearbox, Nigel apparently happy to stay there studying form, followed by Piquet, Berger, Alesi and Andrea de Cesaris. The second Jordan had started 11th and was being driven superbly. It was nearly as good an effort as Patrese's. By lap seven, Riccardo was seventh and looking for a way past Andrea, having gained ten places!

With the tyre stops, things changed at the front. Most of the runners were on Goodyear's softer C compound and Senna was the first to come in for a new set on lap 15. His stop was slow, taking 9.9s, and by the time he rejoined he was down to fifth, behind Mansell, Piquet, Berger and Alesi — and only just ahead of de Cesaris. In fact Andrea valiantly tried to get by the McLaren as they plunged down to Eau Rouge at some 170 mph. Ayrton would have none of it though, controversially weaving around in front of the Jordan in a successful effort to keep Andrea behind.

On the very next lap Nigel came in for a smooth 7.4s stop. Not brilliant, but 2.5s quicker than Senna's and, on lap 18, he was back in front, two places ahead of Ayrton as Piquet stopped for new Pirellis. On lap 20 Mansell led Alesi by some five seconds with Senna third, Piquet fourth, de Cesaris fifth and the incredible Patrese sixth (after a 17.8s tyre stop by Gerhard Berger, who spun on rejoining the track). On lap 22 Nigel was out. With the race in his pocket, he slowed as he approached the chicane, being passed by Alesi and Senna before rolling to a standstill. As in Canada, an electrical defect had immobilised his engine and gearbox. What ghastly luck. Mansell took his misfortune extremely well, but the sad fact was that it had made his chances of becoming the 1991 World Champion doubly difficult.

Now his rival Ayrton Senna was second,

Pro-Gachot graffiti was everywhere, on T-shirts, racing cars and even on the track itself. Emanuele Pirro negotiates a message of support.

chasing the new leader (the fourth of the race) Jean Alesi — and on lap 23 Riccardo Patrese had passed de Cesaris to take fourth. Ayrton wasn't overworried, because he knew that Alesi had started the race on the harder Goodyear Bs in the hope of going through non-stop and that he was close enough to wait until Jean's tyres inevitably deteriorated. But, on lap 26, he struck a problem. As in Brazil he lost gears. No first. No second. Only third to sixth. Before long he was 11 seconds behind Alesi with Piquet, Patrese and de Cesaris tight up behind him. McLaren, Benetton, Williams and Jordan nose-to-tail in the bright sunlight. It was

Andrea de Cesaris enjoyed the race of his career, at one point threatening Senna's lead. Here, he plans his strategy with Jordan designer Gary Anderson.

a marvellous sight!

On lap 30 Patrese momentarily passec Piquet to take third, only to skate wide at Le Combes with fading brakes. One lap later we had the sad sight of Alesi getting out of a smoking Ferrari. Jean's first chance of victor with the Prancing Horse had exploded and M Lombardi's team had clearly got a lot to d before their main race of the year, on home tur at Monza in two weeks' time. So now a ver lucky Senna was back in the lead with a nev sight in his mirrors. It was Andrea de Cesaris' Jordan! The rejuvenated Italian, the man wh had driven in the most Grands Prix withou winning (159), was having the best race of hi career and looked as though he might be abou to end his unwanted record. He was pushin Senna very hard indeed. For 11 stirring laps h kept up the pressure until, on lap 42 with onl two to go, his Ford HB V8 let go, having bee on the verge of overheating for several laps Hardly surprising, for its radiators were blocke by rubber fragments. The Italian's retiremen gave the struggling Senna his 32nd Grand Pri win and fourth successive Belgian victory. U to second went Patrese! Incredible. Riccard had passed a gripless, Pirelli-disenchante Piquet on lap 34 but, with a sensational si points almost in his grasp, Riccardo also los gears. Only it was worse for him than Ayrton because he only had fifth left.

So the frustrated Berger, who'd charged u from ninth after his tardy tyre stop, seethin inwardly at his down-on-power engine finished second to give McLaren its second one two of the year. Lucky, but they finished and th others didn't. The Benettons of Piquet an Moreno were third and fourth and little Robert set his first fastest lap (1m 55.161s, 134.806 mp — 0.07s slower than Prost's 1990 record) Riccardo Patrese, who deserved so much more finished a very disappointed fifth and Mar Blundell deservedly took his first Worl Championship point (and Brabham-Yamaha's with a fine sixth position after a sturdy drive.

Like I said, it was a Belgian Grand Prix t remember. And the exciting postscript wa Jordan designer Gary Anderson's confiden statement that "we should go even better a Monza!"

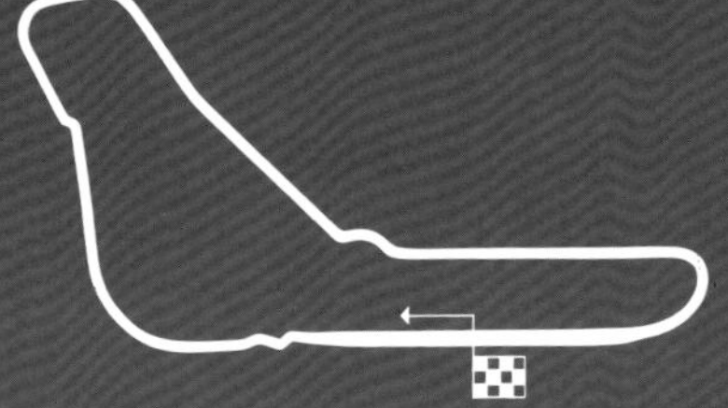

ITALY

September 8 1991 Circuit: Monza

Despite Ferrari's disappointing weekend, the locals still didn't need much persuasion to invade the track. Somewhere in the middle of the flag-waving fanatics, Mansell, Senna and Prost celebrate their 1-2-3.

It was a strange Monza this year. Usually the historic track, rich with memories of the Grand Prix greats who have raced there since the 1920s, has a vibrant atmosphere generated by the fabled *tifosi* — for whom Formula One is a religion, in which Ferrari is God. But this year, depressed by the general recession and the fact that their idolised team was in the doldrums, their numbers were dramatically down and things were curiously low-key. Except for the opportunism, disloyalty, deviousness, back-stabbing and politicking which, sadly, dominated the pre-race proceedings.

Paddock conversation was monopolised by a messy situation involving the Benetton and Jordan teams, and the man who had so sensationally made the news two weeks earlier in Belgium — Michael Schumacher. Whilst no contract had been signed, Eddie Jordan vehemently insisted that letters of intent had been exchanged agreeing that the brilliant young Mercedes-Benz protege would become a member of his team whilst Mercedes was

''Who shall we sign this week?'' After all the political and legal mayhem, Ford's Michael Kranefuss and Benetton's Tom Walkinshaw confer at Monza.

The first Monza chicane is a tight squeeze, reminiscent of the Surrey section of the M25 during the first few moments after the start (right).

getting ready for its anticipated return to Grand Prix racing. He was sure that confirmatory legalities would be completed before the Italian race. But others thought differently. The result? Between Spa and Monza Roberto Moreno was fired by Benetton, and Schumacher was appointed to take his place. Jordan tried, but failed, to get an injunction to block the move and Moreno successfully took separate legal action and obtained substantial compensation. Feelings naturally ran high amidst an atmosphere of confusion and outrage. It's said that all's fair in love, war and business, but these contentious happenings left a nasty taste in most mouths and did the image of Formula One no good at all.

When the dust settled the two likeable, and blameless, drivers had changed places. Schumacher was to drive for Benetton (he signed a multi-year contract) and Moreno, on a one-race basis, for Jordan. The final pieces in the jigsaw did not fall into place until 8.00 am on Friday. When they did, everyone thankfully transferred their attention to what they'd really come for — the racing.

As a result of the modifications to Silverstone, the Italian Grand Prix would now become the fastest of all. With its 200 mph plus straight, ultra-fast Lesmo bends and the dauntingly quick 180-degree Parabolica, Monza is a power circuit which is extremely demanding on engines. But the three chicanes, built to slow things down, also make it hard on brakes, and its overall characteristics make it exhausting for the drivers — especially if it is hot, which it usually is. In fact, say the Goodyear technicians, it is the toughest track of the year. But, on the plus side, its width provides plenty of passing opportunities.

This was the race where Nigel Mansell, at minimum, had to finish ahead of Ayrton Senna if he was to keep his championship hopes alive.

TEAM ANALYSIS

McLAREN

Three lightweight cars for first time. Six satisfying points for Senna. Nine for team. Perfect. Ayrton takes 59th pole and leads race despite unremitting pressure from Mansell and Patrese. Yields to Patrese, lap 26, but regains lead when Riccardo spins next lap (gearbox problem). Passed by Mansell, lap 34, and immediately pits for superb 5.9s tyre stop. Rejoins fifth. Catches and passes Schumacher, Berger and Prost to finish second only half a second ahead of Alain. Sets fastest (record) lap (1m 26.601s, 150.756 mph). Championship lead reduced to nonetheless commanding 18 points. Berger starts third and finishes fourth, complaining of dodgy handling (goes off three times) and lack of power. Team's constructors' championship lead down by one point (to 15).

TYRRELL

The 300th Grand Prix for Uncle Ken's team is not a good one. Despite having no specific problems with their cars, Modena and Nakajima start only 13th and 15th. Stefano (who became a father on race morning) battles with Morbidelli until lap 33, when he retires with engine problem. Naka makes no progress, retiring from 15th, lap 25, when throttle sticks open after going through gravel.

WILLIAMS

Potential one-two denied by repetition of semi-automatic gearbox failure. Mansell starts unlucky second, with demon lap slowed by traffic. Riccardo fourth on grid after being quickest on Saturday morning. Both then harry Senna for 18 laps, after which Nigel waves Patrese by to intensify pressure on Ayrton. Riccardo takes lead, lap 26, only to spin when transmission plays up. Continues third but retires, lap 28 (gearbox failure). Nigel resumes attack and forcefully passes Senna, lap 34, going away non-stop to win his first Italian GP and 20th in all. He is now 18 points behind Senna, and team is 15 behind McLaren — so the championships are feasible, but not probable.

BRABHAM

Team confirms use of Judd V10 engines in 1992. Usual pre-qualification domination, with Blundell first and Brundle second, followed by highest-ever qualification for Mark (11th). Martin starts 19th. Blundell attacks when fuel load lightens and finishes 12th (one lap down, 0.013s behind Comas!) with fifth fastest lap of race. Martin spins twice on full tanks and stops three times for tyres — but still finishes 13th, on same lap as Mark, with excellent third fastest lap of race.

FOOTWORK

"We are up against it with the DFR engine," says Jack Oliver. He is proved right when both his Italian drivers fail at their home race — Caffi does not pre-qualify, Alboreto fails to qualify.

LOTUS

Team's hopes for success after finding good race set-up not realised. With Johnny Herbert again honouring Japanese F3000 commitments, Michael Bartels returns but fails to qualify. Mika Häkkinen starts 25th and finishes 14th in first Italian GP (four laps down), despite persistent misfire.

FONDMETAL

After massive crash in pre-race Monza tyre-tests, Grouillard pre-qualifies third when team goads him into action. Then qualifies 26th for his fourth race of the year. Advances to 12th by lap 33 but retires, lap 47, with gear selection problems and resultant engine failure.

"If Senna signs for Footwork, Prost goes to Ligier, Mansell retires and..." JJ Lehto contemplates the future during qualifying.

LEYTON HOUSE

An encouraging Monza test (seventh fastest and 226 reliable laps) followed by another disappointing GP. Capelli blows three engines on Saturday (!) but qualifies 12th with Friday time. Spends most of race with Piquet and is up to seventh, laps 36-42. Finishes eighth (full distance), despite crossing sand trap trying to keep ahead of Nelson on late charge after tyre stop. Gugelmin starts 18th with Friday time. Pits on lap seven to change ECU (misfire). Resumes last. With tyre blisters, no clutch and cut foot, he too crosses a sand trap before finishing 15th (four laps down) after an eventful race.

AGS

Gabriele Tarquini tries to pre-qualify new Tyrrell-like JH27 but engine expires on first lap. Also fails to pre-qualify JH26, as does Fabrizio Barbazza.

BENETTON

An incredible meeting! Team creates uproar by firing Roberto Moreno and controversially contracting Michael Schumacher as his successor, fending off unsuccessful litigation by Jordan team. Schumacher then demonstrates that his brilliance in Belgium was no fluke by again qualifying seventh (in strange car and on Pirelli qualifiers for first time) — behind only the McLarens, Williams-Renaults and Ferraris. Drives stunning non-stop race. In points-position every lap except first. Fourth laps 28-33 and finishes fifth — in his first full-distance GP and only his second F1 race. Nelson Piquet starts his 200th GP eighth on grid (behind Schumacher), amidst rumours that he is to be fired for bad-mouthing team. Races strongly behind Schumacher but stops for tyres when sixth, lap 35. Resumes eighth and charges. Sets second fastest lap of race, lap 39, on new rubber. Catches and passes Capelli and de Cesaris to finish sixth — subsequently saying that "Schumacher drives like Gilles Villeneuve."

DALLARA

For team's home GP, Pirro and Lehto start 16th and 20th. Emanuele down to 19th after lap 21 tyre stop but recovers well to finish tenth (one lap down). JJ charges to excellent 12th, lap 21. Down to 17th, lap 27 (tyres). Back to 12th, lap 35, but retires, lap 36, with suspension damage caused by driving to pits with rear puncture.

MINARDI

Pier-Luigi Martini again qualifies well (tenth), with Morbidelli 17th (Friday time after another armco-bashing session on Saturday). Martini spins out of race lap nine. Gianni drives confidently and well to finish ninth (one lap down). Team to lose Ferrari engines in 1992.

LIGIER

A mixed-bag meeting. Boutsen and Comas start 21st and 22nd. Thierry hits early-braking Brundle on lap two, spins and retires angrily. Comas loses clutch and has locking rear brakes but soldiers on to finish tenth, a whisker ahead of Mark Blundell.

FERRARI

The Prancing Horse fails to please the *tifosi*. After

Unceremoniously ditched by Benetton, Roberto Moreno sported a set of Jordan's leprechaun-flavoured overalls for the weekend. The Brazilian's long-term F1 future was uncertain, however. After qualifying well, an early spin didn't help his cause.

castigating "gutless and complacent" management, Alain Prost qualifies fifth, one place ahead of Jean Alesi. Prost fastest in Sunday warm-up (full tanks?), but passed by Alesi at start. Back to fifth, lap two, when Jean motocrosses over first chicane gravel trap. Fourth after Patrese retirement. Passes Berger to take second, lap 34, when Senna tyre-stops, but loses place back to Ayrton, lap 46, and finishes third (first finish in last four races). After victories every season since 1980, Ferrari has yet to win a 1991 race. Alesi charges to 12th, lap 28, following lap two nose and tyre changes but retires, lap 30, when engine fractures.

LARROUSSE-LOLA

Suzuki fails to qualify for second successive race after two spectacular engine blow-ups. Bernard starts 24th. Retires from 17th, lap 22, with identical failure.

COLONI

Team decides not to replace tired engine and can't even start it for the unfortunate Chaves to attempt to pre-qualify.

JORDAN

Team spends pre-race week trying to stop Benetton from poaching Schumacher. Roberto Moreno appointed as replacement on one-race basis after litigation fails. Roberto rises to occasion superbly by qualifying ninth, driving car for first time. Then sadly spoils it all by locking brakes and sliding out of contention at Variante Ascari on lap three. Andrea de Cesaris starts 14th before driving another excellent non-stop race on home track. Sixth laps 36-47 but caught and passed by charging (new tyres) Piquet on lap 48. Finishes seventh (full distance) after praiseworthy drive which restores team's morale.

LAMBORGHINI

Van de Poele again fails to qualify (29th). Larini does so (23rd). Relieved to finish for second time in '91 — albeit 16th (five laps down).

With an 18-point deficit after Senna's successive victories in Hungary and Belgium, he simply couldn't afford to let the gap increase. Things had gone well for Williams in the pre-race Monza tyre tests, with Mansell and Patrese topping the times. Since then, McLaren had made significant advances and there were confident expectations of a good race. It turned out to be even better than we'd anticipated.

In glorious weather the McLaren and Williams men dominated the two qualifying sessions. Senna took his 59th pole position with Mansell only just failing to beat him, despite having to swerve in and out of traffic at hair-raising speed on his quickest lap. Berger was third and Patrese fourth to complete a symmetrical pattern, with a mere 0.2s covering the four of them. To the dismay of the gloomy *tifosi*, Prost and Alesi were only fifth and sixth in their Ferraris. They were followed by the two Benettons, the fastest of which was Michael Schumacher's! The incredible newcomer, in a strange car and having to familiarise himself with Pirelli tyres, had comfortably outqualified his new team-mate, thrice World Champion Nelson Piquet (who was about to drive in his 200th Grand Prix). Ironically it was the other new driver/car combination which was next on the grid — Roberto Moreno in the Jordan which Schumacher would have driven but for his somewhat unexpected move.

It wasn't the best of weekends for Minardi. Pier-Luigi Martini (followed here by Nakajima and Moreno) was an early spinner, and the future was clouded by the confirmation of Scuderia Italia's engine deal with Ferrari. Minardi would have to look elsewhere in '92.

So the scene was set for a great race, with the two championship contenders on the front row of the grid. We weren't to be disappointed. Senna knew he had to lead from the start. If the two beautifully-balanced Williams, with their Renault power, got ahead they'd be long gone. He did just that, edging into the snake-like chicane ahead of Mansell, Berger, Patrese, Alesi (up to fifth) and Prost, who had Schumacher and Piquet right behind him. Alesi was the first to break the pattern, with an impetuous attempt to pass Berger on the second lap. That took him over the gravel trap and down to last after a stop for a new nose and tyres. He charged back to 12th but retired on lap 30 (engine). On lap seven Patrese surged past Berger to take third and now began a magnificent sight — Ayrton Senna driving as hard as he knew to resist the combined efforts of the two Williams men to dislodge him from his precarious lead.

For 18 glorious laps the trio drove round together with Nigel trying to get by Ayrton and Riccardo trying to pass Nigel! Marvellous. On lap 19 Mansell waved his team-mate by. British hearts sank. Was he in trouble? No he wasn't. "The car was very difficult to drive on full tanks and it was sliding a lot when I was following Ayrton closely. So I let Riccardo pass. After all we were in Italy and I knew he'd give Ayrton a hard time while I took a breather!" He sure did. For six breathtaking laps the man from Padova drove with his front wing virtually under Senna's gearbox and, on lap 26, his pressure did the trick. Into the lead went Riccardo — the first time that an Italian had led his own Grand Prix since Riccardo himself had done so in 1983 (Brabham-BMW). Now the *tifosi* woke up with a massive roar of approval — if it couldn't be a Ferrari, an Italian would do!

With Patrese having succumbed to gearbox failure, Senna holds off the determined Mansell. The Brazilian holds an advantage of at least two centimetres at this point ...

But, sadly, not for long. Hardly any time at all in fact. On the very next lap, at the Ascari bends where he'd taken the lead, Riccardo slid off and down to a scrabbling third as he rejoined the track just ahead of the battling Berger and Prost. But those who thought he'd overdone it misjudged him. It was the dreaded Williams semi-automatic gearbox malfunctioning again. "I didn't catch third when I was braking for the Variante Ascari," said Riccardo, "and it went into the gear when I was going into the corner, locked the rear wheels and I spun. I got away but then the gearbox broke completely." He was out of the race. What awful luck. So now, with Senna back in the lead ahead of Mansell, pursued by Berger, Prost, Schumacher (a magnificent, seemingly relaxed fifth) and Piquet it wasn't just the *tifosi's* hearts that sank. So did those in British chests. Because if the Williams' transmission, which had given so much trouble in the past, had afflicted Patrese, why shouldn't it do the same to Mansell?

It didn't though. Nigel closed up on Senna and gave him just as hard a time as Riccardo had. Harder in fact, because the front tyres of the less well-balanced McLaren were going off. On lap 34 at the Ascari bends Mansell drew alongside Senna, doggedly sat out the corner and superbly took a lead that he was never to lose. And that was the signal for the canny Senna immediately to stop for new Goodyears. "My tyres were gone. I knew if I didn't stop I'd lose places and not be able to get them back." His tyre stop took just 5.93s and when he rocketed out of the pit lane he was in fifth place, having been passed by Prost, Berger (who'd been taken by Alain when he'd gone off at Ascari and filled the Ferrari's cockpit with stones!) and the mightily impressive Schumacher.

The manner of his transfer may have been controversial, but there was no denying Benetton's logic in acquiring the services of Michael Schumacher. Fifth place was pretty good for starters.

On fresh rubber Senna charged, grimly determined to finish as close as possible to Mansell, who was now some 16 seconds ahead. Every place he gained would make Nigel's championship gain smaller. It took him three laps to catch and pass Schumacher's non-stop Benetton, and another four to reel in Berger, who gave no trouble, moving over in deference to team orders. Now it was lap 41 of 53 and Prost was six seconds ahead. No problem! Ayrton's 41st lap was his and the race's fastest — a new lap record in 1m 26.061s (150.756 mph). It cut deeply into the gap. Lap 46 saw the McLaren head the Ferrari. Alain hadn't got the grunt and, aiming to finish for the first time in four races, let Senna through. But there was no way that Ayrton was going to catch Mansell and he didn't.

It was the first time that Mansell, darling of the *tifosi*, had won in Italy and his 20th Grand Prix victory was one of his best. He'd driven a forceful, non-stop race of tactical brilliance, using his team-mate to pressure Senna before simply outdriving the World Champion. But Senna too had driven with the cunning and skill that are his hallmarks. Against a rival of equal ability in a superior car he'd conducted a brilliant damage-limitation campaign which had succeeded. ''Second place has reduced our future problems. Every race from now on adds more pressure to Nigel as he cannot afford not to finish.'' But nor really, when you thought about it, could Ayrton! Every remaining race could be a cliffhanger.

Alain Prost duly got the finish he'd striven for, only half a second behind Senna as he crossed the line a comfortable 11 seconds ahead of Berger. But, in spite of the brilliance of Mansell and Senna, for me the man of the race was Michael Schumacher. He'd endured more than a week of intense psychological pressure through his move from Jordan to Benetton, over which his hands were clean. His drive was his first in anger for his new team and his first Grand Prix finish. He was racing on Pirelli tyres for the first time. It was his first Grand Prix at Monza and he'd finished fifth, beaten only by four of the world's top drivers. To beat a determined Piquet, never having put a wheel wrong, was quite magnificent. Benetton may not have covered itself in glory in the way it got him, but it wouldn't have any regrets!

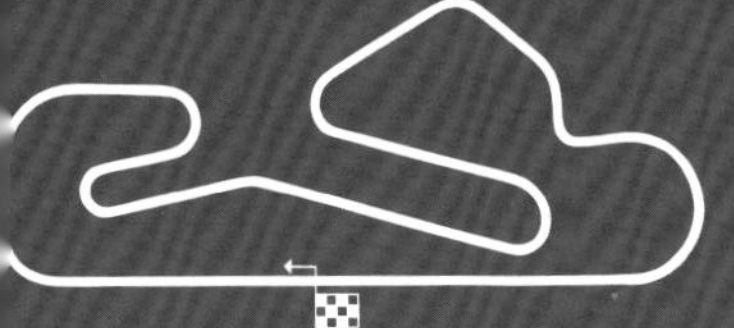

PORTUGAL

September 22 1991 Circuit: Estoril

Before the pit lane drama, Patrese and Mansell stroke along at a comfortable pace, leaving the McLarens in their wake.

As the Grand Prix scene assembled at Estoril for round 13 of the World Championship, speculation about the outcome of the series was intense. Ayrton Senna was leading the drivers' contest by a comfortable 18 points, but Nigel Mansell had regained the initiative with his superb win in Italy. During the season he had arguably lost some 37 points due to car problems, whereas Senna had lost only 11. Surely it was time for the Brazilian's luck to turn? Or was his prophesy at Phoenix that reliability would win the 1991 championship going to be proven true? Ironically it was to be an unprecedented occurrence, unconnected with reliability, that would further strengthen Senna's position in Portugal.

Sunny Estoril is one of Grand Prix racing's better locations, popular with everyone who goes there. The spectacular, 2.7-mile circuit, which is situated in the mountainous, rock strewn, coastal area near the most westerly point in Europe, has a long (190 mph) straight and a variety of corners which bring out the best in a driver. It is demanding, hard on tyres, brakes and the drivers' stamina, and calls for skill in finding the best compromise between downforce for the corners and minimum drag for the straight. The facilities at the track may be a bit primitive, but when there's time to relax the area's glorious sandy beaches and excellent restaurants provide a lot of consolation!

Unlike all too many circuits these days, Estoril has places where passing is possible but getting pole position is no less important than anywhere else. Gerhard Berger was the quickest in Friday's rain-shortened qualifying session, and his 1m 13.221s lap seemed certain to keep him there on Saturday. Mansell briefly displaced Senna from second place but the Brazilian took it back and, with six minutes to go, it looked like an all-McLaren front row. Bad news for Mansell and Williams. But then, dramatically to change the situation, came the incredible Riccardo Patrese who, the next day, would be starting his 221st GP.

Riccardo had stopped out on the circuit with an electrical problem in his race car. Angrily returning to the pits he faced the prospect of starting fourth. But even as he marched back the Williams mechanics were changing the set-up on Mansell's spare car for Riccardo to take over. With so little time left he was justifiably reluctant to go out in a strange car and drive immediately at ten-tenths. ''I'll give it a go,'' he said. ''If it's handling well when I exit the last corner, I'll go for it.'' It was and he did — 1m 13.001s was his time and it gave him his seventh career pole! So now there was the intriguing prospect of the two World Championship contenders, Senna and Mansell, starting third and fourth on row two behind their team-mates and ahead of the persistently disappointing Ferraris of Prost and Alesi. ''The first five seconds after the red turns to green will be the most interesting and will set the scene for the race which, I think, will be all about tactics,'' said Mansell. He never spoke a truer word!

Sunday was hot, sunny and dry. Mansell and Patrese were fastest in the warm-up followed by Berger and Prost. Senna was only sixth. Interesting! And sure enough, just as Nigel had forecast, the start of the 71-lap race was sensational. Unlike his three previous 1991 pole positions Patrese got away well. As Mansell left the grid, he booted his Williams-Renault, twitched in front of Senna and dived inside

''OK. This is what we do. We hide his wheel nuts in your sidepod. You just cruise along in the top three, and try not to laugh too loud when he stops for tyres.'' Senna and crew discuss tactics.

Berger to follow Riccardo round turn one! Both Senna and Berger took a dim view of Nigel's forcefulness and criticised him for it after the race, but he didn't hit either of them and was safely into second. They'd have tried to do exactly the same!

Behind the fighting four at the front, Jean Alesi had moved ahead of his Ferrari team-mate and Pier-Luigi Martini had started a superb drive by blasting past Mauricio Gugelmin's Leyton House to seventh. What was to be a riveting and very significant race was well and truly on.

Williams had a plan and Riccardo followed it. "The first part was to pull away from the McLarens. Then, when we had a comfortable lead I slowed down, let Nigel pass and have his race." Selfishness is no part of Patrese's nature and he had promised to help Mansell win the championship before the race had even begun. And that he did. On lap 18 Nigel moved ahead and looked set for victory, for the two Williams cars clearly had an edge over the McLarens, of which Berger's was first, six and a half seconds behind Patrese and two ahead of Senna. Alesi, Prost, Martini and Capelli were next but, good as their fight for the places was, everyone's attention was at the front.

It was the tyre stops that transformed the race — and destroyed Mansell's hopes. When Berger came in on lap 27 Senna moved up to third, Alesi and Prost to fourth and fifth. On lap 29 it was Senna's turn and his stop was the fastest of the race; 5.04s was all it took, but so close were the two Ferraris that he rejoined in fifth place.

Lean spell. Stefano Modena posted another retirement as Tyrrell failed to trouble the scorers for the eighth consecutive race.

Benetton's latest sidepod tweak apparently played havoc with the aerodynamics.

TEAM ANALYSIS

McLAREN

Contrasting results but progress in both championships. Senna, below usual qualifying form, starts third. Makes conservative tyre choice for race (hard Bs on left: soft Cs on right). Is aggressively passed by Mansell at start (to Ayrton's displeasure) and races fourth for 26 laps. Down to fifth after lap 28 tyre stop (5.04s!). Benefits from Mansell/Berger retirements to finish second after failing to catch Patrese. Resultant six-points increase championship lead to seemingly unbeatable 24 points with only three races to go. Re-signs to drive for McLaren in 1992. Berger heads Friday times but starts second after Patrese's sensational Saturday pole lap. Like Senna, Gerhard ousted by thrusting Mansell at start. Third until lap 27 tyre stop. Recovers to second (passing Senna), lap 35, and sets about chasing Patrese but retires, lap 35 (engine electrics). Team's championship lead over Williams down to 11 points.

TYRRELL

Lacklustre Spain amidst rumours that team losing Honda engines and Braun sponsorship and being merged with Jackie Stewart's racing organisation in 1992. Modena starts 12th (''no grip'') and Nakajima a miserable 21st, complaining of stomach problems (just like 1991). Stefano never higher than 11th and retires from 12th, lap 57, when engine fails due to one of own visor rip-offs blowing into air intake. Satoru drives to exhausted 13th.

WILLIAMS

Team wins 50th GP in atmosphere of gloom. In closing minutes of qualifying Riccardo Patrese takes sensational pole position in hastily set-up spare car, having angrily walked in half a lap after electrical problem stops race chassis. Mansell starts fourth but rockets past Senna and Berger into second at first corner. Happily follows Patrese before taking lead on lap 18, as planned. Stays there until disastrous lap 30 tyre stop when signalled out before right rear wheel nut on. Unsurprisingly wheel departs when Mansell does. Nigel rejoins, 17th and lapped. Drives magnificently, including fastest lap (record 1m 18.179s, 124.467 mph) to unlapped sixth, lap 47, but is black-flagged, lap 50, and disqualified for having car worked on in pit lane. Riccardo drives on to well-deserved, untroubled fifth GP win. Mansell now heartbreaking 24 points behind seemingly uncatchable Senna, but team gap to McLaren constructors' lead reduced to 11 points.

BRABHAM

Brundle pre-qualifies fastest despite suspension collapse. Blundell second. Both qualify — Mark 15th, Martin 19th. Blundell retires from 20th, lap 13, with, very disturbingly, another rear suspension failure. Brundle finishes 12th.

FOOTWORK

After pre-qualifying fourth Alboreto starts 24th with revised aerodynamics. Then races to 15th (three laps down) for team's first 1991 finish. Caffi again fails to pre-qualify and seems destined for chop.

LOTUS

Johnny Herbert again returns to team. Qualifies 22nd but retires, lap two, when clutch explodes. Mika Häkkinen starts 26th and races at rear of field to finish 14th (three laps down), greatly inconvenienced by constant need to hold head up with hand on high-G corners.

FONDMETAL

Ninth failure to pre-qualify by Olivier Grouillard.

LEYTON HOUSE

Team more than worried about future following arrest of Japanese owner Akira Akagi, allegedly involved in massive financial scandal. In trying circumstances, drivers do very well to qualify seventh (Capelli's best of year) and ninth (Gugelmin). Ivan drives excellent race. Up to strong fifth, lap 40, following lap 28 tyre stop, but loses nosecone assembly, lap 64, and goes off. Rejoins with new unit. Classified 17th and last, seven laps down. After bad start Gugelmin climbs to eighth, lap 29, but is delayed by Mansell pit lane fracas at lap 31 tyre stop. Rejoins 12th and finishes praiseworthy seventh, one lap down.

AGS

Both drivers use new JH27, but Tarquini does not qualify and Barbazza does not pre-qualify.

BENETTON

Team's 150th race — Ford's 350th. Not bad for either. Piquet (rumoured to be joining Ferrari in '92, if Prost leaves) qualifies 11th, one place behind astounding new team-mate Michael Schumacher (driving for first time at Estoril). Both drivers make two Pirelli tyre stops before finishing fifth (Piquet) and sixth — both full distance. Schumacher's second successive points finish in first three Grands Prix. Piquet up to fifth in championship.

DALLARA

Closely-matched qualifying performances by Pirro and Lehto see them start 17th (Emanuele) and 18th. Neither finishes. JJ retires from 20th, lap 15, after struggling with faulty gear linkage. Pirro out when 16th, lap 17 (engine).

MINARDI

A very heartening meeting for the financially-strapped Italian team. As usual Pier-Luigi Martini qualifies well in eighth. Gianni Morbidelli 13th on grid (and fifth fastest in Sunday warm-up). Martini races strongly to fourth, lap 40, and stays there to equal his previous career-best finish at Imola. By finishing ninth Morbidelli gives team best-yet 1991 result.

LIGIER

Ligier's drearily unsuccessful 1991 uplifted by rumour that team will be joined by Alain Prost in 1992 (in non-driving capacity). Thierry Boutsen and Erik Comas start 20th and 23rd. Erik, very happy with his car, finishes 11th, one lap down. Considerably less so, Thierry races to 16th (three

Fine tuning. The Williams FW14 was now unquestionably the class of the field; McLaren's constructors' title was under increasing threat.

laps down), complaining about "absolutely no grip."

FERRARI

Team's disarray intensified by rumour that Prost will retire at end of season to join Ligier in non-driving role. Alesi openly comments on lack of leadership. In cars which handle badly on low fuel load, Alain qualifies fifth and Jean sixth (adversely affected by departure of race engineer Maurizio Nardon). Prost car catches fire during Sunday warm-up. Alesi passes Prost at start. Jean and Alain then race together until lap 30 when fourth-placed Prost tyre-stops. Alain rejoins seventh and climbs to third, lap 38, before retiring, lap 40, when engine expires. Down to sixth in championship. Alesi overshoots pit for lap 31 tyre stop when second and takes over 16 seconds for change, rejoining fifth. Third by lap 40. Has job to stay ahead of Martini's Ferrari-engined Minardi but does so to finish third. What will team do to pull itself together?

LARROUSSE-LOLA

Aguri Suzuki starts 25th but Eric Bernard, affected by family bereavement, fails to qualify. Suzuki retires from 20th and last, lap 41, with transmission failure after unsuccessfully battling with Häkkinen and hiccoughing engine.

COLONI

At home event Pedro Chaves sadly maintains his pre-qualification failure record. But, amazingly, the team is bought by an Italian shoe manufacturer — hopefully with the intention to improve it... massively.

JORDAN

Team delightedly announces deal to use Yamaha engines for four years, commencing 1992. Andrea de Cesaris qualifies disappointed 14th. Moreno 16th for last Jordan race before being replaced in Spain by F3000 ace Alessandro Zanardi. Andrea down to 16th after lap 25 tyre stop. Fights up to fine sixth, laps 42-46, but, delayed in second tyre stop by stuck wheel, drops to 13th. Nevertheless finishes fine eighth (one lap down). Moreno drives to tenth (one lap down) in spite of being delayed by Mansell's lost-wheel shambles at lap 31 tyre stop.

LAMBORGHINI

No joy again. Both Larini and van de Poele fail to qualify.

When Mansell came to a standstill for his new Goodyears on lap 30, he had a commanding enough lead for James Hunt, in the TV commentary box with me, to remark that he should make a calm and deliberate stop of ten seconds if need be. It was less than ten seconds, 7.75s to be exact, and Nigel momentarily looked good as he started to race out of the pit lane, seemingly sure of the fifth win that would reduce Senna's championship lead by at least six points. But he wasn't! For suddenly he was sitting, distraught, in a stationary Williams three-wheeler, stranded in the outer pit lane. He had been let out before the right rear wheel nut had been secured.

Whoever was responsible for an enormously stressful situation, it was irrelevant. The damage was done. A new wheel was fitted frantically (the original one had hurtled off, knocked down two of the Tyrrell mechanics ready for Nakajima's stop and ended up in the Jordan garage), and Nigel was on his way — 17th and lapped. Now if there's a gritty, gutsy fighter in Formula One it's Nigel Mansell, and he reached right down into himself to recover. With Patrese now in the lead, Senna second, Berger third Prost fourth and Alesi fifth, after a terrible tyre stop, Nigel charged.

On lap 33 he unlapped himself as Patrese emerged from his tyre stop still in the lead. On lap 36 he put up the fastest lap of the race, a new record in 1m 18.179s (124.467 mph), and by lap 47 he had caught and passed nine of his rivals, including Modena, Gugelmin, Piquet, Schumacher and de Cesaris, to get back into the points at sixth. By my reckoning he was on target for third place at the end of the race, for Alesi, Martini and Capelli, ahead of him, were close together and he was lapping fast enough to take them all. But it was not to be. On lap 50 the black flag went out. He had been disqualified for having his car worked on in the pit lane. It was his second Portuguese disqualification for pit lane transgressions in three years (he had been excluded in 1989 when he reversed his Ferrari after overshooting his tyre-crew). ''No complaints,'' said Frank Williams. ''We broke the rules.'' But bitter, bitter gall for poor Mansell, who had lost ten seemingly certain points through no fault of his own. ''I drove my best. I got into the lead and did everything perfectly. I can't comment on the

''Can I have power-steering for the next round?'' Martin Brundle (right) shows signs of the effort required to guide a Brabham-Yamaha into 12th place.

The new AGS JH27 had its first proper run, though the end result was pretty much the same. Tarquini (pictured) failed to qualify, and Barbazza didn't even get that far.

CAMEL

pit stop — I went but I was only on three wheels. I am happy if the team wins, but I am just too upset to say any more.'' Hardly surprising.

In the meantime there had been two other very notable retirements. Gerhard Berger, who had moved up to second past Senna on lap 35 to try and wear Patrese down, went out when his Honda V12 became a V11. Alain Prost had departed from third when his Ferrari engine called it a day. Senna had tested Patrese's resolve and car worthiness by pushing as hard as he could but, realising that both Riccardo and the Williams were happy, decided to settle for second and six valuable points.

With the realisation that only miracles in the last three races would keep the championship alive, things frankly went a bit flat after Mansell's exclusion. But there was still a lot going on. Jean Alesi was third, though his place looked anything but secure. Right behind him, driving superbly, was little Pier-Luigi Martini in his Minardi-Ferrari, and he was only just ahead of Capelli's Leyton House which, in turn, was being challenged by Nelson Piquet's Benetton-Ford.

Poor Capelli's season had been even worse than Mansell's and, like Nigel, he was again to suffer in Portugal. In a strong fifth place and set for only his third finish of the season, Ivan had his nosecone assembly drop off and put him out of the race. Up to fifth went Piquet and up to sixth went the brilliant newcomer Michael Schumacher in his Benetton — in the points for the second time in his first three Grands Prix!

Life is a funny thing. So intent had everyone been on the Mansell fracas and its effect on the championship that they had almost lost sight of Patrese's quite superb drive. But the fact was that he had totally overwhelmed Ayrton Senna and his McLaren. Riccardo drove a faultless and selfless race and he more than deserved the victory that was his. ''When I left my pit stop I was still in the lead and I must say that it was quite easy to win. After the stop everything I did was just to control Ayrton. There were no problems at all, the car was really perfect.'' Maybe so, Riccardo, but it took *you* to get the best out of it. Very well done!

They say you make your own luck, but once again an apparently blameless Mansell had drawn the short straw and once again Senna had finished where it mattered — well up in the points, now with an even bigger championship lead. ''I think I am as near to another title as I could be,'' said Ayrton. ''Right now, with three races remaining, I only need to make six or seven points even if Mansell wins all three races — which is a hard job for him. So I think we are nearly there. Still, every race is a different story and you never know!''

No, you don't, but now Mansell had an even bigger mountain to climb if he was to achieve his ambition. Stranger things had happened in Grand Prix racing but not much, surely?

''Ligier? You can't be serious?'' Alesi (left) and team-mate Prost discuss the latest paddock gossip, as speculation grew that the thrice World Champion might be on the verge of leaving Ferrari.

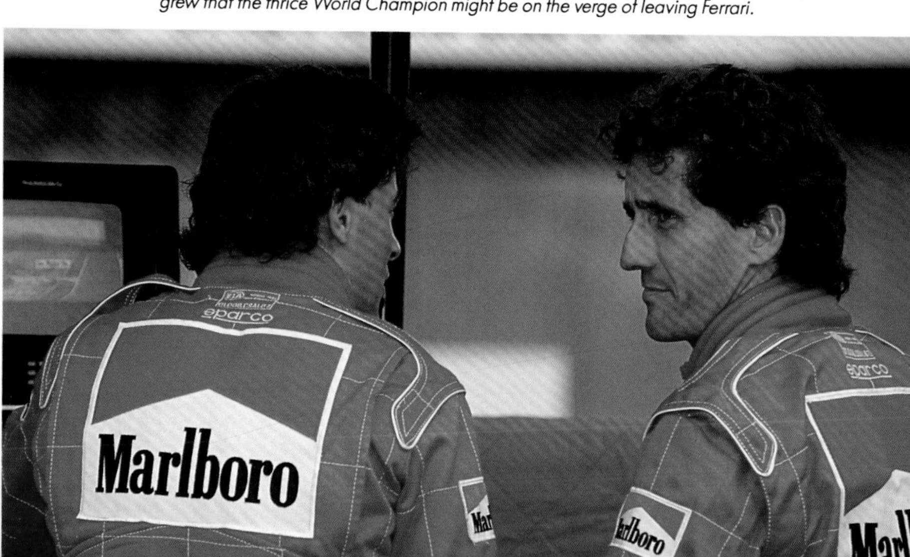

SPAIN

September 29 1991 Circuit: Barcelona

"I'm sorry. Green overalls are part of the contract." Jordan team manager Trevor Foster apologises to European F3000 graduate Alessandro Zanardi, who did a competent job on his F1 debut, finishing ninth.

This time, no day-long drive from Lisbon down to Jerez. Instead, a diagonal flight to the top right corner of the Iberian Peninsula. Because, after being held at four different locations since 1951, the Spanish Grand Prix was moving back to its spiritual home — the magnificent city of Barcelona. Not to the glorious Montjuich Park circuit of the 1970s, but to an entirely new state-of-the-art location at Montmelo, on the outskirts of the city.

And what a location! Some £40m had been spent on building a superb 2.95-mile, 15-corner circuit with all the infrastructure that it needed to be the best in the world. When it's finished! There just hadn't been time to complete it before work for the 1992 Barcelona Olympics took precedence. Two gigantic storms prior to Thursday's familiarisation practice hadn't helped either, but on the day everything that mattered was ready.

"A really interesting design — I like it," said Ayrton Senna. "I think it's fantastic," said

Michael Schumacher. ''It's alright, but it's not *my* kind of circuit,'' said Gerhard Berger. Pirelli thought it was great — its tyres were performing extremely well — but Goodyear wasn't so happy. The smooth surface was causing virtually no wear and was making it very difficult to heat up harder compounds. Emergency action would be needed!

There was much, much more to talk about than the new circuit and how ghastly the Barcelona traffic was. After Nigel Mansell's tyre-changing débâcle in Portugal, Ayrton Senna was now 24 points ahead of the Englishman in the championship and really seemed to have it made for the third time in four years. More than anything, he wanted to go to Honda's home race in Japan with the championship in the bag. To stop that happening, Mansell had to finish at least four points ahead of the Brazilian in Spain. Realistically, that meant he had to win.

Considering the crushing points-loss blow that he'd suffered in Portugal, Nigel was in incredibly good form. ''I don't hold anybody responsible. What happened was very, very unfortunate. We'll just do the best job we car — I'm not going to give up yet.'' He certainly didn't! In Friday's qualifying session he was second fastest to a rejuvenated Gerharc Berger, with Senna third and Patrese fourth. Bu what would happen on Saturday? Two things. The first? With a change in the weather, the track was slower. The second? Trying desperately to get on the front row of the grid, Senna blew his Honda V12 asunder, liberally coating a main corner with Shell oil anc effectively terminating the final qualifying session at half-time.

So the vital Spanish Grand Prix would see the same four on the two front rows of the grid as ir Portugal — but in a significantly different order. Berger had his first pole position since Phoenix 1990, with Mansell alongside him. Senna anc Patrese sat on row two ahead of the amazing Michael Schumacher's Benetton and Alair Prost's Ferrari. Remembering how Mansell hac disposed of Senna and Berger in Portugal, there were few who couldn't see him in the lead by the first corner in Spain. But he wasn't. After

While Prost (left) and Patrese (right) look fit for another 65 laps, winner Mansell looks like he could do with a fortnight's holiday in Hawaii.

Wednesday's storm it had been dry, but Sunday morning was wet. Alarmed at the comparative success of the Pirelli runners (seven of the top 15 on the grid), Goodyear had flown in two sets per car of its softest D compound on Saturday night. But in the wet warm-up, in which Mansell was fastest by a convincing 1.7s, nobody even tried them. Vitally, that was to affect the race.

At two o'clock, when the GP began in front of some 70,000 people (a bit different to Jerez!), the track was damp but drying out. Prost wanted to start on slicks but his team wouldn't agree. Michele Alboreto did so and reaped a rich reward — until he had to retire. But as the 26 surged towards turn one it was Berger in the lead with Senna second — ahead of Mansell! "Both Riccardo and I were on the slippery side of the track and we lost out," said Nigel. He was right, for a wheelspinning Patrese was down to eighth. Schumacher, Alesi and Pirro were ahead of him and Prost was 12th after being baulked by his team-mate.

With no respect for his elders, Schumacher was past Mansell and pushing Senna for second on lap two. Time for Nigel to get going! He did. With an inspired Berger now nearly four seconds ahead he took Schumacher for third and closed right up on Senna as Prost shot into his pit for new Goodyear slicks — the softer Ds. Just the job they were too. Alain rejoined 19th — last but four. Seven laps later he was fourth!

On lap five we had one of the most thrilling sights I've ever seen in Grand Prix racing. After sitting behind Senna, looking for an opportunity to pass, Mansell exited the 155 mph pit corner right under the McLaren's rear wing. He pulled out of Senna's slipstream and drew level with him on the long main straight. At 195 mph, neither of them yielded. Literally inches apart, with sparks flying from their ground-effect skid plates, they grimly held on, wheel to wheel. But at the first turn Nigel had the inside line. Senna had to concede the corner. It was a perfect demonstration of how Formula One drivers justify their salaries.

Berger was now nearly nine seconds away with Alesi fourth, having an outstanding drive. Patrese had passed Schumacher to fifth and

McLarens to the fore. Berger and Senna got the jump at the start, but their lead was about as secure as Coloni's future.

TEAM ANALYSIS

McLAREN
Almost the worst possible result, after bringing seven cars (yes, *seven*!) in effort to maximise both championship situations before Japan. Berger takes first pole position since Phoenix 1990 with Senna third on grid after massive engine blow-up on Saturday. Gerhard leads until long (16.6s) lap nine stop for tyres and removal of brake air-scoop masking tape. Down to fifth. Regains lead laps 12-20. Passed by Mansell, lap 21. Retires from second, lap 34 (engine electrics — his seventh 1991 DNF). Senna loses second to Mansell, lap five. Fits Goodyear's harder Cs on left and Ds on right in lap nine stop. Spins down to seventh, lap 14. Up to third, laps 34-37, but passed by Patrese and Alesi as result of wrong tyre choice. Finishes fifth with championship lead cut to 16 points. Team down to second in constructors' championship, one point behind Williams.

TYRRELL
Another unimpressive race. Modena and Nakajima qualify 14th and 18th, complaining of handling problems. Even worse in wet warm-up (26th and 23rd). Stefano spins down to last on lap one and, after *five* tyre stops finishes 16th, 1.3s and one place ahead of Nakajima, who has three tyre stops. Both three laps down.

WILLIAMS
Wonderful result after grisly Portugal. Knowing that he needs to win to keep championship alive, a pressured but relaxed and cheerful Nigel Mansell, blaming nobody for his Portuguese misfortune, takes second on grid with Patrese fourth. Nigel, fastest in warm-up by 1.7s, has ugly altercation with Berger and Senna in drivers' briefing. Down to fourth at start but passes Schumacher, Senna and Berger to lead on lap nine before tyre stop. Down to fifth but leads again, lap 21. Stays there for magnificent fifth 1991 win (21st in all) which keeps championship open, 16 points behind Senna. Riccardo Patrese drives fine race too. Drops to eighth after poor start but leads on lap ten before tyre stop. Down to tenth. During great recovery passes Senna to third lap 38. Posts fastest and record lap of race (1m 22.837s, 128.188 mph), successfully fighting to stay ahead of Alesi. Finishes third. Team takes constructors' championship lead from McLaren by one point. Roll on Japan!

BRABHAM
Following usual pre-qualifying one-two, Blundell and Brundle start 12th and 11th after team's best 1991 practice so far. Martin up to excellent sixth, lap six, car and Pirelli tyres both suiting circuit. Collides with Lehto and spins, lap 18, but, despite engine cutting out and two tyre stops, finishes tenth, two laps down. Blundell loses 11 places on lap one ("I made a mistake"). Up to fine 11th, lap 11, after lap three stop for slicks. Collides with Pirro, lap 12, and damages suspension. Second tyre stop from 12th, lap 36. Engine blows when 14th, lap 50. With Martin setting four fastest laps and Mark three, team feels car now on pace, but very impressive Blundell shattered to learn he won't be retained for 1992. Well-funded Japanese Akihiko Nakaya is to join in his place.

FOOTWORK
After pre-qualifying third, Michele Alboreto starts from 24th on slicks. Benefiting from tyre choice, charges up to 12th by lap four. Then collides with Häkkinen and pits for new nose. Rejoins last but, with overheating engine, retires from lapped 19th, lap 24. Alex Caffi once again fails to pre-qualify.

LOTUS
Michael Bartels again substitutes for Johnny Herbert but fails to qualify after destroying car in Friday accident. Mika Häkkinen qualifies 21st before retiring from excellent tenth, lap six, when hit by Alboreto.

FONDMETAL
Ex-AGS driver Gabriele Tarquini replaces Grouillard as result of row between Olivier and team owner. He likes car. Team likes him. Pre-qualifies and qualifies well (22nd in strange car, for first GP since Monaco). Races impressively to his first finish since Phoenix — 12th, two laps down.

LEYTON HOUSE
Ivan Capelli again qualifies well in eighth but out, lap two, after colliding with Pirro. Gugelmin, 13th on grid, stops for slicks, lap eight. Charges up to sixth, lap seven, before tyre stop. Recovers from 18th to equal his best '91 finishes (France and Portugal) in seventh, one lap down.

AGS
In team's last expected 1991 GP, neither Olivier Grouillard (replacing Gabriele Tarquini, see Fondmetal), nor Fabrizio Barbazza pre-qualify.

BENETTON
Designer Rory Byrne rejoins team from Reynard. After destroying tub in Thursday familiarisation practice, Michael Schumacher, again in dazzling form, qualifies best-yet fifth, five places ahead of Nelson Piquet. Saucily passes Patrese and Mansell to third, lap one, and pushes Senna for second. To pits from fourth for slicks, lap six. Back to third, lap 12. Spins down to sixth lap 21. Tyre-stops, lap 30, and recovers from eighth to finish sixth — in the points for the third time in his first four GPs. Also sets four fastest laps in another outstanding race. Piquet second fastest in warm-up. Patchy race with wet settings, three tyre stops and electrical problem. Runs as high as fifth and as low as 18th. Finishes 11th, two laps down.

DALLARA
Team proudly announces use of Ferrari engines in 1992. Pirro and Lehto qualify ninth and 15th. Both have race collisions: Pirro with Capelli, lap two; Lehto with Brundle, lap 18. JJ impressively up ten places to fifth, lap 34, but down to eighth after tyre stop. Finishes eighth, one lap down. Emanuele pits after Capelli collision and notches up three fastest laps on way to finishing 15th, three laps down. A good day for Dallara and Judd.

Into the unknown. Booted out by Fondmetal, Olivier Grouillard took refuge at AGS...albeit for just one hour on Friday morning. It was to be the Italian-owned French team's final appearance of the season.

MINARDI
Only 16th and 19th on grid for Morbidelli and Martini. Gianni runs ninth three laps from end, collides with Zanardi and hits team-mate Martini. Finishes 14th, three laps down. Pier-Luigi, 11th at time of impact, finishes 13th, two laps down, on three wheels and brake disc!

LIGIER
Demoralising race. Boutsen (25th) and Comas share back row of grid. Thierry collides with Bernard, lap one, and retires. Erik up to sensational sixth in damp conditions, laps 8-9, but falls back as track dries. Retires with electrical problems, lap 37, after earlier stop to change ECU.

FERRARI
With Prost's future intentions unclear, team typically favours Alesi – notably with new V12 exhaust system. Prost qualifies sixth, one place ahead of Jean. Alain tries to start on slicks but team refuses to fit them. Baulked by Alesi, makes bad start. Down to 12th. In for tyres, lap three. Down to 19th. Then fairly slices through field up to fourth, lap 11. Second to Mansell, lap 34, and finishes there, 11 seconds down, for highest place since France. "I could have won if I'd started on slicks..." Jean Alesi tyre-stops from fourth, lap ten. Rejoins eighth. When running fifth, lap 28, given ten-second stop-go penalty for weaving at start. This effectively costs him 32 seconds. Blazes back in ninth place and charges. Catches and passes Senna for fourth, lap 50, and pushes Patrese for third – but fails. After four fastest laps, finishes fourth (22.7s behind Mansell) for team's best race since France.

LARROUSSE-LOLA
Amidst heightened rumours of imminent merger with AGS, Aguri Suzuki does not qualify. Eric Bernard starts 23rd but collides with Boutsen and retires on lap one.

COLONI
Pedro Chaves, frustrated and angry through lack of miles and non-payment of retainer, refuses to drive. So, once again, no Coloni after Friday morning.

JORDAN
F3000 star Alessandro Zanardi replaces Roberto Moreno as team's fifth 1991 driver. De Cesaris qualifies 17th, with Sandro 20th for first GP. After long, lap four, stop for tyres and roll-bar adjustment Andrea up to eighth, laps 16-22, only for engine to cut and cause retirement. After lap seven tyre stop, Zanardi finishes praiseworthy ninth – despite colliding with Morbidelli and spinning, lap 63.

LAMBORGHINI
Further failures to qualify by Larini and van de Poele.

Fazed not at all by his rivals' past record, Schumacher had some fun in the opening laps. His efforts eventually netted him a third consecutive points finish.

Martin Brundle and JJ Lehto were a storming seventh and eighth. Once again though, tyre changes were to transform the situation. With the canny Prost, who'd changed first of all, charging through the field, Berger came in on lap eight. By the time his mechanics had changed him to Ds and taken the masking tape off his brake shrouds, he'd been stationary for 16.6 too-long seconds and he was down to fifth. Mansell was leading. Senna, Patrese and Alesi were next. Erik Comas was an incredible sixth thanks to the damp conditions, which suited his Ligier. Prost was seventh.

We held our breath at the end of lap nine as the leaders came in together. Not unnaturally, the Williams men made very, very sure that they got it right this time and Senna was back on the track well before Nigel. "It was a great stop though," said Mansell. "This time I left with all four wheels!" And when he did he was in fifth place behind new leader Riccardo Patrese (yet to stop), Senna, Berger and Alesi. Ayrton took the lead when Riccardo came in for tyres but, to our surprise, he waved Berger through on lap 12. Was he implementing some devious plan? No he wasn't. To be blunt he'd cocked it up! Against Goodyear's advice he'd asked for the harder Cs on his replacement left wheels and, with reduced grip, he was already paying the price. McLaren wasn't worried though. If Berger won and Mansell was second, Senna would be champion. But on lap 13 Ayrton suffered again for his mistake. He spun! In turn 15. . .at some 150 mph. Mansell and Schumacher missed him by inches as they shot past to take second and third. Prost did so comfortably as he took fourth and, at the end of lap 14, Senna was seventh behind Piquet and Martin Brundle. Out of the points!

Not for long though because he quickly disposed of Brundle and Alesi. But, on lap 21, the worst thing possible happened to Ayrton. Mansell passed Berger to take the lead — and ten points if he stayed there. Which he seemed very likely to do, for his Williams-Renault was performing faultlessly and Nigel was obviously going to be very careful indeed! He needed to be, because Berger wasn't about to give him

Appreciation of dress sense was not a condition of admission to Benetton's flamenco party. For male visitors, a 1970s second division footballers' haircut was compulsory...

Until a fatal accident involving spectators curtailed the 1975 Spanish GP, Barcelona was its spiritual home. Although the Circuit de Catalunya lacked Montjuich Park's charisma, the brand new facility was still mighty impressive.

Displeased with Olivier Grouillard, Fondmetal recruited Gabriele Tarquini for the rest of the season. The charming Italian rewarded the team's faith with 12th place.

any relief and the Austrian had got the irrepressible Schumacher right up his exhaust pipe. Leastways until Michael spun off in his enthusiasm — down to sixth behind Prost (now third), Senna and Alesi. Then, in five laps, two more dramatic happenings. The mercurial Alesi had to charge into his pit, stop for ten seconds, and rip out again — a 'stop-go' penalty for "weaving at the start" said the stewards. Down to ninth from fifth went Jean. But out altogether from second went Berger, on lap 34. Once again his Honda V12 had lost cylinders and, for the seventh time in 14 races, Gerhard retired. "Why does it always seem to happen to me and not to Ayrton?" he must have wondered.

On the 40th lap of 65, Mansell was leading Prost by 16.5s and Patrese had caught and passed Senna to take third. Ayrton was struggling. "After the spin, the left-hand tyres were blistered. I couldn't go quicker." Not only did Alesi also catch and adventurously pass him to take fourth on lap 50 but a rapidly recovering Schumacher looked like doing so too (he didn't). But at the end of a great race the question was whether Alesi was going to make Ferrari's day by taking third place from Patrese. He was gaining on the Italian but Riccardo knew the score. "I had to push very hard to keep him behind but the car was responding well and I was able to do it." Fastest lap of the race was the result (1m 22.837s, 122.188 mph). Plus four points for Riccardo and Williams.

If anyone had forecast before the race began that Nigel Mansell (who'd had a slanging match with his new 'chum' Ayrton Senna in the drivers' briefing, and who'd been driving with a twisted ankle from a football match the evening before) would win his fifth GP of the year, that Senna would finish only fifth and that the Ferraris of Prost and Alesi would be second and fourth, I'd have doubted it. But now the championship would be going to Japan unresolved. Maybe even to Australia. Nigel had reduced the gap to 16 points and, with first and third places, Williams had moved ahead of McLaren in the constructors' contest by a single point.

Now the pressure was really on Senna, McLaren and Honda, especially the latter. Anything could happen in Japan!

JAPAN

October 20 1991 Circuit: Suzuka

Missing person: as champion Senna, winner Berger and the consistent Patrese acknowledge the packed grandstands, the podium is conspicuously devoid of Jean-Marie Balestre. The Frenchman's FISA presidency was over, and successor Max Mosley prefers a low-profile approach to the job.

The Japanese Grand Prix at Suzuka, near Nagoya on Honshu Island, does not have a happy history. In 1987, Nigel Mansell had a mammoth accident during practice and was unable to start. Both 1989 and 1990 were marred by collisions between Alain Prost and Ayrton Senna, acrimoniously resolving two World Championships. And Suzuka 1991, having seen Ayrton Senna win his third title in the most laudable way, also saw the emotional and intense Brazilian publicly disgrace himself after the race with a foul-mouthed verbal attack on deposed FISA president Jean-Marie Balestre.

Tension was high when the teams arrived in Japan after a three-week lay-off. In Spain, Nigel Mansell's brilliant victory had prevented Senna from achieving his ambition to go to Honda's homeland as world champion. Similarly, the Williams team's success in Spain had wrested the lead in the constructors' contest from McLaren. In the country where

Sixth place wasn't exactly seismic news, but Stefano Modena's efforts brought Tyrrell its first point for quite some time.

At last! Alex Caffi finally qualified for a race, on the same weekend that Footwork announced that it would not be retaining the Italian's services in 1992 (right).

face means so much, the Woking outfit arrived a bit short of it. But, typically, it hadn't been idle since the last race. Neil Oatley's design team had further honed its car's aerodynamics and made beneficial suspension changes. Shell had formulated yet *another* performance-enhancing fuel. And, at Waco, Honda had made its V12 engine lighter and even more powerful. Would Williams, Renault and Elf have done as much? For Suzuka they'd have had a job. The circuit, with its theme park and hotels, is owned by Honda and, uniquely amongst the Formula One teams, is used all year long by McLaren for testing Honda's latest developments.

People who regard the Italians, Brazilians and the Silverstone crowd as being the ultimate enthusiasts clearly haven't been to Japan. Over four million Grand Prix-crazy people applied for tickets in 1991, with a ballot deciding the lucky 100,000 or so who actually got them. The organisation is no less intense. Mindful of the controversy caused by the end-of-lap chicane which had brought Prost and Senna together in 1989, they had tried to improve things by moving it some 30 metres down the road. In doing so, however, they'd made it even tighter and even more ludicrous. But, apart from that, Suzuka remained a fine circuit of which the drivers approve. Riccardo Patrese regards it as one of the three best in the world (with Imola and Spa). It is very testing, has just about every kind of corner, and requires perfect chassis balance. But in the race, apart from the chicane, it has another major defect. It is virtually impossible to pass — which is why the notorious 1989 collision happened. So, as in Monaco and Hungary, being on the front row of the starting grid and being best-placed to reach the first corner ahead is vital.

With the World Championship at stake, that is why Senna and Mansell strove even harder than usual to be there. Senna was. Mansell wasn't. But Ayrton wasn't in his 60th pole position. That was Gerhard Berger's honour — for the second race in succession. Ever since the

Footwork
BLAUPUNKT

TEAM ANALYSIS

McLAREN

Perfect team result marred by emotional and degrading post-race tirade by Senna. Substantial peformance increase achieved since Spain. Revised aerodynamics and front suspension, more power from lighter Honda V12 and improved Shell fuel. Berger and Senna dominate qualifying — first and second both days. Gerhard takes second successive pole position. After clean start which allays fears of repeat of 1990 first-corner collision (Senna and Prost), Berger builds ten-second lead over Senna by lap ten. With championship safe after Mansell's lap ten retirement, Senna charges and takes lead, lap 18. Lap 19 tyre stop (ten seconds) drops Gerhard to third. Back to second lap 24. Senna sets fastest lap (1m 41.532s, 129.195 mph) but, with seemingly certain 33rd win, offers victory to Berger after radio consultation with team boss Ron Dennis, in appreciation of Gerhard's championship help during season. Moves over at last corner to give Berger his first McLaren win in 31 races. Senna, now 1991 world champion and the youngest-ever three-times winner, then gravely sullies his image by obscenely vilifying former FISA president Jean-Marie Balestre after admitting that his 1990 championship resulted from his deliberately colliding with Prost at Suzuka. Team's superb third one-two of year returns McLaren to head of constructors' championship by commanding 11 points.

TYRRELL

Despite higher-revving Honda V10 engines and revised suspension, Modena and Nakajima qualify only 14th and 15th. Having run seventh, laps 14-20, Satoru spins out of his last Japanese GP when suspension breaks, lap 31. Modena battles with Brundle from lap one. Loses seventh to Martin, lap 21, and has bird hit helmet but finishes sixth for first Tyrrell point since Canada.

WILLIAMS

Team suffers from failure to match McLaren's post-Spain development progress. Mansell, only 0.03s off Senna qualifying time, starts third, failing to make vital front row by one place. Closely challenges Senna for nine laps but, in McLaren turbulence at Turn One, lap ten, has recurrence of practice braking problem and spins out of race to end his championship challenge. Patrese starts fifth after Friday spin and Saturday throttle problem. Takes lead, laps 22-23, when McLarens tyre-stop but down to third after own lap 23 stop. Unable to challenge due to gearbox problem (yet again), finishes third. Team now 11 points behind McLaren in constructors' championship with only one race left.

BRABHAM

Lighter, more powerful Yamaha V12 no help to Mark Blundell, who has oil leak and fails to pre-qualify for the first time. Martin Brundle pre-qualifies fastest before qualifying 19th (inconsistent Pirelli tyre problems). Battling with Modena up to seventh, lap 21. Tenth after lap 23 tyre stop but finishes fifth, one lap down, after "one of the best drives I've ever had!" A psychological boost for Martin before joining Benetton in 1992.

Hollow shells. Ferrari was still suffering, the ongoing turmoil shortly to be complicated further by the sacking of Alain Prost ....

FOOTWORK

New underbody for Hart V8 engine helps both Caffi and Alboreto to pre-qualify, second and third. Michele fails to qualify but Alex does so, 26th, for first GP drive of season. Handicapped by lack of racing miles is happy to finish tenth, two laps down. Team to use Mugen (Honda) V10 in 1992.

LOTUS

With revised rear suspension, Häkkinen and Herbert qualify 21st and 23rd. Mika spins out of race, lap four. Johnny retires from 11th, lap 31 (broken earth wire).

FONDMETAL

Tarquini pre-qualifies fourth and starts second race for team 24th in spare car after hurting knee in Friday off. In pain, races doggedly to 11th, three laps down.

LEYTON HOUSE

Ivan Capelli nobly helps financially-strapped team he had been with since 1987. Stands down to enable Mercedes-Benz protégé Karl Wendlinger to take his place. The Austrian qualifies 22nd (12th fastest in Sunday warm-up), but is nerfed out of race by a spinning de Cesaris on lap two. Gugelmin has very early, lap six, tyre stop (understeer problem). Rejoins 19th and grapples with continuing understeer to finish eighth out of 11, one lap down after a second tyre stop.

AGS

nable to afford long trips, team withdraws from last two ıces of season.

BENETTON

fter winning last two Japanese GPs team hopes for hat-ick – but fails. Schumacher qualifies ninth (top Pirelli) fter destroying Piquet's race car in Saturday crash. Vearing neck brace in race, up to sixth laps 10-21. To fifth ıps 22-27. Down to sixth after lap 27 tyre stop and races vith Martini and Brundle until retiring, lap 35 (engine), fter another very impressive drive. 1990 winner Nelson quet qualifies tenth but starts from back after having a amaged front wishbone rosejoint replaced on grid. yre-stops, lap 20, and races strongly from 14th to finish eventh, one lap down, after struggling to get by Erik Comas.

DALLARA

disastrous race. After qualifying 12th and 16th, JJ Lehto nd Emanuele Pirro are both taken out by a spinning ndrea de Cesaris on lap two.

MINARDI

xcellent qualifying performances put Martini (after riday crash) and Morbidelli seventh and eighth on rid. Having avoided de Cesaris/Lehto/Pirro/Wendlinger ıp two fracas Gianni seventh, laps 10-13. Tyre stops ıp 14. Rejoins ninth but retires with broken wheel earing, lap 16. Pier-Luigi has fine race before lap 40 etirement. Sixth laps 1-9. Fifth laps 10-20 and fourth ntil lap 22 tyre stop. Fights back to fifth, laps 28-39, vhen broken clutch cuts electrics. He and team eserved better.

LIGIER

Only 17th and 20th on grid for Boutsen and Comas. Both dvance, sandwiching Nakajima, reaching ninth and 1th, lap 21. Comas pushes hard to reach excellent eventh, lap 24, but retires with broken alternator, lap 42. Boutsen finishes ninth (one lap down), delayed by fading oil pressure after tyre stop.

FERRARI

Amidst frenzied speculation about his future Alain Prost starts fourth, two places ahead of Alesi with both some two seconds off the pace. Doing his best in too-slow car Alain finishes fourth to raise his record points total to 699.5. Alesi engine grenades itself on lap one. No wonder Alain wants out! A very sad reflection on such a historically great team.

LARROUSSE-LOLA

Amidst continuing rumours of future merger with AGS, Gérard Larrousse team's awful 1991 gets worse. Eric Bernard breaks leg in Friday morning crash. Suzuki qualifies 25th for first GP since Italy but retires from 15th place on home track on lap 27 (electrics).

COLONI

Consistently unimpressive team amazingly makes it to Suzuka. 1990 F3 champion of Japan, F1 first-timer Naoki Hattori, substitutes for disenchanted Pedro Chaves. In duff car, adorned with $250 sponsorship signatures, unsurprisingly fails to pre-qualify.

JORDAN

Bertrand Gachot, released from gaol after his sentence was dramatically reduced on appeal, hastens to Suzuka but fails to renew Jordan drive. With growing confidence, Alessandro Zanardi qualifies 13th and is sixth in Sunday warm-up. Excellent eighth, laps 3-6, but retires, lap eight, when gearbox jams in second. Andrea de Cesaris starts 11th but spins out, lap two, whilst trying to pass Morbidelli, taking Lehto, Pirro and Wendlinger with him!

LAMBORGHINI

Economising with only a few mechanics. With no grip, insufficient power and hopelessly off the pace, both Larini and van de Poele fail to qualify.

Following in the footsteps of Mercedes SWC colleague Michael Schumacher, Karl Wendlinger had a short GP debut for Leyton House, becoming involved in the lap two accident provoked by Andrea de Cesaris.

likeable Austrian had joined McLaren at the beginning of 1990, he had been overawed by the redoubtable Senna. In 1990 he'd also been too big for the car, but now both problems were behind him and he was far more like the Berger of old — cheerful, relaxed and blindingly fast. He set a 1m 34.700s, over two seconds faster than Senna's 1990 pole, 0.1s faster than Senna in 1991 and 0.2s quicker than third-fastest Mansell. That tenth between Nigel and Senna was to make all the difference in the race. The GP seemed certain to be between the two McLaren men and Mansell, because Patrese was fifth on the grid, sandwiched between the Ferraris of Prost and Alesi, and the latter three were some two seconds off the pace. To emphasise that top drivers in the same team achieve almost identical results, the Minardi-Ferraris of Martini and Morbidelli were next up, followed by the Benetton-Fords of Michael Schumacher and Nelson Piquet.

Not satisfied with their increasing presence in F1, the Japanese are looking to tackle other sports ... such as synchronised umbrella wielding.

Senna had been conducting his usual psychological warfare before the race. "I gave way to Mansell's forceful tactics in Portugal and Spain but I won't be so timid here." (Talk about the pot calling the kettle black.) But he was wasting his time trying to intimidate the gritty Nigel. Ironically Ayrton, second on the grid was on the "dirty" right side of the track which had so inflamed his feelings in 1990, when he had been in pole position there. So, as the lights turned to green, the watching world held its breath. But this time, thank heavens, there was a clean start. Out in front it was Berger, followed by his team-mate and Mansell with Patrese fourth ahead of the two Ferraris.

Jean Alesi's race didn't last long. Just half a lap in fact, as his V12 exploded him out of contention. And with Prost's car just not fast enough, all Alain could do was to try and finish well up in the points. Which he did. But the McLaren men had a plan. Whoever was ahead at the beginning of the race would be helped by the other. It didn't matter to Senna whether he finished first or second, provided he was ahead of Mansell. And that is where he was. So he let Gerhard pull away. Nigel was right behind Ayrton's McLaren most of the time, but there was no way he could get past in the sweeping curves where, thanks to the Williams's superior handling, he was quicker. On the exit from the chicane, Senna's Honda V12 had more grunt than Nigel's Renault V10. Stalemate. Until the beginning of lap ten.

As the two championship contenders braked from some 180 mph to enter Turn One the front of Mansell's car jinked to the left, rode over the kerb and was gone, into the run-off area's deep gravel, where he stayed. The 1991 World Championship had been decided at exactly the same place as in 1990 — but, thankfully, very differently. "I'd been putting the pressure on Ayrton, not pushing too hard, when, at Turn One, the brake pedal went soft and I just couldn't slow down sufficiently." Nigel had done his best but it wasn't enough. Senna was champion and the youngest-ever triple winner of the title. A magnificent achievement.

Now, with no worries about the championship, he could go for his 33rd Grand

Head start: Berger and Senna protect their interests at the green light as Mansell holds on to third place.

Prix victory, to the delight of his countless Japanese fans. And he did! Berger was ten seconds ahead, but his early pace had taken the edge off his tyres. Lap by lap the gap decreased. Lap 13: six seconds. Lap 16: 2.3. On lap 17 they were together and next time around the brilliant Brazilian took the lead. All over bar the cheering? Not at all! Berger came in for a new set of soft-compound Goodyear Cs on lap 19. After an over-long ten second stop he rejoined third behind Patrese, who took the lead on lap 22 when Senna changed tyres (in a searing 5.8s!). But, on lap 24, after Riccardo had stopped, the McLarens were back in front with Senna in the lead by 3.3s. With Prost fourth, not gaining and not being caught, it was the battle for the last two points places that was getting everybody's attention. After the tyre stops it was a glorious tussle between Pier-Luigi Martini's Minardi, Michael Schumacher's Benetton-Ford, Martin Brundle's Brabham-Yamaha and Stefano Modena's Tyrrell-Honda. Three nationalities and four constructors. It was good to see! On lap 35 Schumacher's engine gave up after another fine drive by the young German and, on lap 40, Martini's clutch did the same thing, severing the electrics and leaving Brundle and Modena to fight for fifth. Which Martin got after "one of the best drives I've ever had!" It was his first points finish since Japan 1989 (fifth for Brabham-Judd), and it was richly deserved. As was Modena's single point, after a drought that had lasted since his second place in Canada.

On lap 39 out of 53 Senna set the fastest lap of the race (1m 41.532s, 129.195 mph), over two seconds faster than his 1990 lap record. On lap 45 he was 3.3 seconds ahead of his friend and team-mate. Berger had an engine problem. "I was going absolutely flat out when it made a big noise. I thought I was out again but then it got OK. I watched the gears and the revs and it seemed alright, so I was able to keep going quickly." His reward for his season-long selfless help for Senna to win the championship was about to come. "Do you want me to let Gerhard through?" Senna asked team boss Ron Dennis over the car-to-pit radio. Yes, he did,

In his best drive of the season, the Benetton-bound Martin Brundle hauled his Brabham to fifth place.

replied Ron. To his great credit Ayrton did so — and it can't have been easy, for him of all people, voluntarily to have conceded victory. Moving over at the very last corner he let Gerhard sweep inside him to take his first victory in a McLaren after 31 races with the team — by just 0.3s!

And then he spoiled everything. Having driven a superb and generous race, having won his third title in four years, having become the youngest ever three-times world champion and having helped put McLaren back in the lead of the constructors' championship, he erupted. In the hearing of his Honda engine suppliers who, like the stunned crowd listening to him over the public address system, venerated him, he launched into an abusive tirade, laced with obscenities, against the ex-president of FISA, Jean-Marie Balestre. As he did so he revealed for the first time that his 1990 championship had been won at Suzuka by his deliberately taking Prost off. Outrage about alleged injustices by the president had clearly been boiling inside him ever since the 1989 and 1990 happenings at Suzuka. It all came pouring out in a torrent of bitterness and invective. He may have relieved his feelings but, as a man and a world champion, it did him incalculable harm displaying, as it did, an arrogant belief that only he was right and that, in his determination to win, he was prepared "to go for it regardless of the consequences." The possible results of which don't bear thinking about.

It takes all sorts to make a world, and we've certainly got all sorts in Formula One! By the next Grand Prix, the best of the year in Adelaide, where hopefully the sun would be shining and where the Australian atmosphere would certainly be more than agreeable, maybe the nasty taste of Suzuka would have left our mouths. In all probability, that seemed doubtful.

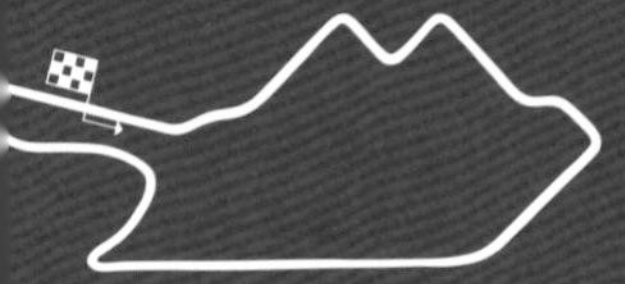

AUSTRALIA

November 3 1991 Circuit: Adelaide

As Alain Prost contemplated the benefits of being a pedestrian, Gianni Morbidelli stepped in at Ferrari with impressive results, the young Italian finishing in the points.

When we first went to Australia in 1985, no one was surprised by the clear blue sky, blazing sunshine and scorching temperature. We all knew that Australia was like that all the time, didn't we? We gulped a bit when 1986's pre-race days were deluged with torrential rain, and we were badly rattled in '89 when the race had to be stopped on lap three because of near flooding. It was eventually restarted to run the full two hours, but our blind belief that the weather down under was always wonderful had been severely shaken!

But, as they say in Oz, no worries for 1991! After all, Adelaide is the state capital with the lowest annual rainfall in Australia. That may well be so, but this year we seemed to get it all on race day! The sad result was that the Grand Prix ended up being the shortest in the history of the World Championship. Never before had so many people from all over the world put so much time, effort and money into a meeting for so little return.

Adelaide is a lovely city in glorious surroundings, and its street circuit is the finest

In the '60s, this would have been a tablecloth in an English seaside fish and chip restaurant; nowadays, it's the height of Adelaide fashion (below).

Sayonara, Naka-san. Japan's first full-time GP driver prepares to start his final race. Unfortunately for Satoru Nakajima, he posted the first retirement.

there is. Not a glamorous practical joke like Monaco nor an inappropriate fabrication like Phoenix, but a realistic, natural venue formed from everyday roads. Its 2.35-mile lap surrounds parkland on the edge of the city, has just about every kind of corner, from tight hairpins to virtually flat out sweepers, and incorporates the near 200 mph Jack Brabham straight. Even on race day it can be reached in minutes from any of the city's excellent hotels, and the organisation and administration are immaculate. Add to all that the friendliness, cheerfulness, hospitality and sheer enthusiasm of the thousands of Australians who live and go there for the race, and it is no wonder that their Grand Prix is universally judged to be the best of the year.

There was an incredulous atmosphere there on the pre-race Wednesday though, when the news broke that Alain Prost had been fired by Ferrari. Fired? Yes, fired. Alain had spoken out once too often about his beliefs that his employers hadn't done enough to develop their excellent 1990 car and that the three-man Maranello management committee couldn't manage its way out of a paper bag. ''He is a disruptive influence and his presence in Adelaide would have made the situation in the team unbearable,'' said team manager (and committee member) Claudio Lombardi. Who was right and who was wrong was irrelevant. The world's most successful Grand Prix driver had driven his last race for the sport's most charismatic team. Exit Prost, enter Gianni Morbidelli, Minardi team member and Ferrari test driver, scarcely believing his luck. A drive for Maranello at the age of 23! No one knew what was going to happen to Alain, but it didn't seem unreasonable to assume that there'd be some writs flying about and that he'd bob up again somewhere. Maybe even in the Williams team, with Renault's blessing, said some.

Come Thursday and the early start of race proceedings, however, and the gossip died down, to be replaced by conjecture about what was going to happen on Sunday. The drivers' championship may have been decided but the constructors' contest hadn't. Could Williams, 11 points behind McLaren, pull it off against the odds? Could three-times world champion, and last year's winner, Nelson Piquet shine in his last drive for Benetton (and, maybe, his last ever GP)? Would Morbidelli impress, racing the Ferrari he knew so well from testing? And there were a lot of curious eyes looking at Bertrand Gachot, back on the scene after his early release from gaol in England, to drive for Lola in place of the injured Eric Bernard. Plenty to think about!

Being used only once a year, Adelaide is always faster on day two than it is on the Friday. Whilst it certainly wasn't sunny enough to worry overmuch about the dreaded hole in the ozone layer, it was plenty hot enough for the track to be in prime condition and for, surprise, surprise, Ayrton Senna to go even faster than he had for his 1990 pole position. Nearly one and a half seconds quicker in fact. With all the extra rubber now put down on the low-grip tarmac, the second qualifying session's times could be sensational!

Saturday morning was dull and overcast with heavy cloud cover and odd spots of rain.

Andrea de Cesaris practises not being able to see where he is going, which came in handy on Sunday.

Gerhard Berger was quickest, 1m 14.314s, but then it really rained. The afternoon's qualifying session looked like being a washout but, with the rain stopped, the warm track suddenly dried with 15 minutes to go. What a scramble to get out and try to improve yesterday's times!

Out of the 30 who attempted only nine failed — and Senna wasn't one of them. With yet another of his mega-laps he went round in 1m 14.041s, three tenths of a second faster than Berger and eight tenths faster than Mansell, who was third quickest. Nigel shrugged his shoulders philosophically. ''McLaren, Honda and Shell are two steps ahead of Williams, Renault and Elf on the development road. We can't live with them on power.'' At Nigel's

TEAM ANALYSIS

McLAREN
Ideal end to superb season. Exploiting Honda power superiority Senna takes 60th pole position (1m 14.041s, 114.202 mph) with Berger third on grid to achieve team's third successive front row. Senna leads, hotly pursued by Mansell, until dangerously wet race stopped and abandoned after 16 laps. Berger spins down to third, lap three, but sets fastest lap (1m 41.141s, 83.602 mph) before spinning out of race, lap 15. With results based on lap 14 positions, Senna achieves 33rd GP victory with Berger third and team winning constructors' championship for fourth successive (seventh in all) year. Just as Ayrton prophesied before the first race at Phoenix, reliability was the key to success. With it, McLaren had enjoyed another magnificent year.

TYRRELL
Another poor result in team's last race with Honda power. Modena starts ninth after major confrontation with wall on Saturday, which writes off car. Finishes tenth in presumed last race for team. Satoru Nakajima, no lover of street circuits, qualifies 24th for last GP before retirement. Hits Boutsen's Ligier, lap three. Replaces nosecone but retires from 26th, lap five, after losing control at Esses. Then joins Fuji TV technicians at circuit to put finishing touches to hour-long programme honouring the conclusion of his 14-year career.

WILLIAMS
At Nigel Mansell's request, team brings reactive suspension car to Adelaide for race-conditions evaluation. Results very encouraging but Nigel decides to use normal car on Sunday after qualifying third in it. Patrese fourth on grid. Mansell drives inspired race, harrying Senna in dangerous, virtually sightless, conditions. Repeatedly tries, but fails, to take lead until ''the car just went left on me.'' Into the wall. With Nigel still in car, race stopped. Riccardo down to eighth, lap one, but up to fifth, lap six. When race abandoned Mansell classified second and Patrese fifth after racing with debris jammed under his Williams. Team hopes for constructors' championship dashed but Renault pleased with best-ever Grand Prix season.

BRABHAM
Last race for team with Yamaha engines before it is reconstituted and moved to Milton Keynes. After pre-qualifying fastest Martin Brundle, with brake problem, fails to qualify for first time since Austria '85. Mark Blundell second in pre-qualifying and 17th on grid for last Brabham race. In poor-handling car finishes first Australian GP 17th (one lap down), after two 360 degree spins.

FOOTWORK
An encouraging end to a character-building season. Thanks to new undertray and determined driving, Michele Alboreto pre-qualifies second and starts 15th. Alex Caffi pre-qualifies fourth and is 23rd on grid for second race of season, his last with the team. Michele spins out of contention, lap 16, but classified 13th (full distance) when race stopped. Caffi classified 15th (one lap down). Team optimistic that Mugen V10 engines will greatly improve performance in 1992, although they will still have to pre-qualify.

LOTUS
In last race with Judd V8 engines, Johnny Herbert and Mika Häkkinen qualify 21st and 25th — with Mika being lucky to get away with major side-swipe of Esses wall on Saturday. Johnny goes off in Sunday warm-up but is OK and races to excellent 11th (full distance). Mika 19th (one lap down). Very underfinanced team justified in feeling satisfied with ninth place in constructors' championship.

FONDMETAL
New car built to replace Japanese GP write-off but, sadly for Tarquini, suspension collapses at end of pre-qualifying and prevents him getting through. All the way to Australia for 11 laps and 26 miles! Team hopes for 1992 return with two drivers and different engine, but will have to continue pre-qualifying.

COLONI
Team rounds off what must have been a uniquely unsuccessful Grand Prix season by having Naoki Hattori, five seconds off the pace, make it 15 failures to pre-qualify in 15 attempts.

JORDAN
Calamitous two days of practice followed by happy ending. Zanardi crashes three times (one of them caused by suspension defect) and de Cesaris destroys car on Saturday but both qualify — eighth (Andrea) and 16th. Only one spare nosecone left for race, out of six brought, but no need for it. Both drivers very sensibly race with great caution. De Cesaris finishes eighth and Zanardi ninth (both full distance). No points but, in last race before switching from Ford to Yamaha power, team achieves constructors' championship objective by finishing excellent fifth in first year, after Tyrrell also fails to score.

LAMBORGHINI
Eric van de Poele fails to qualify for last race with team before switching to Brabham for 1992. Nicola Larini qualifies well (19th), but is involved with Alesi/Schumacher lap five collision and crashes out of race. Team future unknown, but will have to pre-qualify in 1992 if it continues.

LEYTON HOUSE
Mauricio Gugelmin qualifies 14th. Karl Wendlinger 26th on grid for his second GP despite major problems changing gear (too tall for car). Gugelmin loses control when hits standing water on lap 14. Spins inside pit wall and hits two marshals who are mercifully not badly hurt. Classified 14th (one lap down). Wendlinger impressively progresses from 26th to 16th by lap six. To pits to correct

If the F1 season was to be extended to 30 races, Roberto Moreno might get to drive for every team in the course of the year. At Adelaide, he took over Morbidelli's vacated Minardi.

misfire lap seven. Rejoins 21st and last. Classified 20th (two laps down) after a first Australian GP that he will long remember! Much-liked Ivan Capelli, with March/Leyton House since 1987, given special trophy and emotional send-off after race. Team's future unknown but rumours suggest link with Mercedes-Benz.

AGS
Team fails to appear following withdrawal after Spain. Future intentions unclear.

BENETTON
Departing Nelson Piquet strongly criticises team for alleged lack of car development before qualifying fifth. Michael Schumacher sixth on grid, 0.2s slower using Series VI Ford HB V8 engine with revised valve gear. Michael charges strongly. Passes Nelson to fourth, lap two. Then harries Berger for third. Down to fifth behind Piquet, lap five. Hit by Alesi's Ferrari when trying to repass Nelson and obliged to retire. Piquet has 360 degree spin, lap six, but finishes fourth in last race for team. With no drive for '92 his future unknown but says "see you next year!"

DALLARA
With team using Judd V10 engines for last time, JJ Lehto qualifies 11th and Emanuele Pirro 13th. Pirro drives storming last race for team. Up to ninth, lap one, and to seventh, lap six. Chases Morbidelli for sixth-place half-point but misses it by 1.2s, finishing seventh. Lehto down to 15th, lap one. Recovers to finish 12th (full distance).

MINARDI
As result of Gianni Morbidelli's move to Ferrari, Roberto Moreno joins his third 1991 team, qualifying 18th with Friday time in strange car which he finds very uncomfortable. Miserably races to 16th, one lap down. Pier-Luigi Martini starts tenth. Down to 12th in foul conditions, lap one, and then to 17th, lap four. Out, lap nine, when hits standing water on Jack Brabham straight and helplessly nose-dives into wall. Team's last race with Ferrari power. Lamborghini engines come in for 1992.

LIGIER
Last race for detested Lamborghini-powered car. 1989 winner Thierry Boutsen ("but I was in a Williams then!") qualifies 20th, with team-mate Erik Comas 22nd for his first Australian GP. Thierry hit by Nakajima on lap five and retires. "I can't wait for the (Renault-powered) JS 37!" Under circumstances, Comas does well to finish 18th (one lap down).

FERRARI
What a casino, as they say on the continent! Uproar and consternation amidst the whole Grand Prix scene when Ferrari announces on Wednesday that it has fired Alain Prost for continually rubbishing the car and the management in public. Team manager Claudio Lombardi says "Prost has been a disruptive influence and his presence in Adelaide would have made the situation in the team unbearable." Visiting airline chief, and ex-Ferrari world champion, Niki Lauda says "Alain got what he deserved" but pit-lane opinions mixed. Meanwhile, Prost stays in Port Douglas, Queensland, and understandably fails to show saying "the matter is in the hands of my lawyers." A very sad ending to what was, in 1990, a very successful partnership. Whither Prost? Nobody knows. Ferrari test driver and Minardi team member Gianni Morbidelli drafted into Maranello team and qualifies well at eighth in familiar car after big "off" on Friday. Then, in truly daunting conditions, has superb drive to finish sixth and score half-point in first Ferrari race. Jean Alesi, dispirited by Prost's departure, qualifies seventh. Hits Boutsen's Ligier, lap six, and zaps into back of Schumacher's Benetton, causing inevitable retirement. With no win for first season since '86, team finishes distant third in constructors' championship.

LARROUSSE-LOLA
Appalling end to appalling season. Bertrand Gachot, after successful appeal for early release from UK gaol, joins Larrousse-Lola for one race after failing to regain place in Jordan team. In strange car, unsurprisingly fails to qualify. Aguri Suzuki (to join Footwork-Mugen team in 1992) destroys car in massive Friday crash and fails to qualify sole remaining Lola on Saturday.

request Williams had brought its reactive suspension car to Adelaide, partly to do some race-conditions development and partly in the hope that its smooth ride and aerodynamic benefits would help compensate for their comparative lack of power. But it didn't. Not enough anyway. So, for the third race in succession, there were two McLarens on the front row of the grid ahead of Mansell and Patrese, third and fourth. The odds against Nigel matching Senna's six wins and Williams finishing 12 points ahead of McLaren to gain the constructors' championship were formidable.

The traditional half-hour warm-up, which finishes four hours before the race to allow plenty of time for work on the cars, was dry but, at 10.45, the rain started. At 13.15, 45 minutes before the race was due to begin, there was such a ferocious increase in the amount of water bucketing out of the skies that Adelaide airport was closed. And the rest of Australia was suffering almost drought conditions!

At 13.30 the parade lap began with the news that the latest forecast said the rain would stop at 14.00 and be followed by more later. It didn't stop though. This was to be the baptismal race for Goodyear's new, asymmetric tread design. And didn't they need it!

Bertrand Gachot returned to F1 with Larrousse, replacing the injured Eric Bernard. Bertrand discovered that prison can dull your competitive edge; he failed to qualify.

From his hard won pole position, and with the invaluable benefit of a clear track in front of him, Senna led by nearly 3.5s at the end of the first of the scheduled 81 laps. Not that there was the remotest chance of them doing 81 laps. It would be another two-hour race, like 1989. Berger was second, just ahead of Mansell. The Benettons of Piquet and Schumacher were fourth and fifth, followed by the Ferraris of Alesi and Morbidelli, with Riccardo Patrese down from fourth on the grid to eighth. In conditions which had to be seen to be believed, Schumacher got ahead of Piquet into fourth on lap two and, when Berger slid sideways on lap three, Mansell got past him into second. But how anybody stayed on the track was beyond me. With rivers of water running across it, vision totally obscured by the giant roosters of spray thrown up by the wide, pumping tyre treads of the cars ahead, and with some 700 horsepower to feed down to the waterlogged tarmac, they were indeed heroes.

Satoru Nakajima, the man who had set the fastest lap on his way to finish fourth in 1989's atrociously similar race, was the first to go. He had already rammed Thierry Boutsen's Ligier and come in for a new nosecone when he went off on lap five. Then, on the main straight, Alesi collided with Schumacher to take himself, Michael and the nearby Nicola Larini out of the race. On lap eight Pier-Luigi Martini, motoring flat out down the same Jack Brabham straight at some 170 mph, suddenly had his Minardi snap sideways and plough straight into the concrete wall as he aquaplaned off. Things were looking very serious indeed, with no sign of the rain abating and with marshals and incident trucks frantically trying to clear debris off the circuit.

Up at the front Nigel Mansell, driving a typically courageous race, was practically glued to Senna's wing, but totally unable to see enough to get by — even if he'd had the grunt to do so. Berger was third, but not close enough to get to grips with the Williams, Piquet fourth, Patrese fifth and Morbidelli an excellent sixth. On lap 13 with, unsurprisingly, nobody passing anybody but 19 of the original 26 starters still gingerly feeling their way round the track, Gerhard Berger set the fastest lap of the race,

Ayrton Senna got away first and went on to win the shortest race in Grand Prix history, taking full advantage of the fact that his rivals couldn't see their own nosecones in his spray.

''Sorry punters, that's your lot.'' After dropping several hints that the race would restart, the organisers finally took the decision to call the whole thing off.

1m 41.141s. An incredible 83.602 mph average for the 2.4 miles, in absolutely unspeakable conditions.

Then Mansell went off. Heavily. ''I don't know what happened. I was following in Ayrton's tracks and the car just went left on me. It might have aquaplaned or I might have hit something, but it went totally out of control and I went straight into the wall.'' If it happened to Nigel it could happen to any of the other 12 who were left. On lap 16, with Senna frantically gesticulating for the race to be stopped, race director Roland Bruynseraede had seen enough. Out went the red flag as Berger spun off, as did the even more experienced Michele Alboreto.

So what now? With some cars on the track in their grid positions to restart, and with the rest in their garages, it was far from clear. Riccardo Patrese stormed furiously off to race control to remonstrate with the officials. McLaren boss Ron Dennis diplomatically intimated that he would not be willing to let his valuable drivers start again in the appalling conditions and virtually every driver was vociferously against doing so.

After three ''10 minute'' boards had been shown to keep the proceedings alive, a bedraggled Bruynseraede held out the red flag again. The 1991 Australian Grand Prix had been abandoned after 16 laps — the shortest ever World Championship race was over with half points being awarded to the top six finishers. In accordance with the rules, the results were based on the positions at the end of lap 14 — so even though Mansell and Berger were out of the race they were classified second and third ahead of Nelson Piquet, Riccardo Patrese (who had been charging round with debris jammed under his car) and the particularly worthy Gianni Morbidelli.

McLaren had easily won its fourth successive constructors' championship, and deservedly so, but almost everyone involved — the drivers, their teams, the officials and spectators — felt frustrated and cheated. What surely would have been a superb race had literally been washed away. And, needless to say, it was dry enough to hold it an hour later!

Whether the race should have been started at all will long be a matter of contention but at least, mercifully, no one had been badly hurt. Everyone just quietly drifted away to think about and work for the 1992 season. It wasn't all that far away!

REVIEW OF 1991

In attempting concisely to review a Grand Prix year which lasted for nine months, visiting five continents, it is difficult to know where to start. Formula One is about far more than just the drivers. It is also about the cars, their engines and tyres, the fuels, the circuits, the teams, the sponsors, the organisers, the politics, the rules, the races and a host of other things.

But when, in years to come, memories of '91 are recalled they will surely revolve around just four words — Senna, Mansell, Williams and McLaren. Because those two drivers and teams dominated a cliff-hanging championship that stirred passions. Thank heavens Nigel Mansell decided not to retire! His gutsy driving and gritty refusal to accept defeat turned what would have been an Ayrton Senna whitewash into an enthralling contest between two very different personalities.

After the first four races Senna had made history by winning all of them. He had 40 championship points to Mansell's six — mainly due to the repeated failure of Williams's semi-automatic gearbox. Nine races into the series, Mansell had closed the gap to a mere eight points following his superb hat-trick of victories in France, Britain and Germany. Then Senna pulled away again thanks to the success of a concentrated McLaren-Honda development programme. Ayrton could have clinched his third world title in Spain, but Mansell's inspired fifth win unclinched it. So, for the third year in succession, race 15, in Japan, looked likely to resolve the issue. With memories of the Senna/Prost collisions in 1989 and '90 and the subsequent bitter recriminations, our hearts were in our mouths.

We needn't have worried, because this time there were no problems. As is often the case, a race of exciting promise failed to deliver. Mansell, needing to win, spun out of third place leaving Senna generously to donate victory to his co-operative team-mate Gerhard Berger... and to become the sport's youngest-ever three times world champion. By so doing he joined, statistically, the truly greats — Juan-Manuel Fangio (five times), Jack Brabham, Jackie Stewart, Niki Lauda, Nelson Piquet and Alain Prost. However, his right to be regarded as highly as them will be contested after his frank admission, following the '91 Japanese GP, that his 1990 collision with Prost at Suzuka resulted from his pre-race decision to "go for the lead at the first corner regardless of the consequences." To risk causing very high speed collisions between his following rivals because he resented FISA's decision not to change the pole position on the grid demonstrated arrogant ruthlessness and a disturbing disregard for his fellow drivers.

One man and his pooch found a neat way to avoid the traffic jams at Magny-Cours. Dogs are of course banned in the paddock, which — according to some unkind souls — didn't explain the presence of the Ligier JS35B ...

Nigel Mansell's third second place in the championship was far more to do with his car than him. Throughout the season he drove with brilliance and dogged determination. In my opinion, there was nothing between him and Senna in terms of driving ability. It was indeed

New faces: Max Mosley's nomination as FISA presidential candidate came as a surprise to many, not least long-time incumbent Jean-Marie Balestre. On October 9, Mosley became the first Englishman to hold the post.

tough that he lost so many points through the failure of his Williams's semi-automatic gearbox but, in the words of the old cliché, "to finish first, first you've got to finish!"

It was the same in the constructors' contest. After Monaco, McLaren headed the gearbox-stricken Williams team by a daunting 38 points. But in Germany they lost the lead for the first time in 40 races — to Williams. For one race only, because they were back at the top in Hungary. But they sank to second again in Spain, by a single point, before convincingly regaining the lead in Japan. The constructors' battle may not have the glamour of the drivers' championship, but in many ways it is even more important. Certainly it is to the sponsors, the teams and their many suppliers. So it was fitting that it wasn't resolved until the last GP of the year. Australia hosts what is generally regarded as being the most enjoyable Grand Prix and it deserved to hold the championship decider. But it was McLaren's impressive third one-two of the season in Japan that virtually guaranteed them a seventh richly deserved title. They and their Honda and Shell collaborators simply did the job better than anyone else.

But whilst McLaren and Williams were the stars, there were 16 other teams that were trying just as hard. Some were successful, most weren't. In such a financially demanding sport it never ceases to amaze me that so many of them are able to keep going. That they do so is a tribute to their enthusiasm and their ability to keep their sponsors happy!

As I see it there were four team levels in 1991. One: McLaren and Williams. Two: Ferrari and Benetton. Three: Jordan and Tyrrell. Four: the rest. Ferrari was an enormous disappointment. In 1990 they had won six races, finished second in the constructors' championship and enabled Alain Prost to finish second to Senna in the drivers' contest. In 1991 they fell apart. Prost's lack of confidence in team manager Cesare Fiorio resulted in the latter being replaced by a management committee. The result was failure, and Prost too, was eventually to be sacked as he continued to be openly critical of the team. With complacency causing insufficient development of their excellent 1990 car, and with a politics-ridden management unable to marshal Ferrari's great strengths, their season was a poor one with not a single win. It is to be hoped that 1992 will see Maranello pull itself together although, sadly, I have to say that I see no sign of it doing so. Especially without Prost.

Benetton failed to live up to expectations too. When the year began, prospects for its new John Barnard-designed car, allied to the Ford HB V8 and a strong driver pairing in Piquet and Moreno, seemed bright. But Barnard left part way through his re-organisation and the team's demoralised personnel, split between two locations, found it hard to develop the car. But Benetton's future looks promising. With the redoubtable Tom Walkinshaw very much in charge, tremendously strong back-up, access to the new Ford V12 engine if it turns out to be better than the V8, and two fine drivers in Martin Brundle and Michael Schumacher, I am optimistic about its chances in 1992.

That Jordan, a brand new organisation, was beaten only by the "Big Four" was a brilliant achievement. Eddie Jordan's Irish charm, business acumen, racing experience and deep knowledge of the sport enabled him to build a superb team which not only raced with great success but was also one of the friendliest in the pit lane. Designer Gary Anderson did a magnificent job, as did commercial manager Ian Phillips, team manager Trevor Foster and all their colleagues. They provided a sympathetic environment which motivated the much-maligned Andrea de Cesaris to show that he was much better than his many detractors had believed, and provided a launch pad for the very impressive Michael Schumacher. The team

SHALL WE SEE THEM AGAIN?

As the soaking crowd drifted away from Adelaide came the sad realisation that, in 1992, we may not be seeing two of Grand Prix racing's truly geat drivers — Alain Prost and Nelson Piquet, both three-times world champions.

Prost's curt dismissal by Ferrari for speaking, in their view, out of turn leaves the amiable Frenchman without a seat for the coming season, unless contracts are to be broken. There is nothing new about that in the Grand Prix world, of course, but any places in teams that Alain would want to go to would cost someone dearly.

In his brilliant 12-year career, Alain has driven for Renault, McLaren and Ferrari to achieve record scores of 44 Grands Prix victories and 699.5 World Championship points. As far as I am concerned he has never been anything other than courteous, considerate, cheerful and objective in his many dealings with me, and I very much hope to be writing about his continued achievements in 1992 or thereafter.

Should he decide to retire he will be greatly missed and long remembered for his driving fluency, his charming personality and his outstanding achievements.

The future of Nelson Piquet is similarly wrapped in mystery with his ''release'' by Benetton and no obvious, acceptable team to go to. In which case I believe he will happily retire to develop his business interests in Brazil where, amongst other things, he owns one of his country's largest tyre dealerships.

With three World Championships from over 200 Grands Prix, wealth and worldwide adulation after a truly memorable career with Brabham, Williams, Lotus and Benetton behind him, he has no need to continue racing but that is what he loves doing above all else.

Should he, too, leave the Grand Prix scene he will be remembered for his love of life, his practical jokes and his outspoken truthfulness as well as for his driving ability. That his great 14-year career seems to have spluttered to a standstill is more than sad. I just hope it has not, but we won't be sure until Kyalami, 1992.

was much affected by Bertrand Gachot's downfall and Schumacher's departure to Benetton, but it still had a wonderful first season. With Yamaha power in 1992 Jordan could be right up there.

Tyrrell, like Ferrari, was a grave disappointment. At the beginning of the year I was confidently expecting them to be able to win races. With *the* chassis of 1990 allied to Honda V10 power, the enthusiastic support of Pirelli and Stefano Modena in the cockpit it seemed a reasonable assumption. But only once during the whole season was the team really in the hunt — at Monaco. Designer Harvey Postlethwaite's departure to Mercedes was a blow from which Tyrrell never recovered. Whether it will be able to do in 1992 is in doubt, with its loss of Honda power.

'The rest' include Ligier, Footwork and Leyton House, which proves that heavy funding and impressive facilities do not necessarily guarantee success in Formula One. Ligier's record can only be described as dismal with its failure to score any points during the whole of 1990 and '91. Will Renault engines, and Renault pressure to succeed, improve things in 1992? They ought to, but only time will tell! In the same way 1991 was a season that the Footwork team (né Arrows) will want to forget. Seemingly unlimited funding from Japan and an exclusive Porsche engine deal looked to be the recipe that would, at last, enable the team to do well. Not so. Porsche's demeaning failure to provide a motor that could get the job done not only did the great Stuttgart concern a lot of harm but dragged the whole team down. Leyton House also failed to impress. Its new car proved to be unreliable and difficult to set up for anything other than ultra-smooth circuits (there aren't many of them!), and owner Akira Akagi's brush with the law in Japan distinctly unsettled the team.

One of these commentators has never won a World Championship. Messrs Barry Sheene, Alan Jones, M Walker and Jackie Stewart enjoy the sunshine that preceded the storm in Adelaide.

So what will be my memories of a wonderful Grand Prix year? Amongst them the very important fact that a change at the top of FISA should result in calmer and more stable direction of the sport in future. The ousting of the much-criticised president, Jean-Marie Balestre, and the elevation of the admirable Max Mosley should replace emotion with logic and dictation with consultation. A very welcome situation.

Plus these snapshots! Senna running out of fuel in Britain and Germany. Nigel Mansell losing his gearbox in Canada and his wheel in Portugal. Michael Schumacher's Grand Prix debut in Belgium. JJ Lehto's unalloyed joy at finishing third in Imola. The outrage in Belgium over Bertrand Gachot's English imprisonment. Riccardo Patrese spinning on Stefano Modena's oil in Monaco. Alain Prost sliding out of the San Marino GP before it had even begun, his tangle with Senna in Germany, his failure to win a race for the first season since 1980 and his eventual acrimonious dismissal. The brilliant success of the Jordan team. Nigel Mansell giving Ayrton Senna a lift on his sidepod after winning the British GP and his meteoric start in Portugal. Senna's selfless donation of victory to Berger in Japan. The abandonment of Australia after just 14 laps. Veteran Riccardo Patrese's wonderful season of success. The fact that Renault's V10 matched Honda's V12. Goodyear's continued dominance of the Grand Prix tyre world. And that breathtaking 195 mph side-by-side race by Mansell and Senna down the main straight in Spain with their joint refusal to yield!

1991. Indeed a year to remember!

1991 FORMULA ONE GRAND PRIX
ROUND ONE

USA

Phoenix, Arizona

March 10, 1991

Circuit Length: 2.312 mls/3.720 km

Laps: 81*

*(Race scheduled for 82 laps, but stopped after two hours)

Mika Häkkinen — star quality in Phoenix.

Official Starting Grid

No.	Driver / Car	Time
1	Senna, *McLaren-Honda*	(1.21.434)
27	Prost, *Ferrari*	(1.22.555)
6	Patrese, *Williams-Renault*	(1.22.833)
5	Mansell, *Williams-Renault*	(1.23.218)
20	Piquet, *Benetton-Ford*	(1.23.384)
28	Alesi, *Ferrari*	(1.23.519)
2	Berger, *McLaren-Honda*	(1.23.742)
19	Moreno, *Benetton-Ford*	(1.23.881)
21	Pirro, *Dallara-Judd*	(1.24.792)
22	Lehto, *Dallara-Judd*	(1.24.892)
4	Modena, *Tyrrell-Honda*	(1.25.065)
7	Brundle, *Brabham-Yamaha*	(1.25.385)
11	Häkkinen, *Lotus-Judd*	(1.25.448)
32	Gachot, *Jordan-Ford*	(1.25.701)
23	Martini, *Minardi-Ferrari*	(1.25.715)
3	Nakajima, *Tyrrell-Honda*	(1.25.752)
34	Larini, *Lamborghini*	(1.25.791)
16	Capelli, *Leyton House-Ilmor*	(1.26.121)
29	Bernard, *Lola-DFR*	(1.26.425)
25	Boutsen, *Ligier-Lamborghini*	(1.26.500)
30	Suzuki, *Lola-DFR*	(1.26.548)
17	Tarquini, *AGS-DFR*	(1.26.851)
15	Gugelmin, *Leyton House-Ilmor*	(1.26.865)
8	Blundell, *Brabham-Yamaha*	(1.26.915)
9	Alboreto, *Footwork-Porsche*	(1.27.015)
24	Morbidelli, *Minardi-Ferrari*	(1.27.042)

Race Classification

Pos.	*Driver*	*No.*	*Nat.*	*Car*	*Laps*	*Time/retirement*
1	Ayrton Senna	1	BR	McLaren-Honda	81	2h 00m 47.828s
2	Alain Prost	27	F	Ferrari	81	2h 01m 04.150s
3	Nelson Piquet	20	BR	Benetton-Ford	81	2h 01m 05.204s
4	Stefano Modena	4	I	Tyrrell-Honda	81	2h 01m 13.237s
5	Satoru Nakajima	3	JPN	Tyrrell-Honda	80	
6	Aguri Suzuki	30	JPN	Lola-DFR	79	
7	Nicola Larini	34	I	Lamborghini	78	
8	Gabriele Tarquini	17	I	AGS-DFR	77	
9	Pier-Luigi Martini	23	I	Minardi-Ferrari	75	Engine
10	Bertrand Gachot	32	B	Jordan-Ford	75	Engine
11	Martin Brundle	7	GB	Brabham-Yamaha	73	
12	Jean Alesi	28	F	Ferrari	72	Gearbox
R	Mika Häkkinen	11	SF	Lotus-Judd	59	Engine
R	Riccardo Patrese	6	I	Williams-Renault	49	Gearbox/spun
R	Roberto Moreno	19	BR	Benetton-Ford	49	Hit Patrese
R	Michele Alboreto	9	I	Footwork-Porsche	41	Gearbox
R	Ivan Capelli	16	I	Leyton House-Ilmor	40	Gearbox oil pump
R	Thierry Boutsen	25	B	Ligier-Lamborghini	40	Electrics
R	Gerhard Berger	2	A	McLaren-Honda	36	Fuel pump
R	Nigel Mansell	5	GB	Williams-Renault	35	Gearbox
R	Mauricio Guglemin	15	BR	Leyton House-Ilmor	34	Gearbox
R	Mark Blundell	8	GB	Brabham-Yamaha	32	Spun off
R	Emanuele Pirro	21	I	Dallara-Judd	16	Clutch
R	Gianni Morbidelli	24	I	Minardi-Ferrari	15	Gearbox
R	JJ Lehto	22	SF	Dallara-Judd	12	Clutch
R	Eric Bernard	29	F	Lola-DFR	4	Engine

Fastest lap: Alesi, on lap 49, 1m 26.758s, 95.936 mph/154.394 km/h

Drivers' World Championship

Pos.	*Driver*	*Total*
1	Ayrton Senna	10
2	Alain Prost	6
3	Nelson Piquet	4
4	Stefano Modena	3
5	Satoru Nakajima	2
6	Aguri Suzuki	1

Constructors' World Championship

Pos.	*Team*	*Total*
1	McLaren	10
2	Ferrari	6
3	Tyrrell	5
4	Benetton	4
5	Lola	1

Non Qualifiers

No.	*Name*	*Car*
26	E Comas	Ligier-Lamborghini
10	A Caffi	Footwork-Porsche
18	S Johansson	AGS-DFR
12	J Bailey	Lotus-Judd

Non Pre-Qualifiers

No.	*Name*	*Car*
33	A de Cesaris	Jordan-Ford
31	P Chaves	Coloni-DFR
14	O Grouillard	Fomet-DFR
35	E van de Poele	Lamborghini

1991 FORMULA ONE GRAND PRIX
ROUND TWO

BRAZIL

Autodromo José Carlos Pace,

Interlagos, São Paulo

March 24, 1991

Circuit Length: 2.687 mls/4.325 km

Laps: 71

Ayrton Senna — a home win … at last!

Official Starting Grid

No.	Driver	Car	Time
1	Senna	*McLaren-Honda*	(1.16.392)
6	Patrese	*Williams-Renault*	(1.16.775)
5	Mansell	*Williams-Renault*	(1.16.843)
2	Berger	*McLaren-Honda*	(1.17.471)
28	Alesi	*Ferrari*	(1.17.601)
27	Prost	*Ferrari*	(1.17.739)
20	Piquet	*Benetton-Ford*	(1.18.577)
15	Gugelmin	*Leyton House-Ilmor*	(1.18.664)
4	Modena	*Tyrrell-Honda*	(1.18.847)
32	Gachot	*Jordan-Ford*	(1.18.882)
29	Bernard	*Lola-DFR*	(1.19.291)
21	Pirro	*Dallara-Judd*	(1.19.305)
33	de Cesaris	*Jordan-Ford*	(1.19.339)
19	Moreno	*Benetton-Ford*	(1.19.360)
16	Capelli	*Leyton House-Ilmor*	(1.19.517)
3	Nakajima	*Tyrrell-Honda*	(1.19.546)
*30	Suzuki	*Lola-DFR*	(1.19.832)
25	Boutsen	*Ligier-Lamborghini*	(1.19.868)
22	Lehto	*Dallara-Judd*	(1.19.954)
23	Martini	*Minardi-Ferrari*	(1.20.175)
24	Morbidelli	*Minardi-Ferrari*	(1.20.502)
11	Häkkinen	*Lotus-Judd*	(1.20.611)
26	Comas	*Ligier-Lamborghini*	(1.21.168)
17	Tarquini	*AGS-DFR*	(1.21.219)
8	Blundell	*Brabham-Yamaha*	(1.21.230)
7	Brundle	*Brabham-Yamaha*	(1.21.280)

**Failed fuel pressure on the grid*

Race Classification

Pos.	Driver	No.	Nat.	Car	Laps	Time/retirement
1	Ayrton Senna	1	BR	McLaren-Honda	71	1h 38m 28.128s
2	Riccardo Patrese	6	I	Williams-Renault	71	1h 38m 31.119s
3	Gerhard Berger	2	A	McLaren-Honda	71	1h 38m 33.554s
4	Alain Prost	27	F	Ferrari	71	1h 38m 47.497s
5	Nelson Piquet	20	BR	Benetton-Ford	71	1h 38m 50.088s
6	Jean Alesi	28	F	Ferrari	71	1h 38m 51.769s
7	Roberto Moreno	19	BR	Benetton-Ford	70	
8	Gianni Morbidelli	24	I	Minardi Ferrari	69	
9	Mika Häkkinen	11	SF	Lotus-Judd	68	
10	Thierry Boutsen	25	B	Ligier-Lamborghini	68	
11	Emanuele Pirro	21	I	Dallara-Judd	68	
12	Martin Brundle	7	GB	Brabham-Yamaha	67	
13	Bertrand Gachot	32	B	Jordan-Ford	63	Fuel pick-up
R	Nigel Mansell	5	GB	Williams-Renault	59	Gearbox
R	Erik Comas	26	F	Ligier-Lamborghini	50	Spun off
R	Pier-Luigi Martini	23	I	Minardi-Ferrari	47	Spun off
R	Mark Blundell	8	GB	Brabham-Yamaha	34	Engine
R	Eric Bernard	29	F	Lola-DFR	33	Clutch
R	JJ Lehto	22	SF	Dallara-Judd	22	Alternator
R	Andrea de Cesaris	33	I	Jordan-Ford	20	Engine cut out/spun off
R	Stefano Modena	4	I	Tyrrell-Honda	19	Gearshift
R	Ivan Capelli	16	I	Leyton House-Ilmor	16	Engine
R	Satoru Nakajima	3	JPN	Tyrrell-Honda	12	Spun off
R	Mauricio Gugelmin	15	BR	Leyton House-Ilmor	9	Driver unwell; withdrew
R	Gabriele Tarquini	17	I	AGS-DFR	0	Spun off
DNS	Aguri Suzuki	30	JPN	Lola-DFR	0	Fuel pressure

Fastest lap: Mansell, on lap 35, 1m 20.436s, 120.278 mph/193.570 km/h.

Drivers' World Championship

Pos.	Driver	Total
1	Ayrton Senna	20
2	Alain Prost	9
3=	Riccardo Patrese	6
3=	Nelson Piquet	6
5	Gerhard Berger	4
6	Stefano Modena	3
7	Satoru Nakajima	2
8=	Aguri Suzuki	1
8=	Jean Alesi	1

Constructors' World Championship

Pos.	Team	Total
1	McLaren	24
2	Ferrari	10
3=	Benetton	6
3=	Williams	6
5	Tyrrell	5
6	Lola	1

Non Qualifiers

No.	Name	Car
9	M Alboreto	Footwork-Porsche
10	A Caffi	Footwork-Porsche
12	J Bailey	Lotus-Judd
18	S Johansson	AGS-DFR

Non Pre-Qualifiers

No.	Name	Car
14	O Grouillard	Fomet-DFR
31	P Chaves	Coloni-DFR
34	N Larini	Lamborghini
35	E van de Poele	Lamborghini

1991 FORMULA ONE GRAND PRIX
ROUND THREE

SAN MARINO

Autodromo Enzo & Dino Ferrari, Imola

April 28, 1991

Circuit Length: 3.132 mls/5.040 km

Laps: 61

Eric van de Poele — unlucky not to score.

Official Starting Grid

Driver	Car	Time	No.
Senna	McLaren-Honda	(1.21.877)	1
Patrese	Williams-Renault	(1.21.957)	6
Prost	Ferrari	(1.22.195)	*27
Mansell	Williams-Renault	(1.22.366)	5
Berger	McLaren-Honda	(1.22.567)	2
Modena	Tyrrell-Honda	(1.23.511)	4
Alesi	Ferrari	(1.23.945)	28
Morbidelli	Minardi-Ferrari	(1.24.762)	24
Martini	Minardi-Ferrari	(1.24.807)	23
Nakajima	Tyrrell-Honda	(1.25.345)	3
de Cesaris	Jordan-Ford	(1.25.491)	33
Gachot	Jordan-Ford	(1.25.531)	32
Moreno	Benetton-Ford	(1.25.655)	19
Piquet	Benetton-Ford	(1.25.809)	20
Gugelmin	Leyton House-Ilmor	(1.25.841)	15
Lehto	Dallara-Judd	(1.25.974)	22
Bernard	Lola-DFR	(1.25.983)	29
Brundle	Brabham-Yamaha	(1.26.055)	7
Comas	Ligier-Lamborghini	(1.26.207)	26
Suzuki	Lola-DFR	(1.26.356)	30
van de Poele	Lamborghini	(1.26.550)	35
Capelli	Leyton House-Ilmor	(1.26.602)	16
Blundell	Brabham-Yamaha	(1.26.778)	8
Boutsen	Ligier-Lamborghini	(1.26.998)	25
Häkkinen	Lotus-Judd	(1.27.324)	11
Bailey	Lotus-Judd	(1.27.976)	12

*Spun off on final parade lap

Race Classification

Pos.	Driver	No.	Nat.	Car	Laps	Time/retirement
1	Ayrton Senna	1	BR	McLaren-Honda	61	1h 35m 14.750s
2	Gerhard Berger	2	A	McLaren-Honda	61	1h 35m 16.425s
3	JJ Lehto	22	SF	Dallara-Judd	60	
4	Pier-Luigi Martini	23	I	Minardi-Ferrari	59	
5	Mika Häkkinen	11	SF	Lotus-Judd	58	
6	Julian Bailey	12	GB	Lotus-Judd	58	
7	Thierry Boutsen	25	B	Ligier-Lamborghini	58	
8	Mark Blundell	8	GB	Brabham-Yamaha	58	
9	Eric van de Poele	35	B	Lamborghini	57	Fuel pump
10	Erik Comas	26	F	Ligier-Lamborghini	57	
11	Martin Brundle	7	GB	Brabham-Yamaha	57	
12	Mauricio Gugelmin	15	BR	Leyton House-Ilmor	55	Engine
13	Roberto Moreno	19	BR	Benetton-Ford	54	Gearbox/engine
R	Stefano Modena	4	I	Tyrrell-Honda	41	Engine
R	Andrea de Cesaris	33	I	Jordan-Ford	37	Gear linkage
R	Bertrand Gachot	32	B	Jordan-Ford	37	Damage caused by earlier spin
R	Ivan Capelli	16	I	Leyton House-Ilmor	24	Spun off
R	Eric Bernard	29	F	Lola-DFR	17	Engine
R	Riccardo Patrese	6	I	Williams-Renault	17	Electrics/engine
R	Satoru Nakajima	3	JPN	Tyrrell-Honda	15	Transmission
R	Gianni Morbidelli	24	I	Minardi-Ferrari	10	Gearbox
R	Jean Alesi	28	F	Ferrari	2	Slid off
R	Aguri Suzuki	30	JPN	Lola-DFR	2	Spun off
R	Nelson Piquet	20	BR	Benetton-Ford	1	Spun off
R	Nigel Mansell	5	GB	Williams-Renault	0	Collided with Brundle
DNS	Alain Prost	27	F	Ferrari	0	Spun off before start

Fastest lap: Berger, on lap 55, 1m 26.531s, 130.290 mph/209.682 km/h

Drivers' World Championship

Pos.	Driver	Total
1	Ayrton Senna	30
2	Gerhard Berger	10
3	Alain Prost	9
4=	Riccardo Patrese	6
4=	Nelson Piquet	6
6	JJ Lehto	4
7=	Pier-Luigi Martini	3
7=	Stefano Modena	3
9=	Mika Häkkinen	2
9=	Satoru Nakajima	2
11=	Aguri Suzuki	1
11=	Jean Alesi	1
11=	Julian Bailey	1

Constructors' World Championship

Pos.	Team	Total
1	McLaren	40
2	Ferrari	10
3=	Benetton	6
3=	Williams	6
5	Tyrrell	5
6	Dallara	4
7=	Minardi	3
7=	Lotus	3
9	Lola	1

Non Qualifiers

No.	Name	Car
9	M Alboreto	Footwork-Porsche
10	A Caffi	Footwork-Porsche
17	G Tarquini	AGS-DFR
18	F Barbazza	AGS-DFR

Non Pre-Qualifiers

No.	Name	Car
14	O Grouillard	Fomet-DFR
21	E Pirro	Dallara-Judd
31	P Chaves	Coloni-DFR
34	N Larini	Lamborghini

1991 FORMULA ONE GRAND PRIX
ROUND FOUR

MONACO

Circuit de Monaco,

Monte Carlo

May 12, 1991

Circuit Length: 3.328 mls/2.068 km

Laps: 78

Stefano Modena — first front row start.

Official Starting Grid

No.	Driver	Car	Time
1	Senna	McLaren-Honda	(1.20.344)
4	Modena	Tyrrell-Honda	(1.20.809)
6	Patrese	Williams-Renault	(1.20.973)
20	Piquet	Benetton-Ford	(1.21.159)
5	Mansell	Williams-Renault	(1.21.205)
2	Berger	McLaren-Honda	(1.21.222)
27	Prost	Ferrari	(1.21.455)
19	Moreno	Benetton-Ford	(1.21.804)
28	Alesi	Ferrari	(1.21.910)
33	de Cesaris	Jordan-Ford	(1.22.764)
3	Nakajima	Tyrrell-Honda	(1.22.972)
21	Pirro	Dallara-Judd	(1.23.022)
22	Lehto	Dallara-Judd	(1.23.023)
23	Martini	Minardi-Ferrari	(1.23.064)
15	Gugelmin	Leyton House-Ilmor	(1.23.394)
25	Boutsen	Ligier-Lamborghini	(1.23.431)
24	Morbidelli	Minardi-Ferrari	(1.23.584)
16	Capelli	Leyton House-Ilmor	(1.23.642)
30	Suzuki	Lola-DFR	(1.23.898)
17	Tarquini	AGS-DFR	(1.23.909)
29	Bernard	Lola-DFR	(1.24.079)
8	Blundell	Brabham-Yamaha	(1.24.109)
26	Comas	Ligier-Lamborghini	(1.24.151)
32	Gachot	Jordan-Ford	(1.24.208)
9	Alboreto	Footwork-Porsche	(1.24.606)
11	Häkkinen	Lotus-Judd	(1.24.829)

Race Classification

Pos.	Driver	No.	Nat.	Car	Laps	Time/retirement
1	Ayrton Senna	1	BR	McLaren-Honda	78	1h53m 02.334s
2	Nigel Mansell	5	GB	Williams-Renault	78	1h 53m 20.682s
3	Jean Alesi	28	F	Ferrari	78	1h 53m 49.789s
4	Roberto Moreno	19	BR	Benetton-Ford	77	
5	Alain Prost	27	F	Ferrari	77	
6	Emanuele Pirro	21	I	Dallara-Judd	77	
7	Thierry Boutsen	25	B	Ligier-Lamborghini	76	
8	Bertrand Gachot	32	B	Jordan-Ford	76	
9	Eric Bernard	29	F	Lola-DFR	76	
10	Erik Comas	26	F	Ligier-Lamborghini	76	
11	JJ Lehto	22	SF	Dallara-Judd	75	
12	Pier-Luigi Martini	23	I	Minardi-Ferrari	72	
R	Mika Häkkinen	11	SF	Lotus-Judd	64	Oil leak/caught fire
R	Gianni Morbidelli	24	I	Minardi-Ferrari	49	Gearbox
R	Mauricio Gugelmin	15	BR	Leyton House-Ilmor	43	Throttle cable
R	Stefano Modena	4	I	Tyrrell-Honda	42	Engine
R	Riccardo Patrese	6	I	Williams-Renault	42	Crashed - Modena's oil
R	Mark Blundell	8	GB	Brabham-Yamaha	41	Crashed - Modena's oil
R	Michele Alboreto	9	I	Footwork-Porsche	39	Engine
R	Satoru Nakajima	3	JPN	Tyrrell-Honda	35	Spun and stalled
R	Aguri Suzuki	30	JPN	Lola-DFR	24	Crashed
R	Andrea de Cesaris	33	I	Jordan-Ford	21	Throttle cable
R	Ivan Capelli	16	I	Leyton House-Ilmor	12	Brake fluid
R	Gabriele Tarquini	17	I	AGS-DFR	9	Gearbox
R	Gerhard Berger	2	A	McLaren-Honda	9	Crashed
R	Nelson Piquet	20	BR	Benetton-Ford	0	Broken suspension/hit by Berger

Fastest lap: Prost, on lap 77, 1m 24.368s, 88.234 mph/142.006 km/h

Drivers' World Championship

Pos.	Driver	Total
1	Ayrton Senna	40
2	Alain Prost	11
3	Gerhard Berger	10
4=	Riccardo Patrese	6
4=	Nelson Piquet	6
4=	Nigel Mansell	6
7	Jean Alesi	5
8	JJ Lehto	4
9=	Pier-Luigi Martini	3
9=	Stefano Modena	3
9=	Roberto Moreno	3
12=	Mika Häkkinen	2
12=	Satoru Nakajima	2
14=	Aguri Suzuki	1
14=	Emanuele Pirro	1
14=	Julian Bailey	1

Constructors' World Championship

Pos.	Team	Total
1	McLaren	50
2	Ferrari	16
3	Williams	12
4	Benetton	9
5=	Tyrrell	5
5=	Dallara	5
7=	Minardi	3
7=	Lotus	3
9	Lola	1

Non Qualifiers

No.	Name	Car
12	J Bailey	Lotus-Judd
18	F Barbazza	AGS-DFR
7	*M Brundle	Brabham-Yamaha
10	**A Caffi	Footwork-Porsche

* Disqualified for failing to take random weight check during qualifying on Thursday.
** No time recorded on Thursday; injured during free practice on Saturday morning.

Non Pre-Qualifiers

No.	Name	Car
14	O Grouillard	Fomet-DFR
31	P Chaves	Coloni-DFR
34	N Larini	Lamborghini
35	E van de Poele	Lamborghini

1991 FORMULA ONE GRAND PRIX
ROUND FIVE

CANADA

Gilles Villeneuve

June 2, 1991

Circuit Length: 2.752 mls/4.430 km

Laps: 69

Eddie Jordan — upsetting the establishment.

Official Starting Grid

No.	Driver / Car	Time
6	Patrese *Williams-Renault*	(1.19.837)
5	Mansell *Williams-Renault*	(1.20.225)
1	Senna *McLaren-Honda*	(1.20.318)
27	Prost *Ferrari*	(1.20.656)
19	Moreno *Benetton-Ford*	(1.20.686)
2	Berger *McLaren-Honda*	(1.20.916)
28	Alesi *Ferrari*	(1.21.227)
20	Piquet *Benetton-Ford*	(1.21.241)
4	Modena *Tyrrell-Honda*	(1.21.298)
21	Pirro *Dallara-Judd*	(1.21.864)
33	de Cesaris *Jordan-Ford*	(1.22.154)
3	Nakajima *Tyrrell-Honda*	(1.22.262)
16	Capelli *Leyton House-Ilmor*	(1.22.443)
32	Gachot *Jordan-Ford*	(1.22.596)
24	Morbidelli *Minardi-Ferrari*	(1.22.993)
25	Boutsen *Ligier-Lamborghini*	(1.23.040)
22	Lehto *Dallara-Judd*	(1.23.040)
*23	Martini *Minardi-Ferrari*	(1.23.125)
29	Bernard *Lola-DFR*	(1.23.260)
7	Brundle *Brabham-Yamaha*	(1.23.516)
9	Alboreto *Footwork-Porsche*	(1.23.529)
30	Suzuki *Lola-DFR*	(1.23.585)
15	Gugelmin *Leyton House-Ilmor*	(1.23.650)
11	Häkkinen *Lotus-Judd*	(1.23.923)
10	Johansson *Footwork-Porsche*	(1.24.433)
26	Comas *Ligier-Lamborghini*	(1.24.460)

*Started from pit lane

Race Classification

Pos.	Driver	No.	Nat.	Car	Laps	Time/retirement
1	Nelson Piquet	20	BR	Benetton-Ford	69	1h 38m 51.490s
2	Stefano Modena	4	I	Tyrrell-Honda	69	1h 39m 23.322s
3	Riccardo Patrese	6	I	Williams-Renault	69	1h 39m 33.707s
4	Andrea de Cesaris	33	I	Jordan-Ford	69	1h 40m 11.700s
5	Bertrand Gachot	32	B	Jordan-Ford	69	1h 40m 13.841s
6	Nigel Mansell	5	GB	Williams-Renault	68	Engine cut out
7	Pier-Luigi Martini	23	I	Minardi-Ferrari	68	
8	Erik Comas	26	F	Ligier-Lamborghini	68	
9	Emanuele Pirro	21	I	Dallara-Judd	68	
10	Satoru Nakajima	3	JPN	Tyrrell-Honda	67	
R	Mauricio Gugelmin	15	BR	Leyton House-Ilmor	61	Engine
R	JJ Lehto	22	SF	Dallara-Judd	50	Engine
R	Stefan Johansson	10	S	Footwork-Porsche	48	Engine
R	Ivan Capelli	16	I	Leyton House-Ilmor	42	Engine
R	Jean Alesi	28	F	Ferrari	34	Engine
R	Eric Bernard	29	F	Lola-DFR	29	Gearbox
R	Alain Prost	27	F	Ferrari	27	Gearbox
R	Thierry Boutsen	25	B	Ligier-Lamborghini	27	Engine
R	Ayrton Senna	1	BR	McLaren-Honda	25	Electrics/alternator
R	Mika Häkkinen	11	SF	Lotus-Judd	21	Spun-off
R	Martin Brundle	7	GB	Brabham-Yamaha	21	Engine
R	Gianni Morbidelli	24	I	Minardi-Ferrari	20	Spun off
R	Roberto Moreno	19	BR	Benetton-Ford	10	Spun, suspension damage
R	Gerhard Berger	2	A	McLaren-Honda	4	Electronics
R	Aguri Suzuki	30	JPN	Lola-DFR	3	Fire/broken fuel line
R	Michele Alboreto	9	I	Footwork-Porsche	2	Engine

Fastest lap: Mansell, on lap 65, 1m 22.385s, 120.284 mph/193.579 km/h.

Drivers' World Championship

Pos.	Driver	Total
1	Ayrton Senna	40
2	Nelson Piquet	16
3	Alain Prost	11
4=	Gerhard Berger	10
4=	Riccardo Patrese	10
6	Stefano Modena	9
7	Nigel Mansell	7
8	Jean Alesi	5
9	JJ Lehto	4
10=	Pier-Luigi Martini	3
10=	Roberto Moreno	3
10=	Andrea de Cesaris	3
13=	Mika Häkkinen	2
13=	Satoru Nakajima	2
13=	Bertrand Gachot	2
16=	Aguri Suzuki	1
16=	Emanuele Pirro	1
16=	Julian Bailey	1

Constructors' World Championship

Pos.	Team	Total
1	McLaren	50
2	Benetton	19
3	Williams	17
4	Ferrari	16
5	Tyrrell	11
6=	Dallara	5
6=	Jordan	5
8=	Minardi	3
8=	Lotus	3
10	Lola	1

Non Qualifiers

No.	Name	Car
8	M Blundell	Brabham-Yamaha
12	J Herbert	Lotus-Judd
17	G Tarquini	AGS-DFR
18	F Barbazza	AGS-DFR

Non Pre-Qualifiers

No.	Name	Car
14	O Grouillard	Fomet-DFR
31	P Chaves	Coloni-DFR
34	N Larini	Lamborghini
35	E van de Poele	Lamborghini

1991 FORMULA ONE GRAND PRIX
ROUND SIX

MEXICO

Autodromo Hermanos Rodriguez

Mexico City

June 16, 1991

Circuit Length: 2.747 mls/4.421 km

Laps: 67*

*(Scheduled for 69 laps but reduced after two aborted starts)

Olivier Grouillard — qualifying sensation.

Official Starting Grid

Driver	Car	Time	No.
Patrese	Williams-Renault	(1.16.696)	6
Mansell	Williams-Renault	(1.16.978)	5
Senna	McLaren-Honda	(1.17.264)	1
Alesi	Ferrari	(1.18.129)	28
Berger	McLaren-Honda	(1.18.156)	2
Piquet	Benetton-Ford	(1.18.168)	20
Prost	Ferrari	(1.18.183)	27
Modena	Tyrrell-Honda	(1.18.216)	4
Moreno	Benetton-Ford	(1.18.375)	19
Grouillard	Fomet-DFR	(1.18.435)	*14
de Cesaris	Jordan-Ford	(1.18.935)	33
Blundell	Brabham-Yamaha	(1.19.064)	8
Nakajima	Tyrrell-Honda	(1.19.092)	3
Boutsen	Ligier-Lamborghini	(1.19.201)	25
Martini	Minardi-Ferrari	(1.19.215)	23
Lehto	Dallara-Judd	(1.19.291)	22
Brundle	Brabham-Yamaha	(1.19.647)	7
Bernard	Lola-DFR	(1.19.785)	29
Suzuki	Lola-DFR	(1.20.049)	30
Gachot	Jordan-Ford	(1.20.050)	32
Gugelmin	Leyton House-Ilmor	(1.20.200)	15
Capelli	Leyton House-Ilmor	(1.20.252)	16
Morbidelli	Minardi-Ferrari	(1.20.322)	24
Häkkinen	Lotus-Judd	(1.20.823)	11
Herbert	Lotus-Judd	(1.20.830)	12
Alboreto	Footwork-Porsche	(1.21.178)	9

*Started from back of grid

Race Classification

Pos.	Driver	No.	Nat.	Car	Laps	Time/retirement
1	Riccardo Patrese	6	I	Willians-Renault	67	1h 29m 52.205s
2	Nigel Mansell	5	GB	Williams-Renault	67	1h 29m 53.541s
3	Ayrton Senna	1	BR	McLaren-Honda	67	1h 30m 49.561s
4	Andrea de Cesaris	33	I	Jordan-Ford	66	Throttle potentiometer
5	Roberto Moreno	19	BR	Benetton-Ford	66	
6	Eric Bernard	29	F	Lola-DFR	66	
7	Gianni Morbidelli	24	I	Minardi-Ferrari	66	
8	Thierry Boutsen	25	B	Ligier-Lamborghini	65	
9	Mika Häkkinen	11	SF	Lotus-Judd	65	
10	Johnny Herbert	12	GB	Lotus-Judd	65	
11	Stefano Modena	4	I	Tyrrell-Honda	65	
12	Satoru Nakajima	3	JPN	Tyrrell-Honda	64	
R	Mark Blundell	8	GB	Brabham-Yamaha	54	Engine
R	Bertrand Gachot	32	B	Jordan-Ford	41	Spun off
R	Aguri Suzuki	30	JPN	Lola-DFR	48	Gearbox
R	Nelson Piquet	20	BR	Benetton-Ford	44	Wheel bearing
R	Jean Alesi	28	F	Ferrari	42	Clutch
R	JJ Lehto	22	SF	Dallara-Judd	30	Engine
R	Michele Alboreto	9	I	Footwork-Porsche	24	Oil pressure
R	Martin Brundle	7	GB	Brabham-Yamaha	20	Lost rear wheel
R	Ivan Capelli	16	I	Leyton House-Ilmor	19	Engine over-revved
R	Alain Prost	27	F	Ferrari	16	Alternator
R	Mauricio Gugelmin	15	BR	Leyton House-Ilmor	15	Engine
R	Olivier Grouillard	14	F	Fomet-DFR	13	Oil line
R	Gerhard Berger	2	A	McLaren-Honda	5	Engine/overheating
R	Pier-Luigi Martini	23	I	Minardi-Ferrari	4	Spun off on Berger's oil

Fastest lap: Mansell, on lap 61, 1m 16.788s, 128.789 mph/207.267 km/h.

Drivers' World Championship

Pos.	Driver	Total
1	Ayrton Senna	44
2	Riccardo Patrese	20
3	Nelson Piquet	16
4	Nigel Mansell	13
5	Alain Prost	11
6	Gerhard Berger	10
7	Stefano Modena	9
8	Andrea de Cesaris	6
9=	Jean Alesi	5
9=	Roberto Moreno	5
11	JJ Lehto	4
12	Pier-Luigi Martini	3
13=	Mika Häkkinen	2
13=	Satoru Nakajima	2
13=	Bertrand Gachot	2
16=	Aguri Suzuki	1
16=	Emanuele Pirro	1
16=	Julian Bailey	1
16=	Eric Bernard	1

Constructors' World Championship

Pos.	Team	Total
1	McLaren	54
2	Williams	33
3	Benetton	21
4	Ferrari	16
5	Tyrrell	11
6	Jordan	8
7	Dallara	5
8=	Minardi	3
8=	Lotus	3
10	Lola	2

Non Qualifiers

No.	Name	Car
10	S Johansson	Footwork-Porsche
17	G Tarquini	AGS-DFR
18	F Barbazza	AGS-DFR
26	E Comas	Ligier-Lamborghini

Non Pre-Qualifiers

No.	Name	Car
21	E Pirro	Dallara-Judd
31	P Chaves	Coloni-DFR
*34	N Larini	Lamborghini
35	E van de Poele	Lamborghini

*Disqualified for failing rear wing height check.

1991 FORMULA ONE GRAND PRIX
ROUND SEVEN

FRANCE

Magny-Cours, Nevers

July 7, 1991

Circuit Length: 2.654 mls/4.271 km

Laps: 72

Andrea de Cesaris — magnificent recovery drive.

Official Starting Grid

No.	Driver / Car	Time	No.	Driver / Car	Time
27	Prost, *Ferrari*	(1.14.789)	6	Patrese, *Williams-Renault*	(1.14.559)
5	Mansell, *Williams-Renault*	(1.14.895)	1	Senna, *McLaren-Honda*	(1.14.857)
28	Alesi, *Ferrari*	(1.15.877)	2	Berger, *McLaren-Honda*	(1.15.376)
19	Moreno, *Benetton-Ford*	(1.16.961)	20	Piquet, *Benetton-Ford*	(1.16.816)
24	Morbidelli, *Minardi-Ferrari*	(1.17.020)	15	Gugelmin, *Leyton House-Ilmor*	(1.17.015)
23	Martini, *Minardi-Ferrari*	(1.17.149)	4	Modena, *Tyrrell-Honda*	(1.17.114)
26	Comas, *Ligier-Lamborgini*	(1.17.504)	33	de Cesaris, *Jordan-Ford*	(1.17.163)
25	Boutsen, *Ligier-Lamborghini*	(1.17.775)	16	Capelli, *Leyton House-Ilmor*	(1.17.533)
3	Nakajima, *Tyrrell-Honda*	(1.18.144)	8	Blundell, *Brabham-Yamaha*	(1.17.836)
12	Herbert, *Lotus-Judd*	(1.18.185)	32	Gachot, *Jordan-Ford*	(1.18.150)
30	Suzuki, *Lola-DFR*	(1.18.224)	14	Grouillard, *Fomet-DFR*	(1.18.210)
7	Brundle, *Brabham-Yamaha*	(1.18.826)	29	Bernard, *Lola-DFR*	(1.18.540)
22	Lehto, *Dallara-Judd*	(1.19.267)	9	Alboreto, *Footwork-DFR*	(1.18.846)

Race Classification

Pos.	*Driver*	*No.*	*Nat.*	*Car*	*Laps*	*Time/retirement*
1	Nigel Mansell	5	GB	Williams-Renault	72	1h 38m 00.056s
2	Alain Prost	27	F	Ferrari	72	1h 38m 05.059s
3	Ayrton Senna	1	BR	McLaren-Honda	72	1h 38m 34.990s
4	Jean Alesi	28	F	Ferrari	72	1h 38m 35.976s
5	Riccardo Patrese	6	I	Williams-Renault	71	
6	Andrea de Cesaris	33	I	Jordan-Ford	71	
7	Mauricio Gugelmin	15	BR	Leyton House-Ilmor	70	
8	Nelson Piquet	20	BR	Benetton-Ford	70	
9	Pier-Luigi Martini	23	I	Minardi-Ferrari	70	
10	Johnny Herbert	12	GB	Lotus-Judd	70	
11	Erik Comas	26	F	Ligier-Lamborghini	70	
12	Thierry Boutsen	25	B	Ligier-Lamborghini	69	
R	Roberto Moreno	19	BR	Benetton-Ford	63	Driver unwell
R	Stefano Modena	4	I	Tyrrell-Honda	57	Gearbox
R	Olivier Grouillard	14	F	Fomet-DFR	47	Oil leak
R	Eric Bernard	29	F	Lola-DFR	43	Puncture
R	JJ Lehto	22	SF	Dallara-Judd	39	Puncture
R	Mark Blundell	8	GB	Brabham-Yamaha	36	Accident
R	Aguri Suzuki	30	JPN	Lola-DFR	32	Clutch
R	Michele Alboreto	9	I	Footwork-DFR	31	Transmission/gearbox
R	Martin Brundle	7	GB	Brabham-Yamaha	21	Gearbox
R	Satoru Nakajima	3	JPN	Tyrrell-Honda	12	Spun off
R	Gianni Morbidelli	24	I	Minardi-Ferrari	8	Spun off
R	Ivan Capelli	16	I	Leyton House-Ilmor	7	Spun, avoiding Morbidelli
R	Gerhard Berger	2	A	McLaren-Honda	6	Engine
R	Bertrand Gachot	32	B	Jordan-Ford	0	Spun off

Fastest lap: Mansell, on lap 49, 1m 19.168s, 120.679 mph/194.215 km/h

Drivers' World Championship

Pos.	*Driver*	*Total*
1	Ayrton Senna	48
2	Nigel Mansell	23
3	Riccardo Patrese	22
4	Alain Prost	17
5	Nelson Piquet	16
6	Gerhard Berger	10
7	Stefano Modena	9
8	Jean Alesi	8
9	Andrea de Cesaris	7
10	Roberto Moreno	5
11	JJ Lehto	4
12	Pier-Luigi Martini	3
13=	Mika Häkkinen	2
13=	Satoru Nakajima	2
13=	Bertrand Gachot	2
16=	Aguri Suzuki	1
16=	Emanuele Pirro	1
16=	Julian Bailey	1
16=	Eric Bernard	1

Constructors' World Championship

Pos.	*Team*	*Total*
1	McLaren	58
2	Williams	45
3	Ferrari	25
4	Benetton	21
5	Tyrrell	11
6	Jordan	9
7	Dallara	5
8=	Minardi	3
8=	Lotus	3
10	Lola	2

Non Qualifiers

No.	*Name*	*Car*
10	S Johansson	Footwork-DFR
11	M Häkkinen	Lotus-Judd
17	G Tarquini	AGS-DFR
18	F Barbazza	AGS-DFR

Non Pre-Qualifiers

No.	*Name*	*Car*
21	E Pirro	Dallara-Judd
31	P Chaves	Coloni-DFR
34	N Larini	Lamborghini
35	E van de Poele	Lamborghini

1991 FORMULA ONE GRAND PRIX
ROUND EIGHT

GREAT BRITAIN

Silverstone

July 14, 1991

Circuit Length: 3.247 mls/5.225 km

Laps: 59

Nigel Mansell — unbeatable on home turf.

Drivers' World Championship

Pos.	Driver	Total
1	Ayrton Senna	51
2	Nigel Mansell	33
3	Riccardo Patrese	22
4	Alain Prost	21
5	Nelson Piquet	18
6	Gerhard Berger	16
7	Stefano Modena	9
8	Jean Alesi	8
9	Andrea de Cesaris	7
10	Roberto Moreno	5
11	JJ Lehto	4
12=	Pier-Luigi Martini	3
12=	Bertrand Gachot	3
14=	Mika Häkkinen	2
14=	Satoru Nakajima	2
16=	Aguri Suzuki	1
16=	Emanuele Pirro	1
16=	Julian Bailey	1
16=	Eric Bernard	1

Constructors' World Championship

Pos.	Team	Total
1	McLaren	67
2	Williams	55
3	Ferrari	29
4	Benetton	23
5	Tyrrell	11
6	Jordan	10
7	Dallara	5
8=	Minardi	3
8=	Lotus	3
10	Lola	2

Official Starting Grid

Driver	Time	No.	No.	Driver	Time
			1	Senna *McLaren-Honda*	(1.21.618)
Mansell *Williams-Renault*	(1.20.939)	5	2	Berger *McLaren-Honda*	(1.22.476)
Patrese *Williams-Renault*	(1.22.109)	6	28	Alesi *Ferrari*	(1.22.881)
Prost *Ferrari*	(1.22.478)	27	20	Piquet *Benetton-Ford*	(1.23.626)
Moreno *Benetton-Ford*	(1.23.265)	19	4	Modena *Tyrrell-Honda*	(1.24.069)
Gugelmin *Leyton House-Ilmor*	(1.24.044)	15	8	Blundell *Brabham-Yamaha*	(1.24.165)
Lehto *Dallara-Judd*	(1.24.141)	22	7	Brundle *Brabham-Yamaha*	(1.24.345)
de Cesaris *Jordan-Ford*	(1.24.169)	33	16	Capelli *Leyton House-Ilmor*	(1.24.587)
Nakajima *Tyrrell-Honda*	(1.24.560)	3	21	Pirro *Dallara-Judd*	(1.24.654)
Gachot *Jordan-Ford*	(1.24.592)	32	24	Morbidelli *Minardi-Ferrari*	(1.25.222)
Boutsen *Ligier-Lamborghini*	(1.25.174)	25	30	Suzuki *Lola-DFR*	(1.25.583)
Bernard *Lola-DFR*	(1.25.537)	29	12	Herbert *Lotus-Judd*	(1.25.689)
Martini *Minardi-Ferrari*	(1.25.583)	23	9	Alboreto *Footwork-DFR*	(1.26.192)
Häkkinen *Lotus-Judd*	(1.25.872)	23			

Race Classification

Pos.	Driver	No.	Nat.	Car	Laps	Time/retirement
1	Nigel Mansell	5	GB	Williams-Renault	59	1h 27m 35.479s
2	Gerhard Berger	2	A	McLaren-Honda	59	1h 28m 17.772s
3	Alain Prost	27	F	Ferrari	59	1h 28m 35.629s
4	Ayrton Senna	1	BR	McLaren-Honda	58	Out of fuel
5	Nelson Piquet	20	BR	Benetton-Ford	58	
6	Bertrand Gachot	32	B	Jordan-Ford	58	
7	Stefano Modena	4	I	Tyrrell-Honda	58	
8	Satoru Nakajima	3	JPN	Tyrrell-Honda	58	
9	Pier-Luigi Martini	23	I	Minardi-Ferrari	58	
10	Emanuele Pirro	21	I	Dallara-Judd	57	
11	Gianni Morbidelli	24	I	Minardi-Ferrari	57	
12	Mika Häkkinen	11	SF	Lotus-Judd	57	
13	JJ Lehto	22	SF	Dallara-Judd	56	
14	Johnny Herbert	12	GB	Lotus-Judd	55	Engine
R	Mark Blundell	8	GB	Brabham-Yamaha	52	Engine
R	Andrea de Cesaris	33	I	Jordan-Ford	41	Accident/suspension failure
R	Jean Alesi	28	F	Ferrari	31	Collided with Suzuki
R	Aguri Suzuki	30	JPN	Lola-DFR	29	Collided with Alesi
R	Thierry Boutsen	25	B	Ligier-Lamborghini	29	Engine
R	Martin Brundle	7	GB	Brabham-Yamaha	28	Throttle cable
R	Michele Alboreto	9	I	Footwork-DFR	25	Gearbox
R	Mauricio Gugelmin	15	BR	Leyton House-Ilmor	24	Chassis vibration/numb right leg
R	Roberto Moreno	19	BR	Benetton-Ford	21	Gearbox
R	Eric Bernard	29	F	Lola-DFR	21	Gearbox
R	Ivan Capelli	16	I	Leyton House-Ilmor	16	Spun off
R	Riccardo Patrese	6	I	Williams-Renault	1	Collision with Berger

Fastest lap: Mansell, on lap 43, 1m 26.379s, 135.325 mph/217.784 km/h

Non Qualifiers

No.	Name	Car
10	S Johansson	Footwork-DFR
17	G Tarquini	AGS-DFR
18	F Barbazza	AGS-DFR
26	E Comas	Ligier-Lamborghini

Non Pre-Qualifiers

No.	Name	Car
14	O Grouillard	Fomet-DFR
31	P Chaves	Coloni-DFR
34	N Larini	Lamborghini
35	E van de Poele	Lamborghini

1991 FORMULA ONE GRAND PRIX
ROUND NINE

GERMANY

Hockenhein-Ring

July 28, 1991

Circuit Length: 4.2265 mls/6.802 km

Laps: 45

Jean Alesi — shrewd tyre choice paid off.

Drivers' World Championship

Pos.	Driver	Total
1	Ayrton Senna	51
2	Nigel Mansell	43
3	Riccardo Patrese	28
4	Alain Prost	21
5	Gerhard Berger	19
6	Nelson Piquet	18
7	Jean Alesi	12
8=	Stefano Modena	9
8=	Andrea de Cesaris	9
10	Roberto Moreno	5
11=	JJ Lehto	4
11=	Bertrand Gachot	4
13	Pier-Luigi Martini	3
14=	Mika Häkkinen	2
14=	Satoru Nakajima	2
16=	Aguri Suzuki	1
16=	Emanuele Pirro	1
16=	Julian Bailey	1
16=	Eric Bernard	1

Constructors' World Championship

Pos.	Team	Total
1	Williams	71
2	McLaren	70
3	Ferrari	33
4	Benetton	23
5	Jordan	13
6	Tyrrell	11
7	Dallara	5
8=	Minardi	3
8=	Lotus	3
10	Lola	2

Official Starting Grid

Driver	Time	No.	No.	Driver	Time
			1	Senna *McLaren-Honda*	(1.37.274)
Mansell *Williams-Renault*	(1.37.087)	5	6	Patrese *Williams-Renault*	(1.37.435)
Berger *McLaren-Honda*	(1.37.393)	2	28	Alesi *Ferrari*	(1.39.042)
Prost *Ferrari*	(1.39.034)	27	20	Piquet *Benetton-Ford*	(1.40.560)
de Cesaris *Jordan-Ford*	(1.40.239)	33	23	Martini *Minardi-Ferrari*	(1.40.998)
Moreno *Benetton-Ford*	(1.40.957)	19	16	Capelli *Leyton House-Ilmor*	(1.41.330)
Gachot *Jordan-Ford*	(1.41.308)	32	4	Modena *Tyrrell-Honda*	(1.41.566)
Nakajima *Tyrrell-Honda*	(1.41.390)	3	15	Gugelmin *Leyton House-Ilmor*	(1.41.735)
Brundle *Brabham-Yamaha*	(1.41.615)	7	21	Pirro *Dallara-Judd*	(1.42.021)
Boutsen *Ligier-Lamborghini*	(1.41.823)	25	22	Lehto *Dallara-Judd*	(1.42.171)
Morbidelli *Minardi-Ferrari*	(1.42.058)	24	*30	Suzuki *Lola-DFR*	(1.42.474)
Blundell *Brabham-Yamaha*	(1.42.216)	8	34	Larini *Lamborghini*	(1.43.035)
Häkkinen *Lotus-Judd*	(1.42.726)	11	26	Comas *Ligier-Lamborghini*	(1.43.364)
Bernard *Lola-DFR*	(1.43.321)	29			

**Started from pit lane*

Race Classification

Pos.	Driver	No.	Nat.	Car	Laps	Time/retirement
1	Nigel Mansell	5	GB	Williams-Renault	45	1h 19m 29.661s
2	Riccardo Patrese	6	I	Williams-Renault	45	1h 19m 43.440s
3	Jean Alesi	28	F	Ferrari	45	1h 19m 47.279s
4	Gerhard Berger	2	A	McLaren-Honda	45	1h 20m 02.312s
5	Andrea de Cesaris	33	I	Jordan-Ford	45	1h 20m 47.198s
6	Bertrand Gachot	32	B	Jordan-Ford	45	1h 21m 10.266s
7	Ayrton Senna	1	BR	McLaren-Honda	44	Out of fuel
8	Roberto Moreno	19	BR	Benetton-Ford	44	
9	Thierry Boutsen	25	B	Ligier-Lamborghini	44	
10	Emanuele Pirro	21	I	Dallara-Judd	44	
11	Martin Brundle	7	GB	Brabham-Yamaha	43	
12	Mark Blundell	8	GB	Brabham-Yamaha	43	
13	Stefano Modena	4	I	Tyrrell-Honda	41	
R	Alain Prost	27	F	Ferrari	37	Left track/unable to find reverse
R	Ivan Capelli	16	I	Leyton House-Ilmor	36	Engine misfire
R	JJ Lehto	22	SF	Dallara-Judd	35	Engine
R	Nelson Piquet	20	BR	Benetton-Ford	27	Engine
R	Satoru Nakajima	3	JPN	Tyrrell-Honda	26	Gearbox
R	Erik Comas	26	F	Ligier-Lamborghini	22	Oil pressure
R	Mauricio Gugelmin	15	BR	Leyton House-Ilmor	21	Gearbox
R	Mika Häkkinen	11	SF	Lotus-Judd	19	Engine
R	Aguri Suzuki	30	JPN	Lola-DFR	15	Engine
R	Gianni Morbidelli	24	I	Minardi-Ferrari	14	Engine
R	Pier-Luigi Martini	23	I	Minardi-Ferrari	11	Spun off on his own oil/engine
R	Eric Bernard	29	F	Lola-DFR	9	Transmission
R	Nicola Larini	34	I	Lamborghini	0	Spun off

Fastest lap: Patrese, on lap 35, 1m 43.569s, 146.913 mph/236.434 km/h

Non Qualifiers

No.	Name	Car
9	M Alboreto	Footwork-DFR
12	M Bartels	Lotus-Judd
17	G Tarquini	AGS-DFR
35	E van de Poele	Lamborghini

Non Pre-Qualifiers

No.	Name	Car
10	A Caffi	Footwork-DFR
14	O Grouillard	Fomet-DFR
18	F Barbazza	AGS-DFR
31	P Chaves	Coloni-DFR

1991 FORMULA ONE GRAND PRIX
ROUND TEN

HUNGARY

Hungaroring

August 11, 1991

Circuit Length: 2.465 mls/3.968 km

Laps:77

Ivan Capelli — rare sighting of a chequered flag.

Official Starting Grid

Driver / Car	Time	No.		No.	Driver / Car	Time
Senna *McLaren-Honda*	(1.16.147)	1		6	Patrese *Williams-Renault*	(1.17.379)
Mansell *Williams-Renault*	(1.17.389)	5		27	Prost *Ferrari*	(1.17.690)
Berger *McLaren-Honda*	(1.17.705)	2		28	Alesi *Ferrari*	(1.18.410)
Pirro *Dallara-Judd*	(1.19.334)	21		4	Modena *Tyrrell-Honda*	(1.19.748)
Capelli *Leyton House-Ilmor*	(1.19.794)	16		7	Brundle *Brabham-Yamaha*	(1.19.976)
Piquet *Benetton-Ford*	(1.19.984)	20		22	Lehto *Dallara-Judd*	(1.20.014)
Gugelmin *Leyton House-Ilmor*	(1.20.024)	15		3	Nakajima *Tyrrell-Honda*	(1.20.565)
Moreno *Benetton-Ford*	(1.20.584)	19		32	Gachot *Jordan-Ford*	(1.20.655)
de Cesaris *Jordan-Ford*	(1.20.805)	33		23	Martini *Minardi-Ferrari*	(1.20.823)
Boutsen *Ligier-Lamborghini*	(1.20.870)	25		8	Blundell *Brabham-Yamaha*	(1.20.954)
Bernard *Lola-DFR*	(1.21.267)	29		30	Suzuki *Lola-DFR*	(1.21.601)
Morbidelli *Minardi-Ferrari*	(1.21.654)	24		34	Larini *Lamborghini*	(1.21.896)
Comas *Ligier-Lamborghini*	(1.22.258)	26		11	Häkkinen *Lotus-Judd*	(1.22.335)

Drivers' World Championship

Pos.	Driver	Total
1	Ayrton Senna	61
2	Nigel Mansell	49
3	Riccardo Patrese	32
4	Gerhard Berger	22
5	Alain Prost	21
6	Nelson Piquet	18
7	Jean Alesi	14
8=	Stefano Modena	9
8=	Andrea de Cesaris	9
10	Roberto Moreno	5
11=	JJ Lehto	4
11=	Bertrand Gachot	4
13	Pier-Luigi Martini	3
14=	Mika Häkkinen	2
14=	Satoru Nakajima	2
16=	Aguri Suzuki	1
16=	Emanuele Pirro	1
16=	Julian Bailey	1
16=	Eric Bernard	1
16=	Ivan Capelli	1

Constructors' World Championship

Pos.	Team	Total
1	McLaren	83
2	Williams	81
3	Ferrari	35
4	Benetton	23
5	Jordan	13
6	Tyrrell	11
7	Dallara	5
8=	Minardi	3
8=	Lotus	3
10	Lola	2
11	Leyton House	1

Race Classification

Pos.	Driver	No.	Nat.	Car	Laps	Time/retirement
1	AyrtonSenna	1	BR	McLaren-Honda	77	1h 49m 12.796s
2	Nigel Mansell	5	GB	Williams-Renault	77	1h 49m 17.395s
3	Riccardo Patrese	6	I	Williams-Renault	77	1h 49m 28.390s
4	Gerhard Berger	2	A	McLaren-Honda	77	1h 49m 34.652s
5	Jean Alesi	28	F	Ferrari	77	1h 49m 44.185s
6	Ivan Capelli	16	I	Leyton House-Ilmor	76	
7	Andrea de Cesaris	33	I	Jordan-Ford	76	
8	Roberto Moreno	19	BR	Benetton-Ford	76	
9	Bertrand Gachot	32	B	Jordan-Ford	76	
10	Erik Comas	26	F	Ligier-Lamborghini	75	
11	Mauricio Gugelmin	15	BR	Leyton House-Ilmor	75	
12	Stefano Modena	4	I	Tyrrell-Honda	75	
13	Gianni Morbidelli	24	I	Minardi-Ferrari	75	
14	Mika Häkkinen	11	SF	Lotus-Judd	74	
15	Satoru Nakajima	3	JPN	Tyrrell-Honda	74	
16	Nicola Larini	34	I	Lamborghini	74	
17	Thierry Boutsen	25	B	Ligier-Lamborghini	71	Engine
R	Pier-Luigi Martini	23	I	Minardi-Ferrari	65	Engine
R	Mark Blundell	8	GB	Brabham-Yamaha	62	Spun/stalled
R	Martin Brundle	7	GB	Brabham-Yamaha	59	Cramp, right foot
R	JJ Lehto	22	SF	Dallara-Judd	49	Engine
R	Nelson Piquet	20	BR	Benetton-Ford	38	Gearbox
R	Eric Bernard	29	F	Lola-DFR	38	Engine
R	Aguri Suzuki	30	JPN	Lola-DFR	38	Engine
R	Emanuele Pirro	21	I	Dallara-Judd	37	Oil pressure
R	Alain Prost	27	F	Ferrari	28	Engine

Fastest lap: Gachot, on lap 71, 1m 21.547s, 108.847 mph/175.173 km/h

Non Qualifiers

No.	Name	Car
9	M Alboreto	Footwork-DFR
12	M Bartels	Lotus-Judd
14	O Grouillard	Fomet-DFR
35	E van de Poele	Lamborghini

Non Pre-Qualifiers

No.	Name	Car
10	A Caffi	Footwork-DFR
17	G Tarquini	AGS-DFR
18	F Barbazza	AGS-DFR
31	P Chaves	Coloni-DFR

1991 FORMULA ONE GRAND PRIX
ROUND ELEVEN

BELGIUM

Circuit de Spa-Francorchamps

August 25, 1991

Circuit Length: 4.3123 mls/6.940km

Laps: 44

Riccardo Patrese — charge of the old brigade.

Drivers' World Championship

Pos.	Driver	Total
1	Ayrton Senna	71
2	Nigel Mansell	49
3	Riccardo Patrese	34
4	Gerhard Berger	28
5	Nelson Piquet	22
6	Alain Prost	21
7	Jean Alesi	14
8=	Stefano Modena	9
8=	Andrea de Cesaris	9
10	Roberto Moreno	8
11=	JJ Lehto	4
11=	Bertrand Gachot	4
13	Pier-Luigi Martini	3
14=	Mika Häkkinen	2
14=	Satoru Nakajima	2
16=	Aguri Suzuki	1
16=	Emanuele Pirro	1
16=	Julian Bailey	1
16=	Eric Bernard	1
16=	Ivan Capelli	1
16=	Mark Blundell	1

Constructors' World Championship

Pos.	Team	Total
1	McLaren	99
2	Williams	83
3	Ferrari	35
4	Benetton	30
5	Jordan	13
6	Tyrrell	11
7	Dallara	5
8=	Minardi	3
8=	Lotus	3
10	Lola	2
11=	Leyton House	1
11=	Brabham	1

Official Starting Grid

Driver / Car	Time	No.	No.	Driver / Car	Time
			1	Senna *McLaren-Honda*	(1.47.811)
Prost *Ferrari*	(1.48.821)	**27**	**5**	Mansell *Williams-Renault*	(1.48.828)
Berger *McLaren-Honda*	(1.49.485)	**2**	**28**	Alesi *Ferrari*	(1.49.974)
Piquet *Benetton-Ford*	(1.50.540)	**20**	**32**	Schumacher *Jordan-Ford*	(1.51.212)
Moreno *Benetton-Ford*	(1.51.283)	**19**	**23**	Martini *Minardi-Ferrari*	(1.51.299)
Modena *Tyrrell-Honda*	(1.51.307)	**4**	**33**	de Cesaris *Jordan-Ford*	(1.51.986)
Capelli *Leyton House-Ilmor*	(1.52.113)	**16**	**8**	Blundell *Brabham-Yamaha*	(1.52.377)
Lehto *Dallara-Judd*	(1.52.417)	**22**	**15**	Gugelmin *Leyton House-Ilmor*	(1.52.623)
Brundle *Brabham-Yamaha*	(1.52.626)	**7**	**6**	Patrese *Williams-Renault*	(1.52.646)
Boutsen *Ligier-Lamborghini*	(1.52.709)	**25**	**24**	Morbidelli *Minardi-Ferrari*	(1.52.896)
Bernard *Lola-DFR*	(1.53.309)	**29**	**12**	Herbert *Lotus-Judd*	(1.53.361)
Nakajima *Tyrrell-Honda*	(1.53.494)	**3**	**14**	Grouillard *Fomet-DFR*	(1.53.628)
Häkkinen *Lotus-Judd*	(1.53.799)	**11**	**21**	Pirro *Dallara-Judd*	(1.53.839)
Comas *Ligier-Lamborghini*	(1.53.847)	**26**			

Race Classification

Pos.	Driver	No.	Nat.	Car	Laps	Time/retirement
1	Ayrton Senna	1	BR	McLaren-Honda	44	1h 27m 17.669s
2	Gerhard Berger	2	A	McLaren-Honda	44	1h 27m 19.570s
3	Nelson Piquet	20	BR	Benetton-Ford	44	1h 27m 49.845s
4	Roberto Moreno	19	BR	Benetton-Ford	44	1h 27m 54.979s
5	Riccardo Patrese	6	I	Williams-Renault	44	1h 28m 14.856s
6	Mark Blundell	8	GB	Brabham-Yamaha	44	1h 28m 57.704s
7	Johnny Herbert	12	GB	Lotus-Judd	44	1h 29m 02.268s
8	Emanuele Pirro	21	I	Dallara-Judd	43	
9	Martin Brundle	7	GB	Brabham-Yamaha	43	
10	Olivier Grouillard	14	F	Fomet-DFR	43	
11	Thierry Boutsen	25	B	Ligier-Lamborghini	43	
12	Pier-Luigi Martini	23	I	Minardi-Ferrari	42	
13	Andrea de Cesaris	33	I	Jordan-Ford	41	Engine/overheating
R	Stefano Modena	4	I	Tyrrell-Honda	33	Oil leak/fire
R	JJ Lehto	22	SF	Dallara-Judd	33	Engine
R	Jean Alesi	28	F	Ferrari	30	Engine
R	Gianni Morbidelli	24	I	Minardi	29	Engine
R	Mika Häkkinen	11	SF	Lotus-Judd	25	Engine
R	Erik Comas	26	F	Ligier-Lamborghini	25	Engine
R	Nigel Mansell	5	GB	Williams-Renault	22	Electrics
R	Eric Bernard	29	F	Lola-DFR	21	Gearbox
R	Ivan Capelli	16	I	Leyton House-Ilmor	13	Engine
R	Satoru Nakajima	3	JPN	Tyrrell-Honda	7	Slid off
R	Alain Prost	27	F	Ferrari	2	Engine
R	Mauricio Gugelmin	15	BR	Leyton House-Ilmor	1	Engine
R	Michael Schumacher	32	D	Jordan-Ford	0	Clutch

Fastest lap: Moreno on lap 40, 1m 55.161s, 134.806 mph/216.948 km/h

Non Qualifiers

No.	Name	Car
10	A Caffi	Footwork-DFR
30	A Suzuki	Lola-DFR
34	N Larini	Lamborghini
35	E van de Poele	Lamborghini

Non Pre-Qualifiers

No.	Name	Car
9	M Alboreto	Footwork-DFR
17	G Tarquini	AGS-DFR
18	F Barbazza	AGS-DFR
31	P Chaves	Coloni-DFR

1991 FORMULA ONE GRAND PRIX
ROUND TWELVE

ITALY

Autodromo Nazionale di Monza

September 8, 1991

Circuit Length: 3.6039 mls/5.80 km

Laps: 53

Michael Schumacher — superstar in the making.

Drivers' World Championship

Pos.	Driver	Total
1	Ayrton Senna	77
2	Nigel Mansell	59
3	Riccardo Patrese	34
4	Gerhard Berger	31
5	Alain Prost	25
6	Nelson Piquet	23
7	Jean Alesi	14
8=	Stefano Modena	9
8=	Andrea de Cesaris	9
10	Roberto Moreno	8
11=	JJ Lehto	4
11=	Bertrand Gachot	4
13	Pier-Luigi Martini	3
14=	Mika Häkkinen	2
14=	Satoru Nakajima	2
14=	Michael Schumacher	2
17=	Aguri Suzuki	1
17=	Emanuele Pirro	1
17=	Julian Bailey	1
17=	Eric Bernard	1
17=	Ivan Capelli	1
17=	Mark Blundell	1

Constructors' World Championship

Pos.	Team	Total
1	McLaren	108
2	Williams	93
3	Ferrari	39
4	Benetton	33
5	Jordan	13
6	Tyrrell	11
7	Dallara	5
8=	Minardi	3
8=	Lotus	3
10	Lola	2
11=	Leyton House	1
11=	Brabham	1

Official Starting Grid

No.	Driver / Car	Time	No.	Driver / Car	Time
1	Senna *McLaren-Honda*	(1.21.114)	5	Mansell *Williams-Renault*	(1.21.247)
2	Berger *McLaren-Honda*	(1.21.346)	6	Patrese *Williams-Renault*	(1.21.372)
27	Prost *Ferrari*	(1.21.825)	28	Alesi *Ferrari*	(1.21.890)
19	Schumacher *Benetton-Ford*	(1.22.471)	20	Piquet *Benetton-Ford*	(1.22.726)
32	Moreno *Jordan-Ford*	(1.23.102)	23	Martini *Minardi-Ferrari*	(1.23.294)
8	Blundell *Brabham-Yamaha*	(1.23.473)	16	Capelli *Leyton House-Ilmor*	(1.23.674)
4	Modena *Tyrrell-Honda*	(1.23.701)	33	de Cesaris *Jordan-Ford*	(1.23.921)
3	Nakajima *Tyrrell-Honda*	(1.24.265)	21	Pirro *Dallara-Judd*	(1.24.282)
24	Morbidelli *Minardi-Ferrari*	(1.24.287)	15	Gugelmin *Leyton House-Ilmor*	(1.24.391)
7	Brundle *Brabham-Yamaha*	(1.24.643)	22	Lehto *Dallara-Judd*	(1.24.725)
25	Boutsen *Ligier-Lamborghini*	(1.25.177)	26	Comas *Ligier-Lamborghini*	(1.25.420)
34	Larini *Lamborghini*	(1.25.717)	29	Bernard *Lola-DFR*	(1.25.871)
11	Häkkinen *Lotus-Judd*	(1.25.941)	14	Grouillard *Fomet-DFR*	(1.26.416)

Race Classification

Pos.	Driver	No.	Nat.	Car	Laps	Time/retirement
1	Nigel Mansell	5	GB	Williams-Renault	53	1h 17m 54.319s
2	Ayrton Senna	1	BR	McLaren-Honda	53	1h 18m 10.581s
3	Alain Prost	27	F	Ferrari	53	1h 18m 11.148s
4	Gerhard Berger	2	A	McLaren-Honda	53	1h 18m 22.038s
5	Michael Schumacher	19	D	Benetton-Ford	53	1h 18m 28.782s
6	Nelson Piquet	20	BR	Benetton-Ford	53	1h 18m 39.919s
7	Andrea de Cesaris	33	I	Jordan-Ford	53	1h 18m 45.455s
8	Ivan Capelli	16	I	Leyton House-Ilmor	53	1h 19m 09.338s
9	Gianni Morbidelli	24	I	Minardi-Ferrari	52	
10	Emanuele Pirro	21	I	Dallara-Judd	52	
11	Erik Comas	26	F	Ligier-Lamborghini	52	
12	Mark Blundell	8	GB	Brabham-Yamaha	52	
13	Martin Brundle	7	GB	Brabham-Yamaha	52	
14	Mika Häkkinen	11	SF	Lotus-Judd	49	
15	Mauricio Gugelmin	15	BR	Leyton House-Ilmor	49	
16	Nicola Larini	34	I	Lamborghini	48	
R	Olivier Grouillard	14	F	Fomet-DFR	46	Engine
R	JJ Lehto	22	SF	Dallara-Judd	35	Puncture
R	Stefano Modena	4	I	Tyrrell-Honda	32	Engine
R	Jean Alesi	28	F	Ferrari	29	Engine
R	Riccardo Patrese	6	I	Williams-Renault	27	Gearbox
R	Satoru Nakajima	3	JPN	Tyrrell-Honda	24	Sticking throttle
R	Eric Bernard	29	F	Lola-DFR	21	Engine
R	Pier-Luigi Martini	23	I	Minardi-Ferrari	8	Spun off/brakes
R	Roberto Moreno	32	BR	Jordan-Ford	2	Spun off/brakes
R	Thierry Boutsen	25	B	Ligier-Lamborghini	1	Spun off

Fastest lap: Senna on lap 41, 1m 26.061s, 150.756 mph/242.619 km/h

Non Qualifiers

No.	Name	Car
9	M Alboreto	Footwork-DFR
12	M Bartels	Lotus-Judd
30	A Suzuki	Lola-DFR
35	E van de Poele	Lamborghini

Non Pre-Qualifiers

No.	Name	Car
10	A Caffi	Footwork-DFR
17	G Tarquini	AGS-DFR
18	F Barbazza	AGS-DFR
31	P Chaves	Coloni-DFR

1991 FORMULA ONE GRAND PRIX
ROUND THIRTEEN

PORTUGAL

Autodromo do Estoril

September 22, 1991

Circuit Length: 2.703 mls/4.350 km

Laps: 71

Pier-Luigi Martini — totally embarrassed Ferrari.

Official Starting Grid

No.	Driver / Car	Time
6	Patrese, *Williams-Renault*	(1.13.001)
2	Berger, *McLaren-Honda*	(1.13.221)
1	Senna, *McLaren-Honda*	(1.13.444)
5	Mansell, *Williams-Renault*	(1.13.667)
27	Prost, *Ferrari*	(1.14.352)
28	Alesi, *Ferrari*	(1.14.852)
15	Gugelmin, *Leyton House-Ilmor*	(1.15.266)
23	Martini, *Minardi-Ferrari*	(1.15.394)
16	Capelli, *Leyton House-Ilmor*	(1.15.481)
19	Schumacher, *Benetton-Ford*	(1.15.578)
20	Piquet, *Benetton-Ford*	(1.15.666)
4	Modena, *Tyrrell-Honda*	(1.15.707)
24	Morbidelli, *Minardi-Ferrari*	(1.15.749)
33	de Cesaris, *Jordan-Ford*	(1.15.936)
8	Blundell, *Brabham-Yamaha*	(1.16.038)
32	Moreno, *Jordan-Ford*	(1.16.080)
21	Pirro, *Dallara-Judd*	(1.16.135)
22	Lehto, *Dallara-Judd*	(1.16.532)
7	Brundle, *Brabham-Yamaha*	(1.16.536)
25	Boutsen, *Ligier-Lamborghini*	(1.16.757)
3	Nakajima, *Tyrrell-Honda*	(1.16.926)
12	Herbert, *Lotus-Judd*	(1.17.015)
26	Comas, *Ligier-Lamborghini*	(1.17.226)
9	Alboreto, *Footwork-DFR*	(1.17.330)
30	Suzuki, *Lola-DFR*	(1.17.434)
1L	Häkkinen, *Lotus-Judd*	(1.17.714)

Drivers' World Championship

Pos.	Driver	Total
1	Ayrton Senna	83
2	Nigel Mansell	59
3	Riccardo Patrese	44
4	Gerhard Berger	31
5=	Alain Prost	25
5=	Nelson Piquet	25
7	Jean Alesi	18
8=	Stefano Modena	9
8=	Andrea de Cesaris	9
10	Roberto Moreno	8
11	Pier-Luigi Martini	6
12=	JJ Lehto	4
12=	Bertrand Gachot	4
14	Michael Schumacher	3
15=	Mika Häkkinen	2
15=	Satoru Nakajima	2
17=	Aguri Suzuki	1
17=	Emanuele Pirro	1
17=	Julian Bailey	1
17=	Eric Bernard	1
17=	Ivan Capelli	1
17=	Mark Blundell	1

Constructors' World Championship

Pos.	Team	Total
1	McLaren	114
2	Williams	103
3	Ferrari	43
4	Benetton	36
5	Jordan	13
6	Tyrrell	11
7	Minardi	6
8	Dallara	5
9	Lotus	3
10	Lola	2
11=	Leyton House	1
11=	Brabham	1

Race Classification

Pos.	Driver	No.	Nat.	Car	Laps	Time/retirement
1	Riccardo Patrese	6	I	Williams-Renault	71	1h 35m 42.304s
2	Ayrton Senna	1	BR	McLaren-Honda	71	1h 36m 03.245s
3	Jean Alesi	28	F	Ferrari	71	1h 36m 35.858s
4	Pier-Luigi Martini	23	I	Minardi-Ferrari	71	1h 36m 45.802s
5	Nelson Piquet	20	BR	Benetton-Ford	71	1h 36m 52.307s
6	Michael Schumacher	19	D	Benetton-Ford	71	1h 36m 58.886s
7	Mauricio Gugelmin	15	BR	Leyton House-Ilmor	70	
8	Andrea de Cesaris	33	I	Jordan-Ford	70	
9	Gianni Morbidelli	24	I	Minardi-Ferrari	70	
10	Roberto Moreno	32	BR	Jordan-Ford	70	
11	Erik Comas	26	F	Ligier-Lamborghini	70	
12	Martin Brundle	7	GB	Brabham-Yamaha	69	
13	Satoru Nakajima	3	JPN	Tyrrell-Honda	68	
14	Mika Häkkinen	11	SF	Lotus-Judd	68	
15	Michele Alboreto	9	I	Footwork-DFR	68	
16	Thierry Boutsen	25	B	Ligier-Lamborghini	68	
17	Ivan Capelli	16	I	Leyton House-Ilmor	64	Broken nose cone
R	Stefano Modena	4	I	Tyrrell-Honda	56	Engine
R	Nigel Mansell	5	GB	Williams-Renault	51	Disqualified
R	Aguri Suzuki	30	JPN	Lola-DFR	40	Gearbox
R	Alain Prost	27	F	Ferrari	39	Engine
R	Gerhard Berger	2	A	McLaren-Honda	37	Engine
R	Emanuele Pirro	21	I	Dallara-Judd	18	Engine
R	JJ Lehto	22	SF	Dallara-Judd	14	Gear linkage
R	Mark Blundell	8	GB	Brabham-Yamaha	12	Rear suspension
R	Johnny Herbert	12	GB	Lotus-Judd	1	Engine/gearbox

Fastest lap: Mansell, on lap 36, 1m 18.179s, 124.467 mph/200.310 km/h

Non Qualifiers

No.	Name	Car
17	G Tarquini	AGS-DFR
29	E Bernard	Lola-DFR
34	N Larini	Lamborghini
35	E van de Poele	Lamborghini

Non Pre-Qualifiers

No.	Name	Car
10	A Caffi	Footwork-DFR
14	O Grouillard	Fomet-DFR
18	F Barbazza	AGS-DFR
31	P Chaves	Coloni-DFR

1991 FORMULA ONE GRAND PRIX
ROUND FOURTEEN

SPAIN

Circuit de Catalunya

Barcelona

September 29, 1991

Circuit Length: 2.949 mls/4.747 km

Laps:65

Gerhard Berger — quickest McLaren ... for once.

Drivers' World Championship

Pos.	Driver	Total
1	Ayrton Senna	85
2	Nigel Mansell	69
3	Riccardo Patrese	48
4=	Gerhard Berger	31
4=	Alain Prost	31
6	Nelson Piquet	25
7	Jean Alesi	21
8=	Stefano Modena	9
8=	Andrea de Cesaris	9
10	Roberto Moreno	8
11	Pier-Luigi Martini	6
12=	JJ Lehto	4
12=	Bertrand Gachot	4
12=	Michael Schumacher	4
15=	Mika Häkkinen	2
15=	Satoru Nakajima	2
17=	Aguri Suzuki	1
17=	Emanuele Pirro	1
17=	Julian Bailey	1
17=	Eric Bernard	1
17=	Ivan Capelli	1
17=	Mark Blundell	1

Constructors' World Championship

Pos.	Team	Total
1	Williams	117
2	McLaren	116
3	Ferrari	52
4	Benetton	37
5	Jordan	13
6	Tyrrell	11
7	Minardi	6
8	Dallara	5
9	Lotus	3
10	Lola	2
11=	Leyton House	1
11=	Brabham	1

Official Starting Grid

Driver / Car	Time	No.	No.	Driver / Car	Time
Berger *McLaren-Honda*	(1.18.751)	2	5	Mansell *Williams-Renault*	(1.18.970)
Senna *McLaren-Honda*	(1.19.064)	1	6	Patrese *Williams-Renault*	(1.19.643)
Schumacher *Benetton-Ford*	(1.19.733)	19	27	Prost *Ferrari*	(1.19.936)
Alesi *Ferrari*	(1.20.197)	28	16	Capelli *Leyton House-Ilmor*	(1.20.584)
Pirro *Dallara-Judd*	(1.20.651)	21	20	Piquet *Benetton-Ford*	(1.20.676)
Brundle *Brabham-Yamaha*	(1.20.677)	7	8	Blundell *Brabham-Yamaha*	(1.20.724)
Gugelmin *Leyton House-Ilmor*	(1.20.743)	15	4	Modena *Tyrrell-Honda*	(1.20.788)
Lehto *Dallara-Judd*	(1.20.967)	22	24	Morbidelli *Minardi-Ferrari*	(1.22.801)
de Cesaris *Jordan-Ford*	(1.21.865)	33	3	Nakajima *Tyrrell-Honda*	(1.22.114)
Martini *Minardi-Ferrari*	(1.22.510)	23	32	Zanardi *Jordan-Ford*	(1.22.580)
Häkkinen *Lotus-Judd*	(1.22.646)	11	14	Tarquini *Fomet-DFR*	(1.22.837)
Bernard *Lola-DFR*	(1.22.944)	29	9	Alboreto *Footwork-DFR*	(1.23.145)
Comas *Ligier-Lamborghini*	(1.23.359)	26	25	Boutsen *Ligier-Lamborghini*	(1.23.553)

Race Classification

Pos.	Driver	No.	Nat.	Car	Laps	Time/retirement
1	Nigel Mansell	5	GB	Williams-Renault	65	1h 38m 41.541s
2	Alain Prost	27	F	Ferrari	65	1h 38m 52.872s
3	Riccardo Patrese	6	I	Williams-Renault	65	1h 38m 57.450s
4	Jean Alesi	28	F	Ferrari	65	1h 39m 04.313s
5	Ayrton Senna	1	BR	McLaren-Honda	65	1h 39m 43.943s
6	Michael Schumacher	19	D	Benetton-Ford	65	1h 40m 01.009s
7	Mauricio Gugelmin	15	BR	Leyton-House Ilmor	64	
8	JJ Lehto	22	SF	Dallara-Judd	64	
9	Alessandro Zanardi	32	I	Jordan-Ford	64	
10	Martin Brundle	7	GB	Brabham-Yamaha	63	
11	Nelson Piquet	20	BR	Benetton-Ford	63	
12	Gabriele Tarquini	14	I	Fomet-DFR	63	
13	Pier-Luigi Martini	23	I	Minardi-Ferrari	63	
14	Gianni Morbidelli	24	I	Minardi-Ferrari	62	Not running; spun off
15	Emanuele Pirro	21	I	Dallara-Judd	62	
16	Stefano Modena	4	I	Tyrrell-Honda	62	
17	Satoru Nakajima	3	JPN	Tyrrell-Honda	62	
R	Mark Blundell	8	GB	Brabham-Yamaha	49	Engine
R	Erik Comas	26	F	Ligier-Lamborghini	36	Electronics
R	Gerhard Berger	2	A	McLaren-Honda	33	Engine
R	Michele Alboreto	9	I	Footwork-DFR	23	Engine
R	Andrea de Cesaris	33	I	Jordan-Ford	22	Electrics
R	Mika Häkkinen	11	SF	Lotus-Judd	5	Spun off
R	Ivan Capelli	16	I	Leyton House-Ilmor	1	Collision with Pirro
R	Thierry Boutsen	25	B	Ligier-Lamborghini	0	Spun off
R	Eric Bernard	29	F	Lola-DFR	0	Hit Boutsen

Fastest lap: Patrese, on lap 63, 1m 22.837s, 128.188 mph/206.299 km/h

Non Qualifiers

No.	Name	Car
12	M Bartels	Lotus-Judd
30	A Suzuki	Lola-DFR
34	N Larini	Lamborghini
35	E van de Poele	Lamborghini

Non Pre-Qualifiers

No.	Name	Car
10	A Caffi	Footwork-DFR
17	O Grouillard	AGS-DFR
18	F Barbazza	AGS-DFR
*31	P Chaves	Coloni-DFR

* *Entry withdrawn*

1991 FORMULA ONE GRAND PRIX
ROUND FIFTEEN

JAPAN

Suzuka International Racing Course

October 20, 1991

Circuit Length: 3.641 mls/5.859 km

Laps: 53

Brundle — bang on form.

Drivers' World Championship

Pos.	Driver	Total
1	Ayrton Senna	91
2	Nigel Mansell	69
3	Riccardo Patrese	52
4	Gerhard Berger	41
5	Alain Prost	34
6	Nelson Piquet	25
7	Jean Alesi	21
8	Stefano Modena	10
9	Andrea de Cesaris	9
10	Roberto Moreno	8
11	Pier-Luigi Martini	6
12=	JJ Lehto	4
12=	Bertrand Gachot	4
12=	Michael Schumacher	4
15=	Mika Häkkinen	2
15=	Satoru Nakajima	2
15=	Martin Brundle	2
18=	Aguri Suzuki	1
18=	Emanuele Pirro	1
18=	Julian Bailey	1
18=	Eric Bernard	1
18=	Ivan Capelli	1
18=	Mark Blundell	1

Constructors' World Championship

Pos.	Team	Total
1	McLaren	132
2	Williams	121
3	Ferrari	55
4	Benetton	37
5	Jordan	13
6	Tyrrell	12
7	Minardi	6
8	Dallara	5
9=	Lotus	3
9=	Brabham	3
11	Lola	2
12	Leyton House	1

Official Starting Grid

No.	Driver	Car	Time
2	Berger	McLaren-Honda	(1.34.700)
1	Senna	McLaren-Honda	(1.34.898)
5	Mansell	Williams-Renault	(1.34.922)
27	Prost	Ferrari	(1.36.670)
6	Patrese	Williams-Renault	(1.36.882)
28	Alesi	Ferrari	(1.37.140)
23	Martini	Minardi-Ferrari	(1.38.154)
24	Morbidelli	Minardi-Ferrari	(1.38.248)
19	Schumacher	Benetton-Ford	(1.38.363)
20	Piquet	Benetton-Ford	(1.38.614)
33	de Cesaris	Jordan-Ford	(1.38.842)
22	Lehto	Dallara-Judd	(1.38.911)
32	Zanardi	Jordan-Ford	(1.38.923)
4	Modena	Tyrrell-Honda	(1.38.926)
3	Nakajima	Tyrrell-Honda	(1.39.118)
21	Pirro	Dallara-Judd	(1.39.238)
25	Boutsen	Ligier-Lamborghini	(1.39.499)
15	Gugelmin	Leyton House-Ilmor	(1.39.518)
7	Brundle	Brabham-Yamaha	(1.39.697)
26	Comas	Ligier-Lamborghini	(1.39.820)
11	Häkkinen	Lotus-Judd	(1.40.024)
16	Wendlinger	Leyton House-Ilmor	(1.40.092)
12	Herbert	Lotus-Judd	(1.40.170)
14	Tarquini	Fomet-DFR	(1.40.184)
30	Suzuki	Lola-DFR	(1.40.255)
10	Caffi	Footwork-DFR	(1.40.402)

Race Classification

Pos.	Driver	No.	Nat.	Car	Laps	Time/retirement
1	Gerhard Berger	2	A	McLaren-Honda	53	1h 32m 10.695s
2	Ayrton Senna	1	BR	McLaren-Honda	53	1h 32m 11.039s
3	Riccardo Patrese	6	I	Williams-Renault	53	1h 33m 07.426s
4	Alain Prost	27	F	Ferrari	53	1h 33m 31.456s
5	Martin Brundle	7	GB	Brabham-Yamaha	52	
6	Stefano Modena	4	I	Tyrrell-Honda	52	
7	Nelson Piquet	20	BR	Benetton-Ford	52	
8	Mauricio Gugelmin	15	BR	Leyton House-Ilmor	52	
9	Thierry Boutsen	25	B	Ligier-Lamborghini	52	
10	Alex Caffi	10	I	Footwork-DFR	51	
11	Gabriele Tarquini	14	I	Fomet-DFR	50	
R	Erik Comas	26	F	Ligier-Lamborghini	41	Alternator
R	Pier-Luigi Martini	23	I	Minardi-Ferrari	39	Clutch
R	Michael Schumacher	19	D	Benetton-Ford	34	Engine
R	Johnny Herbert	12	GB	Lotus-Judd	31	Engine cut out
R	Satoru Nakajima	3	JPN	Tyrrell-Honda	30	Suspension
R	Aguri Suzuki	30	JPN	Lola-DFR	26	Engine
R	Gianni Morbidelli	24	I	Minardi-Ferrari	15	Wheel bearing
R	Nigel Mansell	5	GB	Williams-Renault	9	Brakes/spun off
R	Alessandro Zanardi	32	I	Jordan-Ford	7	Gearbox
R	Mika Häkkinen	11	SF	Lotus-Judd	4	Spun off
R	Andrea de Cesaris	33	I	Jordan-Ford	1	Spun off
R	JJ Lehto	22	SF	Dallara-Judd	1	Spun avoiding de Cesaris
R	Emanuele Pirro	21	I	Dallara-Judd	1	Spun avoiding de Cesaris
R	Karl Wendlinger	16	A	Leyton House-Ilmor	1	Crashed into de Cesaris
R	Jean Alesi	28	F	Ferrari	0	Engine

Fastest lap: Senna, on lap 39, 1m 41.532s, 129.195 mph/207.919 km/h

Non Qualifiers

No.	Name	Car
9	M Alboreto	Footwork-DFR
34	N Larini	Lamborghini
35	E van de Poele	Lamborghini
*29	E Bernard	Lola-DFR

**Injured during practice on Friday*

Non Pre-Qualifiers

No.	Name	Car
8	M Blundell	Brabham-Yamaha
31	N Hattori	Coloni-DFR
**17	O Grouillard	AGS-DFR
**18	F Barbazza	AGS-DFR

***Entries withdrawn*

1991 FORMULA ONE GRAND PRIX
ROUND SIXTEEN

AUSTRALIA

Adelaide

November 3, 1991

Circuit Length: 2.347 mls/3.778 km

Laps:14

Morbidelli — impressive on Ferrari debut.

Official Starting Grid

Driver / Car	Time	No.	No.	Driver / Car	Time
Senna *McLaren-Honda*	(1.14.041)	**1**	**2**	Berger *McLaren-Honda*	(1.14.385)
Mansell *Williams-Renault*	(1.14.822)	**5**	**6**	Patrese *Williams-Renault*	(1.15.057)
Piquet *Benetton-Ford*	(1.15.291)	**20**	**19**	Schumacher *Benetton-Ford*	(1.15.508)
Alesi *Ferrari*	(1.15.545)	**28**	**27**	Morbidelli *Ferrari*	(1.16.203)
Modena *Tyrrell-Honda*	(1.16.253)	**4**	**23**	Martini *Minardi-Ferrari*	(1.16.359)
Lehto *Dallara-Judd*	(1.16.871)	**22**	**33**	de Cesaris *Jordan-Ford*	(1.17.050)
Pirro *Dallara-Judd*	(1.17.342)	**21**	**15**	Gugelmin *Leyton House-Ilmor*	(1.17.344)
Alboreto *Footwork-DFR*	(1.17.355)	**9**	**32**	Zanardi *Jordan-Ford*	(1.17.362)
Blundell *Brabham-Yamaha*	(1.17.365)	**8**	**24**	Moreno *Minardi-Ferrari*	(1.17.639)
Larini *Lamborghini*	(1.17.936)	**34**	**25**	Boutsen *Ligier-Lamborghini*	(1.17.969)
Herbert *Lotus-Judd*	(1.18.091)	**12**	**26**	Comas *Ligier-Lamborghini*	(1.18.112)
Caffi *Footwork-DFR*	(1.18.157)	**10**	**3**	Nakajima *Tyrrell-Honda*	(1.18.216)
Häkkinen *Lotus-Judd*	(1.18.271)	**11**	**16**	Wendlinger *Leyton House-Ilmor*	(1.18.282)

Drivers' World Championship

Pos.	*Driver*	*Total*
1	Ayrton Senna	96
2	Nigel Mansell	72
3	Riccardo Patrese	53
4	Gerhard Berger	43
5	Alain Prost	34
6	Nelson Piquet	26.5
7	Jean Alesi	21
8=	Stefano Modena	10
9=	Andrea de Cesaris	9
10	Roberto Moreno	8
11	Pier-Luigi Martini	6
12=	JJ Lehto	4
12=	Bertrand Gachot	4
12=	Michael Schumacher	4
15=	Mika Häkkinen	2
15=	Satoru Nakajima	2
15=	Martin Brundle	2
18=	Aguri Suzuki	1
18=	Emanuele Pirro	1
18=	Julian Bailey	1
18=	Eric Bernard	1
18=	Ivan Capelli	1
18=	Mark Blundell	1
24	Gianni Morbidelli	0.5

Constructors' World Championship

Pos.	*Team*	*Total*
1	McLaren	139
2	Williams	125
3	Ferrari	55.5
4	Benetton	38.5
5	Jordan	13
6	Tyrrell	12
7=	Minardi	6
8=	Dallara	5
9=	Lotus	3
9=	Brabham	3
11=	Lola	2
12	Leyton House	1

Race Classification

Pos.	*Driver*	*No.*	*Nat.*	*Car*	*Laps*	*Time/retirement*
1	Ayrton Senna	1	BR	McLaren-Honda	14	24m 34.899s
2	Nigel Mansell	5	GB	Williams-Renault	14	24m 36.158s
3	Gerhard Berger	2	A	McLaren-Honda	14	24m 40.019s
4	Nelson Piquet	20	BR	Benetton-Ford	14	25m 05.002s
5	Riccardo Patrese	6	I	Williams-Renault	14	25m 25.436s
6	Gianni Morbidelli	27	I	Ferrari	14	25m 25.968s
7	Emanuele Pirro	21	I	Dallara-Judd	14	25m 27.260s
8	Andrea de Cesaris	33	I	Jordan-Ford	14	25m 35.330s
9	Alessandro Zanardi	32	I	Jordan-Ford	14	25m 50.466s
10	Stefano Modena	4	I	Tyrrell-Honda	14	25m 55.269s
11	Johnny Herbert	12	GB	Lotus-Judd	14	25m 56.972s
12	JJ Lehto	22	SF	Dallara-Judd	14	26m 13.418s
13	Michele Alboreto	9	I	Footwork-DFR	14	26m 14.202s
14	Mauricio Gugelmin	15	BR	Leyton House-Ilmor	13	Crashed in pit lane
15	Alex Caffi	10	I	Footwork-DFR	13	
16	Roberto Moreno	24	BR	Minardi-Ferrari	13	
17	Mark Blundell	8	GB	Brabham-Yamaha	13	
18	Erik Comas	26	F	Ligier-Lamborghini	13	
19	Mika Häkkinen	11	SF	Lotus-Judd	13	
20	Karl Wendlinger	16	A	Leyton House-Ilmor	12	
R	Pier-Luigi Martini	23	I	Minardi-Ferrari	8	Spun off
R	Michael Schumacher	19	D	Benetton-Ford	5	Collision with Alesi
R	Jean Alesi	28	F	Ferrari	5	Collision with Larini
R	Nicola Larini	34	I	Modena-Lamborghini	5	Collision with Alesi
R	Thierry Boutsen	25	B	Ligier-Lamborghini	5	Collision with Nakajima
R	Satoru Nakajima	3	JPN	Tyrrell-Honda	4	Collision with Boutsen

Fastest lap: Berger, on lap 14, 1m 41.141s, 83.602 mph/134.545 km/h

Non Qualifiers

No.	*Name*	*Car*
7	M Brundle	Brabham-Yamaha
29	B Gachot	Lola-DFR
30	A Suzuki	Lola-DFR
35	E van de Poele	Lamborghini

Non Pre-Qualifiers

No.	*Name*	*Car*
14	G Tarquini	Fomet-DFR
31	N Hattori	Coloni-DFR